The Airbnb Launch Blueprint

30 Days to Booked

Eric McDermott

Unjudgeable Press

Contents

To all the aspiring hosts and savvy investors who are ready to seize the opportunity in the booming short-term rental market. May this blueprint equip you with the knowledge, confidence, and actionable strategies needed to transform your vision into a profitable reality. This journey requires dedication, a willingness to learn, and a commitment to excellence, and I am honored to be your guide. May your properties be consistently booked, your guests delighted, and your returns exceed your expectations. This book is a testament to the power of smart planning, meticulous execution, and the entrepreneurial spirit that drives innovation and financial freedom. For those who dare to dream big and work smart, the rewards of the short-term rental industry are within reach. May you build not just successful businesses, but legacies of hospitality and smart investment that stand the test of time and market fluctuations. Your success is the ultimate testament to the principles laid out within these pages.

Preface

The world of short-term rentals, particularly through platforms like Airbnb, has revolutionized how people travel and how savvy individuals generate income. What was once a niche market has exploded into a global phenomenon, offering unparalleled opportunities for those willing to learn and adapt. This book, 'The Airbnb Launch Blueprint: 30 Days to Booked,' is born from years of hands-on experience, from the initial challenges of listing a first property to the complexities of scaling a multi-property portfolio. I've navigated the legal mazes, mastered the art of guest experience, and honed the strategies that turn a vacant property into a thriving income-generating asset. My journey, like many others, was paved with a mix of exhilarating successes and invaluable lessons learned from missteps. I recognized a need for a clear, actionable, and comprehensive guide that demystifies the process, providing a roadmap for anyone looking to enter this lucrative market. This blueprint is designed to accelerate your learning curve, minimize costly mistakes, and empower you to launch a successful Airbnb business within an ambitious yet achievable 30-day timeframe. We'll delve into everything from market analysis and legal compliance to property setup, listing optimization, and operational excellence. Whether you're an entrepreneur seeking a new venture, a real estate investor looking to diversify, or simply someone dreaming of passive income, this book is your essential companion. It's more than just a guide; it's a catalyst for your success in the dynamic world of short-term rentals. Even if you're already actively hosting on Airbnb or managing other short-term rentals, this resource will provide you with advanced strategies, troubleshooting tips, and innovative approaches to elevate your existing business and maximize your profits.

Introduction

Welcome to 'The Airbnb Launch Blueprint: 30 Days to Booked,' your definitive guide to launching and succeeding in the lucrative world of short-term rentals. In today's rapidly evolving travel landscape, the demand for unique, comfortable, and convenient accommodations has never been higher. Platforms like Airbnb have democratized the lodging industry, opening doors for individuals and investors to tap into a significant revenue stream. This book is meticulously crafted for the forward-thinking individual—the aspiring entrepreneur, the seasoned real estate investor, or anyone seeking to build a profitable passive income. You are motivated, you understand the value of smart investment, and you are ready to learn practical, actionable strategies that yield tangible results. We recognize that your time is valuable, and your goals are ambitious. That's why this blueprint is structured to guide you through the entire process, from initial market research and legal navigation to property setup, listing optimization, and seamless operations, all within a focused 30-day launch window. Inside, you'll discover data-driven insights, proven methodologies, and step-by-step instructions, all presented in an authoritative yet accessible tone. We'll explore how to identify high-demand locations, navigate complex regulations, finance your venture, and create listings that capture attention and bookings. Furthermore, we'll equip you with the operational skills to deliver exceptional guest experiences, the key to securing five-star reviews and building a sustainable business. This is not just about listing a property; it's about building a business that provides financial freedom and a fulfilling entrepreneurial journey. Get ready to transform your investment goals into a reality and become a successful host in just 30 days.

Chapter One

Laying the Groundwork: Market Viability and Legal Frameworks

Assessing the Short Term Rental Landscape

The short-term rental market, often exemplified by platforms like Airbnb, presents a dynamic and increasingly significant segment of the hospitality and real estate industries. Understanding the current economic climate is foundational to recognizing the opportunities and challenges inherent in this sector. Globally, there's a discernible shift in how people travel and seek accommodation. The traditional hotel model, while still dominant in many respects, now faces robust competition from the personalized, often more cost-effective, and locally immersive experiences offered by short-term rentals. This trend is fueled by a confluence of factors, including evolving consumer preferences, the rise of remote work, and the desire for unique travel experiences over standardized ones.

Economically, the short-term rental market has demonstrated remarkable resilience and growth. Even in the face of broader economic fluctuations, the demand for flexible and varied accommodation options has remained strong. This is partly due to the inherent adaptability of the model. For travelers, it offers a wider range of price points, amenities, and locations than many traditional hotels. For property owners and investors, it presents a potent avenue for generating income, often at rates significantly higher than long-term rentals, especially in high-demand areas. The ability to monetize underutilized properties, vacation homes, or even spare rooms has opened up income-generating possibilities for a diverse group of individuals, from solo hosts to established real estate investment firms.

The burgeoning opportunity lies in the market's expansion beyond purely leisure travel. Business travel is increasingly embracing short-term rentals, seeking the convenience of a home-like environment, kitchen facilities, and dedicated workspaces. Similarly, the concept of "bleisure" travel, blending business and leisure, further fuels demand. Digital nomads, freelancers, and remote workers actively seek comfortable, connected spaces for extended stays, often extending beyond typical tourist seasons. This diversification of the traveler base creates a more stable and year-round demand, mitigating the seasonality that can affect traditional tourism.

However, it is crucial to approach this market with a data-driven perspective. Enthusiasm for the potential profitability must be tempered with a realistic assessment of market conditions. Not all locations are created equal, and success hinges on thorough research and strategic placement. The term "market trends" encompasses a variety of factors that influence the viability of a short-term rental investment. These include, but are not limited to, local tourism statistics, the presence of universities or business centers attracting longer-term visitors, major event venues, and the general appeal of a region. Occupancy rates, a key performance indicator, can vary dramatically from one city or neighborhood to another, and even from one season to the next within the same locale.

For instance, a property in a bustling metropolitan center known for its cultural attractions and business conferences might command high occupancy and premium nightly rates. Conversely, a property in a more remote or less-visited area, while potentially offering lower acquisition costs, might struggle to achieve consistent bookings without a very specific niche appeal. Understanding these regional differences is paramount. This involves delving into data sources that track travel patterns, average nightly rates, and occupancy levels for short-term rentals within specific geographic areas. Online travel agencies (OTAs) like Airbnb, Vrbo, and Booking.com themselves provide some market data, though often aggregated. More granular insights can be gleaned from specialized short-term rental analytics platforms, which aggregate data from various sources to offer detailed market performance reports.

Profitability in the short-term rental market is not a simple matter of setting a price and waiting for bookings. It is a function of several interconnected variables, including the average daily rate (ADR), occupancy rate, and operational expenses. The ADR is the average amount earned per booked night. The occupancy rate is the percentage of available nights that are actually booked. Profitability is achieved when the revenue generated from these two factors exceeds the total costs associated with operating the rental. These costs can be substantial and include mortgage payments (if applicable), property taxes, insurance, utilities, cleaning fees, maintenance, supplies, booking platform commissions, and potentially property management fees.

A robust understanding of key performance indicators (KPIs) is therefore essential. Beyond ADR and occupancy rate, other vital metrics include:

Revenue Per Available Room (RevPAR): This is a fundamental hospitality metric calculated by multiplying the average daily rate by the occupancy rate. It provides a clear picture of how effectively a property is generating revenue from its available inventory. A higher RevPAR generally indicates a more profitable operation. For example, if a property has an ADR of $150 and an occupancy rate of 80%, its RevPAR would be $120 ($150 0.80). Comparing this RevPAR across different markets or different properties within the same market can offer valuable insights.

Average Booking Value (ABV): This metric calculates the average revenue generated per booking, considering the total revenue and the number of bookings. It can be particularly useful when comparing the financial performance of properties that attract different lengths of stay. A property with longer stays might have a lower ADR but a higher ABV if those longer stays fill occupancy gaps and reduce turnover costs.

Guest Acquisition Cost (GAC): While not always directly tracked by individual hosts on platforms like Airbnb, understanding the cost of acquiring a guest is crucial for long-term strategy. This can include marketing expenses, commission fees paid to booking platforms, and any costs associated with advertising. For hosts focusing on direct bookings, GAC might involve website development, SEO, and social media advertising. Minimizing GAC while maximizing bookings is a key to profitability.

Net Operating Income (NOI): This is a crucial profitability metric that represents the income generated from a property after deducting all operating expenses, but before accounting for debt service (mortgage payments) and income taxes. It provides a pure measure of the property's operational profitability. Calculating NOI allows investors to compare the performance of different properties on an apples-to-apples basis, irrespective of their financing structures.

Return on Investment (ROI): This measures the profitability of an investment relative to its cost. For a short-term rental, ROI can be calculated in various ways, but a common approach is to divide the annual net profit (after all expenses, including debt service) by the total cash invested in the property. A higher ROI signifies a more efficient and profitable investment. Understanding ROI helps in making informed decisions about which properties to acquire and how to manage them for maximum financial return.

Analyzing these KPIs in the context of the current economic climate reveals significant opportunities. For example, during periods of economic uncertainty, travelers may opt for shorter, more local trips or seek accommodations that offer better value for money. Short-term rentals, with their diverse offerings and often competitive pricing compared to multi-room hotel bookings for families or groups, can thrive in such environments. Furthermore, the ongoing trend of remote work means that demand for longer-term stays, often referred to as "monthly stays" on platforms like Airbnb, is robust. These longer bookings can provide a more stable income stream and reduce the frequency of cleaning and turnover, thereby lowering operational costs and improving net profitability.

The "current economic climate" also refers to interest rate environments, inflation, and overall consumer spending power. While rising interest rates can increase the cost of financing property acquisition, they can also make traditional real estate investments less attractive, potentially driving more capital into alternative real estate ventures like short-term rentals, especially if they offer superior returns. Inflation, while increasing operational costs (like utilities and cleaning supplies), also often leads to a greater willingness among travelers to pay higher nightly rates to secure their desired accommodation. The key is to ensure that ADR increases outpace the rise in expenses.

Market potential is directly tied to the demand drivers within a specific region. These drivers can be diverse. For instance, a city with a major university will see consistent demand from visiting families, prospective students, and faculty. A city with a large convention center or a vibrant arts and culture scene will attract business travelers and tourists alike. Proximity to natural attractions like national parks, beaches, or ski resorts will drive seasonal leisure travel. The presence of major employers and corporate travel needs can also create significant demand for business-oriented short-term rentals. Identifying these demand generators is the first step in assessing market potential.

Competition is another critical factor in assessing the short-term rental landscape. In popular markets, the number of listings can be high. This means that simply having a property available is not enough; it must be competitive. Competition can manifest in several ways:

Price Competition: Many hosts will be competing on nightly rates. Understanding competitor pricing, especially for similar properties in the same area, is crucial for setting your own competitive yet profitable rates. This requires ongoing monitoring of the market.

Quality and Amenities Competition: Guests increasingly seek properties that offer a high level of comfort, modern amenities, and a positive aesthetic. Properties that are well-maintained, attractively furnished, and equipped with desired amenities (e.g., fast Wi-Fi, smart TVs, well-equipped kitchens, comfortable bedding) will often outperform those that are not.

Listing Optimization Competition: The effectiveness of a listing's title, description, photos, and responsiveness to inquiries plays a significant role in attracting bookings. Hosts who invest time and effort into optimizing their listings will often capture more of the available market share.

Guest Experience Competition: Reviews are the currency of the short-term rental market. Hosts who consistently provide excellent guest experiences, leading to positive reviews, build a reputation that attracts more bookings and allows them to command higher rates. This includes everything from accurate listing descriptions and smooth check-ins to prompt communication and attention to detail during the stay.

Therefore, assessing the short-term rental landscape involves a multifaceted approach. It requires understanding the macroeconomic factors influencing travel, analyzing granular market data for specific locations, identifying key demand drivers, and evaluating the competitive environment. By thoroughly researching and understanding these elements, aspiring hosts and investors can make informed decisions, identify lucrative opportunities, and set realistic expectations for their short-term rental ventures, laying a solid foundation for success. This detailed assessment forms the crucial first step in the journey of building a profitable and sustainable short-term rental business. It's about marrying enthusiasm with analytical rigor, ensuring that investment decisions are grounded in data and market realities, not just aspiration. This thorough groundwork is what separates short-term rental ventures that merely exist from those that thrive and generate consistent, significant returns.

Identifying HighDemand Locations

The bedrock of a successful short-term rental enterprise is the strategic selection of its physical location. Without a property situated in an area that attracts a consistent flow of potential guests, even the most meticulously appointed and managed rental will struggle to achieve profitability. This fundamental step, therefore, necessitates a deep dive into market research, focusing on understanding what drives demand in specific locales and how to identify emerging hotspots before they become oversaturated. The goal is to place your investment where people want to be, for reasons that translate directly into bookings and revenue.

The initial phase of identifying high-demand locations involves a systematic analysis of tourism statistics. This means looking beyond general notions of popular cities and delving into quantifiable data. Many national and regional tourism boards, as well as city governments, publish annual reports detailing visitor numbers, their origins, and the primary purposes of their trips. Examining these reports can reveal trends that might not be immediately obvious. For instance, a city might appear popular overall, but the data might show that its popularity is heavily skewed towards a specific type of traveler or a particular season. Understanding this granularity is crucial. Are you seeing growth in international tourism, domestic travel, or perhaps a surge in convention attendees? Each of these segments might have different accommodation preferences and spending habits. Platforms like Statista, as well as individual city tourism websites, are invaluable resources here. Look for trends in year-over-year visitor growth. A consistently growing visitor base suggests a healthy and expanding market, which is generally a positive indicator for short-term rental investment. Conversely, stagnant or declining visitor numbers should raise a red flag.

Complementing raw tourism data is an in-depth analysis of local event calendars. Major events – whether they are annual festivals, sporting championships, music concerts, academic conferences, or significant business expos – can dramatically spike demand for accommodation in their surrounding areas. Properties located within a reasonable proximity to venues hosting these events can command premium rates and achieve near-perfect occupancy during event periods. This requires proactive research. Start by identifying the major recurring events in a city or region. Then, investigate the schedules for these events in the upcoming year or two. Are there any new, large-scale events being planned that could attract a significant influx of visitors? Websites like Eventbrite, local convention bureau sites, and even university event listings can be excellent sources of this information. It's not just about the large-scale events; smaller, recurring local events can also contribute to consistent demand, particularly for longer-term stays or for guests seeking a more authentic local experience. For example, a university town will experience consistent demand during graduation weeks, homecoming weekends, and move-in/move-out periods, in addition to the general flow of visiting parents and prospective students.

Proximity to attractions is another non-negotiable factor. These attractions can be diverse, ranging from world-renowned landmarks and museums to natural wonders, theme parks, popular business districts, or even specialized venues like medical centers or universities. Guests booking short-term rentals often prioritize convenience and the ability to easily access the places they wish to visit. A property located within walking distance or a short drive/public transport ride to key attractions will inherently be more desirable. When evaluating a location, map out the prime attractions and consider the travel time from potential rental properties. Online mapping tools like Google Maps are invaluable for this, allowing you to assess walking distances, driving times, and the availability of public transportation routes. Consider what type of attractions are prevalent in an area. Are they primarily tourist-focused, business-oriented, or perhaps geared towards families? This will help you define your target guest.

The efficiency and accessibility of transportation hubs are also critical determinants of a location's demand. Guests, especially those traveling from afar, rely on convenient access to airports, train stations, and major highways. Properties situated in areas that are easily reachable from these hubs, and from which guests can easily navigate the local area, are likely to be more successful. Think about the entire guest journey, from arrival to departure. Is it easy for them to get from the airport to the property? Once at the property, can they easily access public transport to explore the city or reach their destination? Proximity to major interstates, international airports, and well-connected public transit systems (subway, light rail, bus networks) significantly enhances a property's appeal. Moreover, consider the local traffic patterns. A property might be close to an attraction, but if it's located in an area notorious for severe traffic congestion, it could detract from its appeal.

Leveraging online tools and demographic information is essential for forecasting guest demand. The digital age offers a wealth of data that can inform your location selection. Beyond the general tourism statistics, platforms like AirDNA, Mashvisor, and AllThe-Rooms provide granular data on short-term rental performance, including average daily rates (ADR), occupancy rates, booking trends, and competitor analysis for specific neighborhoods and cities. These platforms aggregate data from various booking sites, offering insights into which areas are performing well and why. By analyzing this data, you can identify markets with strong demand and potentially less competition, or conversely, understand the competitive landscape in established markets.

Demographic information can also paint a picture of potential guest demand. Consider the age, income, and lifestyle of the population in and around a potential location. Is it a vibrant city center attracting young professionals and tourists? Is it a family-friendly suburban area with good schools and parks? Is it a retirement community with seasonal visitors? Each demographic group has different travel needs and preferences. Understanding the dominant demographics of an area can help you tailor your property and marketing efforts to attract the right guests. For instance, if an area is heavily populated by young professionals, demand might be higher for modern, well-equipped apartments with good Wi-Fi and proximity to nightlife and business centers. If it's a family-oriented area, demand might be for larger homes with amenities like backyards, proximity to parks, and kid-friendly attractions.

Crucially, you must define your target traveler and ensure your chosen location aligns with their booking potential and the rates you can command. Are you aiming for the business traveler seeking a convenient, home-like environment for longer stays? If so, locations near corporate offices, convention centers, or universities with strong visiting academic communities would be ideal. Are you targeting the leisure traveler looking for a vacation experience? Then, proximity to tourist attractions, entertainment venues, and recreational areas is paramount. For families, factors like safety, proximity to parks, family-friendly attractions, and sufficient space are key. Each target segment will have different priorities when choosing accommodation, and thus different preferences for location.

For example, consider a coastal town. If your target traveler is the summer tourist seeking beach access, then a property right on the beach or within a short walk would be ideal. However, if your target is the off-season traveler interested in hiking and exploring local wineries, a property slightly inland but close to these attractions might be more suitable and potentially more affordable to acquire.

Furthermore, the concept of "demand" isn't static; it evolves. What might be a high-demand location today could become saturated or less desirable in the future due to changes in local economies, new developments, or shifting travel trends. Therefore, an element of forward-thinking is required. Research planned infrastructure projects, new business openings, or upcoming cultural developments that could increase the appeal of a particular area. For instance, a new convention center or a major sports stadium being built could significantly boost demand in its vicinity. Similarly, a city investing in revitalizing its downtown core or developing new public parks can attract more visitors. This foresight can help you get ahead of the curve and invest in areas with potential for future growth.

When evaluating potential locations, don't overlook the importance of seasonality. Some areas experience extreme peaks and troughs in demand throughout the year. While a location with strong seasonal demand can be very profitable during its peak season, it can also lead to periods of zero occupancy and income. Assess whether the seasonality aligns with your financial goals and risk tolerance. Are you looking for consistent year-round income, or can you manage the fluctuations?

Some locations might offer a more balanced demand profile throughout the year due to factors like business travel, university activity, or a mix of attractions that appeal to different travelers at different times.

The process of identifying high-demand locations is an ongoing one. It requires continuous monitoring of market trends, competitor activity, and local developments. Even after acquiring a property, staying informed about changes in the area that could impact demand is crucial for maintaining and enhancing your rental's performance. This diligent research and analysis at the foundational stage will significantly increase your chances of selecting a property in a location that consistently attracts guests, thereby maximizing your investment's potential and laying the groundwork for a thriving short-term rental business. It's about making an informed decision based on data and foresight, rather than just a gut feeling, to ensure your property is positioned for success in the competitive short-term rental landscape. Understanding the ecosystem of a location – the attractions, the events, the transport, and the people who visit – is paramount to unlocking its revenue potential.

Navigating Local Regulations and Compliance

Navigating the intricate web of local regulations and ensuring full compliance is not merely a suggestion; it is an absolute imperative for any aspiring or established short-term rental operator. The regulatory landscape for short-term rentals, often referred to as "Airbnb laws," "vacation rental ordinances," or "homestay rules," is a complex and ever-evolving mosaic that differs dramatically from one municipality to another, and sometimes even within different neighborhoods of the same city. Failure to understand and adhere to these often-specific rules can result in substantial fines, the suspension or revocation of operating permits, and, in severe cases, legal action that could jeopardize your entire investment. Therefore, a thorough and proactive approach to researching and complying with local laws must be an integral part of your foundational strategy, commencing long before you list your property.

The first and most critical step in this compliance journey is to identify the specific governing bodies responsible for short-term rental regulations in your chosen location. This typically involves your city, county, and potentially even state government. Many municipalities have dedicated departments or agencies that oversee hospitality, business licensing, or planning and zoning, which are often the primary points of contact. A good starting point is the official website of the city or county where your property is located. Search for terms like "short-term rental regulations," "vacation rental ordinance," "homestay rules," "business license," or "lodging tax." These searches should lead you to official documents, such as municipal codes, ordinances, and application forms. If the information online is unclear or incomplete, don't hesitate to reach out directly to these departments. A phone call or an email to the city clerk's office, the planning department, or the business licensing division can often provide the most accurate and up-to-date guidance. Some cities even have dedicated short-term rental administrators or ombudsmen whose sole purpose is to assist operators with understanding and navigating these rules.

A common regulatory requirement across many jurisdictions is the necessity of obtaining a business license. This license signifies that you are operating a legitimate business within the municipality. The application process for a business license typically involves providing details about your business structure, contact information, and the physical address of the property. There may be a fee associated with obtaining and renewing this license. Beyond a general business license, many cities also require a specific short-term rental permit or license. This often involves a more detailed application process, which may include property inspections to ensure compliance with safety codes, such as fire safety, smoke detectors, carbon monoxide detectors, and clear exit pathways. Some ordinances may also mandate specific amenities, such as a certain number of fire extinguishers or first-aid kits. The cost and renewal frequency of these permits will vary significantly. For example, some cities might charge an annual fee for a permit, while others may have a one-time application fee with no recurring cost for the permit itself, though business license renewals might still apply.

Zoning laws are another significant area of regulation that can impact short-term rental operations. Zoning ordinances dictate how land can be used within specific districts of a city or county. Some residential zoning areas may prohibit or severely restrict short-term rentals altogether, classifying them as commercial activities that are incompatible with single-family or multi-family residential neighborhoods. Other areas might allow short-term rentals but with specific limitations, such as caps on the number of days a property can be rented out per year, restrictions on the number of guests allowed, or requirements that the primary resident must be present during the rental period (often referred to as "hosted" or "homestay" rentals). It's crucial to understand the zoning classification of your property and whether short-term rentals are permitted in that zone, and if so, under what conditions. Zoning violations can lead to significant penalties, including being forced to cease operations. Researching zoning ordinances usually involves accessing the municipal planning or zoning department's resources, which often include zoning maps and detailed codebooks.

Tax obligations are a critical component of short-term rental compliance that many new hosts underestimate. You will likely be responsible for collecting and remitting various taxes to the relevant government entities. The most common are occupancy taxes, also known as lodging taxes, hotel taxes, or transient occupancy taxes (TOT). These taxes are typically levied on the gross rental income and are paid by the guest, collected by you, and then remitted to the local government. The rates for these taxes can vary widely, from a few percent to over 10% of the rental income. Many platforms like Airbnb and Vrbo have programs that automatically collect and remit these taxes on behalf of hosts in many jurisdictions, but it is your responsibility to verify that this is happening correctly and to understand if there are any taxes that the platform does not cover. In addition to local occupancy taxes, you may also be liable for state sales tax or other forms of tourism taxes. Furthermore, as a business owner, you will also need to consider your income tax obligations. Rental income is taxable, and you will need to report it on your personal or business tax returns. You may also be able to deduct certain expenses associated with operating your short-term rental, such as mortgage interest, property taxes, insurance, utilities, cleaning fees, and maintenance costs. Consulting with a tax professional experienced in real estate or short-term rentals is highly advisable to ensure you are meeting all your tax obligations accurately and taking advantage of all eligible deductions.

Beyond these core regulatory areas, many cities have implemented specific rules tailored to short-term rentals. These can include:

Minimum Stay Requirements: Some ordinances mandate that short-term rentals must have a minimum number of nights, such as two or three consecutive nights, to differentiate them from traditional hotel stays and potentially curb nuisance activity.

Guest Limits: Regulations often specify the maximum number of guests allowed to stay at a property, which can be based on the number of bedrooms, sleeping arrangements, or a fixed number. This is often tied to fire safety and local capacity concerns.

Owner-Occupancy Requirements: As mentioned earlier, some regulations permit short-term rentals only if the primary resident is on the property during the rental period. This is a common approach to maintain the residential character of neighborhoods.

Advertising Restrictions: In some areas, there may be rules about how short-term rentals can be advertised, including requirements to display permit numbers in listings.

Noise and Nuisance Ordinances: While these are general ordinances, they are often more stringently enforced for short-term rentals. Hosts are typically responsible for ensuring their guests comply with local noise restrictions, parking rules, and other community standards. Many cities have "good neighbor policies" or specific complaint hotlines for issues related to short-term rentals.

Safety Standards: Beyond basic fire codes, some jurisdictions may have specific safety requirements for short-term rentals, such as mandatory inspections, specific types of window locks, or requirements for guest contact information to be readily available.

Data Reporting: Some cities require hosts to report rental activity and guest information periodically to the local government. This is often done through a portal managed by the city or a third-party platform.

License Caps and Lotteries: In highly sought-after or heavily regulated markets, cities may implement caps on the total number of short-term rental licenses issued. This can lead to waiting lists or lottery systems for new operators.

The process of researching these regulations should be a continuous one. Laws can change, and new ordinances are frequently introduced in response to evolving markets and community concerns.

Staying informed requires ongoing vigilance. Subscribe to email alerts from your city or county government, follow local news outlets that cover policy changes, and engage with local short-term rental industry associations if they exist. These groups often provide valuable updates and advocacy regarding regulations. When in doubt, always err on the side of caution and seek clarification from the appropriate government agencies. Operating a short-term rental legally and compliantly is not just about avoiding penalties; it's about building a sustainable and reputable business that contributes positively to the community. It fosters trust with guests, neighbors, and local authorities, setting a strong foundation for long-term success.

To effectively navigate this complex landscape, consider developing a checklist of essential compliance items. This might include: obtaining a business license, securing a short-term rental permit, verifying zoning permissions, understanding and implementing guest rules related to noise and waste disposal, ensuring all safety equipment is present and functional, and establishing a system for collecting and remitting taxes. Keep meticulous records of all licenses, permits, tax payments, and communications with regulatory bodies. This documentation is invaluable not only for compliance but also for demonstrating your commitment to operating responsibly should any questions or concerns arise from neighbors or local officials.

Furthermore, understanding the "spirit" behind the regulations is crucial. Many regulations are enacted to address concerns about housing affordability, neighborhood character, public safety, and the impact of short-term rentals on the traditional hospitality industry. By operating your short-term rental in a manner that respects these concerns—by being a good neighbor, prioritizing guest safety, and contributing your fair share in taxes—you are more likely to operate successfully and sustainably in the long run. Building positive relationships with your neighbors, for instance, by introducing yourself and providing them with your contact information in case of any issues, can go a long way in preempting complaints and fostering a harmonious living environment. This proactive community engagement is as vital as understanding the written laws.

It is also worth noting that the definition of "short-term rental" itself can vary. Some jurisdictions might differentiate between a "home-stay" (where the host lives on-site) and an "unhosted" or "full-time" rental (where the host does not live on-site). The rules and permit requirements often differ significantly between these two models. Ensure you understand which category your intended operation falls into and comply with the specific regulations for that category. For instance, if you plan to rent out a room in your primary residence while you are still living there, you will likely face a different set of rules and possibly fewer restrictions than if you are renting out a separate property that you do not occupy.

The due diligence required to master local regulations should be seen as an investment in your business's future. It's an upfront effort that pays dividends by preventing costly fines, legal battles, and reputational damage. It also provides peace of mind, allowing you to focus on providing excellent guest experiences and growing your business, rather than constantly worrying about potential legal repercussions. Always remember that ignorance of the law is never a valid defense. Therefore, treat compliance not as a hurdle, but as a fundamental operational principle, ensuring your short-term rental venture is built on a solid and legally sound foundation.

Financial Modeling Forecasting Your Returns

The preceding discussion has underscored the paramount importance of regulatory compliance, establishing a firm understanding of the legal framework as the bedrock upon which a successful short-term rental business is built. Now, with the legal landscape charted, the focus shifts to the equally critical domain of financial viability. Before a single dollar is committed to a property, or indeed, before even the most exhaustive regulatory research reaches its conclusion, the development of a robust financial model is not merely advisable; it is indispensable. This model serves as your financial compass, guiding you through the decision-making process by projecting the potential income and expenses associated with a short-term rental investment, thereby painting a clear picture of its profitability and return on investment. Without this crucial step, you are essentially navigating blindfolded, leaving your capital vulnerable to unforeseen financial pitfalls.

At the heart of any financial model for a short-term rental property lies the projection of revenue. This is a multi-faceted calculation that begins with understanding two key variables: the Average Daily Rate (ADR) and the projected occupancy rate. The ADR is the average price you expect to charge per night. To determine a realistic ADR, you must conduct thorough market research. Analyze comparable properties in your target area – those with similar amenities, sizes, locations, and levels of finish. Look at their nightly rates on platforms like Airbnb, Vrbo, Booking.com, and any other relevant booking sites. Consider seasonal fluctuations; rates will invariably be higher during peak tourist seasons, holidays, and local event periods, and lower during off-peak times. A well-researched ADR will also account for dynamic pricing strategies, where you adjust rates based on demand, day of the week, and specific events. Avoid simply picking a number; instead, aim for an average that reflects a data-driven approach. For instance, if your research indicates that similar properties charge $150 per night on weekdays, $200 on Fridays and Saturdays, and $250 during a local festival week, you'll need to establish a weighted average based on the anticipated frequency of each rate.

The second crucial element of revenue projection is the occupancy rate. This is the percentage of nights your property is expected to be booked over a given period, typically a year. Again, market research is key. What is the average occupancy rate for comparable short-term rentals in your area? Consider factors like seasonality, local demand drivers (tourism, business travel, events), and the competitive landscape. A newly established listing might initially have a lower occupancy rate as it builds reviews and visibility, while a well-established property with a strong reputation might achieve higher rates. It is prudent to create scenarios: a conservative estimate (e.g., 50-60% occupancy), a realistic projection (e.g., 65-75% occupancy), and an optimistic outlook (e.g., 80%+ occupancy). For example, if your target property is in a popular beach town with a strong summer season but a quieter winter, your annual occupancy rate will reflect this seasonality. If you project an ADR of $175 and a realistic occupancy rate of 70%, your gross annual revenue would be calculated as: $175 (ADR)

365 (days) 0.70 (occupancy rate) = $44,887.50.

However, revenue is only half of the financial equation. The other, often more complex, part is accurately estimating your expenses. These can be broadly categorized into fixed costs (those that remain relatively constant regardless of occupancy) and variable costs (those that fluctuate with bookings).

Fixed costs typically include:

Mortgage Payments: If you are financing the property, your principal and interest payments are a significant fixed cost. Ensure you have the exact figures from your loan agreement.

Property Taxes: These are usually assessed annually but are often paid in installments. Research the specific tax rate for your property's location and current assessed value.

Insurance: Short-term rental insurance is distinct from standard homeowner's insurance and is crucial. Obtain quotes from providers specializing in the short-term rental market. Premiums can vary based on location, property value, and coverage levels.

HOA/Condo Fees: If the property is part of a Homeowners Association or condominium complex, these regular fees are a fixed expense.

Software Subscriptions: You may subscribe to pricing tools, channel managers, or smart lock systems, which often have monthly or annual fees.

Licensing and Permit Fees: As discussed previously, these initial and recurring fees are part of your operational costs.

Variable costs, on the other hand, are directly tied to guest stays and property usage:

Utilities: Electricity, gas, water, and internet costs will increase with occupancy. While not strictly variable in the sense of a per-booking charge, they are highly correlated with usage and thus guest presence. You'll need to estimate based on the property's size, age, and local utility rates, possibly adjusting upwards from typical residential usage.

Cleaning Fees: This is one of the most significant variable costs. You will need to factor in the cost of professional cleaning between each guest turnover. Obtain quotes from local cleaning services that specialize in short-term rentals. The cost will depend on the size of the property and the level of cleaning required.

Supplies: This includes essentials like toilet paper, paper towels, soap, shampoo, coffee, tea, and any welcome amenities. Budget for restocking these items for each guest.

Maintenance and Repairs: Even with careful management, wear and tear are inevitable. Set aside a monthly budget for general maintenance, such as minor plumbing fixes, paint touch-ups, or appliance servicing. Larger, unexpected repairs can also occur, so having a contingency fund is wise.

Guest Turnover Costs: This can include restocking toiletries, replacing linens or towels if they become damaged, and minor amenity replenishment.

Platform Fees: Booking platforms like Airbnb and Vrbo charge service fees, typically a percentage of the booking total. You'll need to account for these as a direct deduction from your revenue.

Property Management Fees: If you hire a property manager, their fees (often a percentage of revenue) will be a significant variable cost.

Taxes (beyond property tax): This includes occupancy taxes (collected from guests but remitted by you) and income taxes. While occupancy taxes are collected from guests, their administration and remittance have associated costs. Your income tax liability will be a percentage of your net profit.

To create a tangible financial model, spreadsheets are your best friend. Many investors build custom spreadsheets, while others leverage templates available online or within accounting software. A typical financial model would include sections for:

1. Property Information: Address, size, number of bedrooms/bathrooms, key amenities.

2. Acquisition Costs (if applicable): Purchase price, closing costs, initial renovation/furnishing budget.

3. Revenue Projections:

Average Daily Rate (ADR) by season/day type.

Projected Occupancy Rate (annual, and potentially monthly to account for seasonality).

Gross Rental Income.

Platform Fees (as a percentage of gross income).

Net Rental Income (Gross Rental Income minus Platform Fees).

4. Operating Expenses:

Mortgage Payment (P&I).

Property Taxes.

Insurance Premiums.

Utilities (estimated monthly averages, potentially adjusted for occupancy).

Cleaning Fees (calculated as cost per cleaning x number of turnovers).

Supplies & Amenities (budgeted monthly).

Maintenance & Repairs (budgeted monthly).

HOA/Condo Fees.

Software/Technology Costs.

Licensing/Permit Renewals.

Property Management Fees (if applicable).

Other miscellaneous operating expenses.

5. Profitability Calculations:

Gross Profit: Net Rental Income - Total Operating Expenses (excluding mortgage interest and depreciation).

Net Operating Income (NOI): Net Rental Income - Total Operating Expenses.

Cash Flow Before Debt Service: NOI.

Cash Flow After Debt Service: NOI - Mortgage Principal & Interest.

Net Profit: Cash Flow After Debt Service - Income Taxes (estimated).

6. Return on Investment (ROI) Metrics:

Cash-on-Cash Return: (Annual Cash Flow After Debt Service / Total Cash Invested) 100%. Total cash invested includes down payment, closing costs, initial renovations, and furnishings. This metric is crucial for understanding the return on the cash you've put into the deal.

Capitalization Rate (Cap Rate): (Net Operating Income / Property Value or Total Investment Cost) 100%. Cap rate is a measure of profitability relative to the property's value, ignoring financing. It's a common metric for comparing real estate investments.

Internal Rate of Return (IRR): A more sophisticated metric that considers the time value of money over the entire holding period of the investment. While more complex to calculate without specialized software, it provides a more comprehensive view of long-term profitability.

Let's illustrate with a hypothetical example. Assume you're considering a property with the following financial parameters:

Purchase Price: $300,000

Down Payment: 20% ($60,000)

Closing Costs: $10,000

Initial Furnishing & Renovation Budget: $20,000

Total Cash Invested: $90,000

Mortgage: $240,000 at 6% interest over 30 years (approx. $1,439 per month P&I)

Annual Property Taxes: $3,600 ($300/month)

Annual Insurance: $1,500 ($125/month)

Annual HOA Fees: $2,400 ($200/month)

Estimated Annual Utilities (total): $3,000 ($250/month)

Estimated Annual Cleaning Costs: $10,000 (assuming $125 per cleaning and 80 turnovers)

Estimated Annual Supplies & Amenities: $2,000 ($167/month)

Estimated Annual Maintenance: $1,800 ($150/month)

Property Management Fee: 15% of gross revenue.

Platform Fees: 3% of gross revenue.

Projected ADR: $180

Projected Occupancy Rate: 70%

Revenue Calculation:

Gross Rental Income = $180　365　0.70 = $46,000.50

Platform Fees = $46,000.50　0.03 = $1,380.02

Property Management Fees = $46,000.50　0.15 = $6,900.08

Net Rental Income = $46,000.50 - $1,380.02 - $6,900.08 = $37,720.40

Expense Calculation:

Mortgage (P&I) = $1,439　12 = $17,268

Property Taxes = $3,600

Insurance = $1,500

HOA Fees = $2,400

Utilities = $3,000

Cleaning Costs = $10,000

Supplies & Amenities = $2,000

Maintenance = $1,800

Total Operating Expenses = $17,268 + $3,600 + $1,500 + $2,400 + $3,000 + $10,000 + $2,000 + $1,800 = $41,568

Profitability Calculation:

Net Operating Income (NOI) = Net Rental Income - Operating Expenses (excluding mortgage P&I for this calculation, as it's a financing cost, not an operating cost in the pure sense for NOI, but we'll use total cash outflow later)

Let's calculate Cash Flow Before Tax: Net Rental Income ($37,720.40) - Operating Expenses (excluding mortgage) ($3,600 + $1,500 + $2,400 + $3,000 + $10,000 + $2,000 + $1,800 = $24,300).

Cash Flow Before Debt Service = $37,720.40 - $24,300 = $13,42
0.40

Cash Flow After Debt Service (Before Tax) = $13,420.40 - $17,268
(Mortgage P&I) = -$3,847.60

In this hypothetical scenario, the property is projected to have a negative cash flow of $3,847.60 annually before considering income taxes. This highlights the critical nature of the financial model. It's not just about identifying potential profits; it's about uncovering potential losses

before you invest.

Let's revisit the ROI metrics with these numbers:

Cash-on-Cash Return: (Annual Cash Flow After Debt Service / Total Cash Invested) 100% = (-$3,847.60 / $90,000) 100% = -4.28%. This indicates a negative return on your invested cash.

This example, while illustrating a negative outcome, emphasizes the power of modeling. It prompts questions: Can the ADR be increased? Can occupancy be improved? Are there ways to reduce expenses, such as finding cheaper cleaning services or optimizing utility usage? Perhaps the initial renovation budget needs to be higher to command a better ADR. Or, maybe the purchase price is too high for the expected returns in that market.

Sensitivity analysis is a vital component of financial modeling. This involves changing one or more variables to see how it affects the overall profitability. For instance, what if the occupancy rate drops to 60%? Or what if cleaning costs increase by 10%? Or if the ADR can be pushed to $190? Running these scenarios helps you understand the risks and the potential upside of your investment. It forces you to think critically about the assumptions you're making. For instance, a sensitivity analysis might reveal that if occupancy drops by 10%, your cash flow turns significantly negative, suggesting that the business model is too reliant on high occupancy. Conversely, a small increase in ADR might dramatically improve profitability, indicating that pricing strategy is a key lever.

It is also crucial to factor in vacancy periods that are not due to low demand but rather to necessary maintenance, upgrades, or personal use. If you plan to use the property yourself for a week or two each year, or if you anticipate a week for deep cleaning and maintenance, these days should be factored into your occupancy calculations, effectively reducing the number of bookable days. For example, if you have 365 days in a year but plan to use it for 7 days and schedule 7 days for maintenance, your maximum bookable days are 351, and your occupancy calculation should be based on this number rather than 365.

Furthermore, don't forget the cost of capital. If you're investing cash, the opportunity cost of that cash is also a consideration. If that cash could have earned 5% in a relatively safe investment, then your short-term rental needs to generate a return significantly higher than that to justify the added risk and effort.

Building a financial model is an iterative process. It requires diligent research, realistic assumptions, and a willingness to adjust based on the data. It's not a one-time exercise; as market conditions change, or as you gain more operating experience with a specific property, you should revisit and update your model. This continuous refinement ensures your financial strategy remains aligned with the evolving realities of the short-term rental market, paving the way for sustainable profitability and a strong return on your investment. The detailed projections created through this financial modeling exercise will also be invaluable when seeking financing from lenders or investors, as it demonstrates a thorough understanding of the business and its potential financial outcomes.

Securing the Right Financing and Insurance

Having meticulously crafted your financial projections and thoroughly understood the regulatory landscape, the next critical step in establishing a successful short-term rental business is to secure the necessary capital and robust insurance coverage. These two pillars are fundamental to both the acquisition of your investment property and its ongoing protection against a myriad of potential risks. Without adequate financing, even the most promising opportunity can remain out of reach, while insufficient insurance can leave your entire investment vulnerable to catastrophic loss.

Financing Your Short-Term Rental Investment

The path to acquiring a property for short-term rental operation typically involves one or a combination of financing strategies. While outright cash purchase is an option for some, the majority of investors rely on debt financing to leverage their capital and increase their potential return on investment. Understanding the nuances of different loan products is paramount to making an informed decision that aligns with your financial goals and risk tolerance.

1. Traditional Mortgages:

For many, the first avenue explored is the traditional residential mortgage. However, it's crucial to understand that purchasing a property with the express intent of operating a short-term rental business can sometimes fall outside the standard guidelines for conventional 30-year fixed-rate mortgages. Lenders often have specific rules regarding owner occupancy and the intended use of the property. If you plan to live in the property for a portion of the year and rent it out when you're not present, this might be permissible under certain owner-occupied loan programs. However, if your sole intention is to purchase the property as an investment and rent it out exclusively to short-term guests, you will likely be subject to investor loan programs.

Investor loans typically come with slightly higher interest rates and often require a larger down payment compared to owner-occupied loans. Expect down payment requirements to range from 20% to 25%, and sometimes even higher, depending on the lender and your financial profile. Creditworthiness plays a significant role, so a strong credit score, a stable income history, and a manageable debt-to-income ratio are essential. It is advisable to shop around with multiple lenders, including banks, credit unions, and mortgage brokers, to compare rates, terms, and fees. Don't hesitate to discuss your specific intent to use the property for short-term rentals upfront, as transparency is key to avoiding issues down the line. Some lenders may have restrictions on the number of days a property can be rented out annually if they classify it under a residential mortgage product.

2. Investment Property Loans (Non-Owner Occupied):

These loans are specifically designed for individuals purchasing properties that will not be their primary residence, and they are the most common route for pure investment properties, including those intended for short-term rentals. As mentioned, expect higher interest rates and larger down payment requirements than for owner-occupied homes. The approval process will heavily scrutinize your financial stability, including your credit history, income, assets, and existing debt obligations. Lenders will also assess the potential rental income of the property, often requiring you to provide market analysis and projected rental figures, which underscores the importance of your earlier financial modeling.

3. Portfolio Loans:

For investors looking to acquire multiple properties, particularly those with a diverse portfolio, portfolio loans can be an attractive option. These loans are secured by the borrower's entire portfolio of investment properties rather than a single property. This can offer more flexibility in terms of loan-to-value ratios and repayment structures. Lenders offering portfolio loans often look at the overall performance of your real estate assets and your experience as an investor. This type of financing is typically sought by more experienced investors and may require a substantial existing portfolio.

4. Hard Money Loans:

Hard money loans are short-term, asset-based loans typically provided by private investors or companies rather than traditional financial institutions. They are characterized by faster closing times and more flexible qualification criteria, making them suitable for situations where speed is critical or traditional financing is not readily available. However, hard money loans come with significantly higher interest rates and origination fees, and they usually have shorter repayment terms (e.g., 6-24 months). These loans are often used to acquire and renovate a property quickly, with the intention of refinancing into a traditional mortgage once the improvements are complete and the property is operational. Given their cost, they are best used strategically for specific situations, such as purchasing a distressed property that requires immediate renovation before it can be rented.

5. Small Business Administration (SBA) Loans:

While not typically for direct property acquisition for short-term rentals, SBA loans can sometimes be utilized indirectly. For instance, if you are establishing a larger hospitality business that includes short-term rental properties as part of a broader service offering, an SBA loan might be applicable for business expansion or working capital. However, direct purchase of a single rental property for passive income is rarely financed through SBA loans.

6. Private Investors and Crowdfunding:

As your investment portfolio grows, you might also consider securing capital from private investors or through real estate crowdfunding platforms. Private investors can provide capital in exchange for
equity in the property or a share of the profits. Crowdfunding platforms allow you to pool funds from multiple smaller investors. Both
options require a well-structured business plan, clear profit-sharing
agreements, and a thorough understanding of securities regulations.

Key Considerations When Securing Financing:

Down Payment: The larger your down payment, the lower your
loan-to-value ratio, which generally leads to better interest rates and
lower monthly payments. It also signifies a stronger commitment to
the investment.

Interest Rates and Fees: Compare interest rates, origination fees,
appraisal fees, closing costs, and any other associated charges from
multiple lenders. A seemingly small difference in interest rate can
translate to thousands of dollars over the life of the loan.

Loan Terms: Understand the repayment period, whether the interest rate is fixed or adjustable, and any prepayment penalties.

Lender Relationship: Building a good relationship with a lender
who understands real estate investments, particularly the short-term
rental market, can be invaluable for future financing needs.

Securing Adequate Insurance Coverage

Once you have secured the financing and are ready to acquire or are
in possession of your short-term rental property, ensuring it is adequately insured is not just a prudent step; it is a contractual necessity
with most mortgage lenders and absolutely vital for protecting your
business from financial ruin. The insurance needs for a short-term
rental property differ significantly from those of a standard homeowner's policy.

1. Landlord Insurance (Dwelling Fire Policy):

A standard homeowner's policy explicitly excludes coverage for commercial activities, including renting out your property on a short-term basis. If a claim arises from an incident occurring while the property is being rented out, your homeowner's insurance will likely deny coverage. Landlord insurance, often referred to as a dwelling fire policy, is designed for property owners who rent out their homes. It typically covers the physical structure of the building against perils like fire, windstorms, and vandalism. It may also offer some liability protection. However, standard landlord policies often have limitations regarding short-term rentals. Many will only cover long-term tenants (typically 30 days or more) and will not provide adequate coverage for frequent guest turnovers and the associated risks of short-term stays.

2. Specific Short-Term Rental Insurance:

This is the most appropriate and comprehensive type of insurance for your venture. Policies specifically designed for short-term rentals acknowledge the unique risks associated with operating a business on your property. These policies usually include broader coverage for:

Property Damage: Covers damage to the dwelling, other structures (like sheds or garages), and personal property (furniture, appliances, fixtures) due to covered events. This often includes accidental damage by guests, which might not be covered under a standard landlord policy.

Loss of Rental Income (Business Interruption): If your property becomes uninhabitable due to a covered event (e.g., a fire), this coverage replaces the rental income you would have earned during the period of repair. This is critical for maintaining cash flow during unexpected downtime.

Liability Protection: This is arguably the most important component for short-term rentals. It protects you financially if a guest is injured on your property and holds you responsible. This can include slip-and-fall incidents, injuries from faulty equipment, or other accidents. Adequate liability coverage is essential, as lawsuits can be financially devastating. Look for policies offering at least $1 million in liability coverage, and consider umbrella policies for even greater protection.

Guest-Caused Damage: Some policies offer specific protection for damage caused by guests, whether accidental or malicious, which is a common concern in short-term rentals.

Contents Coverage: Ensures that your furniture, linens, kitchenware, and other personal belongings within the rental unit are covered against damage or theft.

3. Umbrella Insurance (Excess Liability):

Given the potential for significant liability claims in the short-term rental business, it is highly recommended to supplement your primary short-term rental insurance with an umbrella policy. This provides an additional layer of liability coverage above the limits of your homeowner's, auto, and short-term rental policies. For example, if your short-term rental policy has $1 million in liability coverage, an umbrella policy with an additional $1 million or $2 million can protect you from claims that exceed your primary policy's limits.

4. Commercial Auto Insurance (if applicable):

If you use a vehicle primarily for your short-term rental business (e.g., transporting supplies, meeting guests), you may need commercial auto insurance rather than personal auto insurance. Personal policies often exclude coverage for business-related use of a vehicle.

5. Workers' Compensation (if hiring staff):

If you hire employees directly, such as cleaners or property managers who are not independent contractors, you will likely be required by law to carry workers' compensation insurance. This covers medical expenses and lost wages for employees injured on the job.

Choosing the Right Insurer:

Specialization: Seek out insurance companies that specialize in short-term rental or hospitality insurance. They understand the specific risks and offer tailored policies. Major insurance providers often have specific divisions or partner with agencies that cater to this market.

Policy Comparison: Obtain quotes from multiple specialized insurers. Compare coverage limits, deductibles, exclusions, and premiums carefully. Don't choose solely based on price; ensure the coverage meets your needs.

Policy Review: Thoroughly read and understand your insurance policy. Pay close attention to exclusions, definitions of covered events, and claim procedures. If anything is unclear, ask your insurance agent for clarification.

Disclose Accurate Information: Be truthful and accurate when providing information to your insurer. Misrepresenting the nature of your property's use can lead to denied claims. Clearly state that the property will be used for short-term rentals.

Regular Updates: As your business grows or market conditions change, review your insurance coverage annually to ensure it remains adequate.

By diligently securing the appropriate financing and ensuring comprehensive insurance coverage, you build a robust financial and protective framework for your short-term rental endeavor. This proactive approach not only safeguards your investment but also provides the peace of mind necessary to focus on growing your business and delivering exceptional guest experiences. The capital secured will fund the acquisition and preparation of your property, while the insurance policies act as a critical shield against the inherent risks of operating a hospitality business.

Chapter Two

Crafting Your Winning Property: Design and Setup

Designing For Guest Experience and Reviews

The foundation of any successful short-term rental business is a property that not only meets the basic needs of travelers but actively delights them. In the competitive landscape of vacation rentals, a thoughtfully designed space is often the deciding factor between a one-time guest and a loyal, returning customer who leaves glowing reviews. This section delves into the art and science of crafting an interior that prioritizes the guest experience, directly translating into the positive feedback that fuels bookings and elevates your property's standing. We will explore the crucial design elements that resonate with guests, from the initial impression they receive upon entering to the subtle touches that make their stay memorable and comfortable.

The guest experience begins the moment a potential renter views your listing online, but it is truly cemented when they step through your door. Creating a welcoming and inviting atmosphere is paramount. This starts with an immediate sensory experience. Consider the entryway – it's the first physical interaction a guest has with your property. A clean, well-lit entrance, perhaps with a tasteful welcome mat and a subtle scent, sets a positive tone. Inside, the overall aesthetic should be cohesive and appealing. While trends can be tempting, it's generally best to aim for a timeless design that appeals to a broad range of tastes. Think of a style that feels both current and comfortable, avoiding anything too niche or polarizing. Neutrals often form a solid base, allowing for pops of color and personality through carefully chosen decor.

When selecting furniture, functionality and durability must walk hand-in-hand with comfort and style. For living areas, plush sofas and comfortable armchairs are essential. Guests will spend time relaxing, reading, or socializing here, so investing in quality, supportive seating is non-negotiable. Consider modular or durable fabrics that can withstand frequent use and are easy to clean. Coffee tables and side tables should be strategically placed for convenience, offering surfaces for drinks, books, or devices. In bedrooms, the bed is the centerpiece. A comfortable mattress with good quality linens is arguably the most critical element for a good night's sleep, which directly impacts guest satisfaction. Pillow-top mattresses, memory foam toppers, and a variety of pillow options (firm, soft) cater to different preferences. Crisp, clean, and comfortable bedding – think high thread count cotton or breathable linen – elevates the perceived luxury of the space. Ensure there are sufficient bedside tables with lamps for reading and easily accessible power outlets for charging electronics. Wardrobes or dressers with ample hanging space and drawers are also vital for guests staying more than a night or two.

Color palettes play a significant role in shaping the mood and atmosphere of a space. Lighter, neutral colors like whites, creams, grays, and soft beiges tend to make spaces feel larger, brighter, and more serene – qualities that travelers generally seek in a getaway. These base colors also provide a versatile backdrop that can be enhanced with accent colors through artwork, throw pillows, blankets, or decorative items. Blues and greens often evoke a sense of calm and tranquility, making them excellent choices for bedrooms or relaxation areas. Warmer tones like soft yellows or muted oranges can add a touch of coziness and energy to living spaces, but it's wise to use them judiciously as accents to avoid overwhelming the senses. Consider the natural light available in each room; a room with less natural light might benefit from warmer, lighter hues, while a sun-drenched room can handle deeper or cooler tones.

Lighting is another transformative element that often goes overlooked. A well-lit space enhances the visual appeal and functionality of every area. Layered lighting is key, combining ambient, task, and accent lighting. Ambient lighting, such as overhead fixtures or recessed lighting, provides overall illumination. Task lighting, like reading lamps beside beds or under-cabinet lights in the kitchen, is crucial for functional activities. Accent lighting, such as spotlights on artwork or wall sconces, can highlight architectural features or decorative elements, adding depth and sophistication. Dimmers are a fantastic addition, allowing guests to adjust the brightness to suit their mood, from bright and airy during the day to soft and cozy in the evening.

Natural light should be maximized through the use of sheer curtains or blinds that allow light to filter in while maintaining privacy.

Beyond the fundamental furniture and color choices, numerous amenities and thoughtful touches contribute to an exceptional guest experience. A fully equipped kitchen is a significant draw for many travelers, particularly for longer stays or families. Ensure it includes all the necessary cookware, utensils, dishes, glasses, and basic appliances like a coffee maker, toaster, and microwave. Providing a starter supply of coffee, tea, sugar, and perhaps a local treat can create a memorable "welcome" moment. Similarly, bathrooms should be stocked with essentials such as quality towels, hand soap, toilet paper, and perhaps a small selection of toiletries like shampoo, conditioner, and body wash. A hairdryer is a common and appreciated amenity.

Connectivity is no longer a luxury; it's a necessity. Reliable, high-speed Wi-Fi is absolutely essential. Clearly communicate the Wi-Fi network name and password in an easily accessible location, perhaps on a printed card on the coffee table or kitchen counter. Consider providing a smart TV with access to popular streaming services, or at least ensuring easy access to local channels. For guests who may be working remotely, a dedicated workspace with a comfortable chair and adequate lighting can be a significant differentiator.

Every detail contributes to the overall perception of value and care. This includes maintaining a high standard of cleanliness. Beyond a basic clean, think about those often-missed spots: baseboards, light fixtures, and behind furniture. Fresh, clean linens and towels are a must, and the scent of the property is also important. Avoid overpowering air fresheners; opt for a subtle, pleasant aroma or simply ensure the space is well-ventilated and odor-free. Small decorative touches can make a big impact. Artwork that complements the color scheme, plants (real or high-quality faux) to bring life into the space, and comfortable throws and accent pillows add warmth and personality. Consider the flow of the space. Furniture placement should facilitate easy movement throughout the rooms, avoiding cluttered pathways.

Functionality extends to practical considerations. Ensure there are enough accessible power outlets, especially near beds and seating areas. Coat hooks by the entrance, ample hangers in closets, and a full-length mirror in a convenient location are small but impactful additions. For properties catering to families, consider child-friendly amenities like a portable crib, high chair, or even some basic toys or books. Accessibility should also be a consideration, if feasible, with features like grab bars in bathrooms or a ramp for entry.

Achieving a balance between style, functionality, and bud-get-friendliness is the art of smart interior design for short-term rentals. You don't need to spend a fortune to create a beautiful and inviting space. Focus on versatile, durable pieces that offer good value. Consider sourcing furniture from outlets, consignment shops, or even investing in gently used, high-quality items. DIY projects can also add a personal touch and save money. For instance, painting old furniture can give it a new lease on life, and creating your own artwork can add unique flair.

Guest comfort is the ultimate goal, and this often comes down to those small, thoughtful details. Think about what would make your own stay more pleasant. Perhaps it's having a fully stocked spice rack in the kitchen, extra blankets for chilly evenings, or a selection of books and board games for entertainment. A guest book where visitors can leave notes about their stay can be a charming touch, providing valuable feedback and creating a sense of community. Even the process of check-in and check-out should be as seamless as possible. Clear, concise instructions for entry and departure, perhaps communicated via a digital lock code sent in advance, contribute to a stress-free experience.

When considering larger renovations or furniture purchases, always think about the return on investment. Would an upgraded kitchen make a significant difference in booking rates or nightly prices? Is it worth investing in a premium mattress if reviews consistently mention sleep quality? Data from your booking platform and guest feedback can guide these decisions. Pay attention to what guests praise in their reviews. If multiple guests mention the comfortable sofa or the well-equipped kitchen, you know those elements are working. Conversely, if a recurring theme is a lack of dining space or poor lighting, these are areas to prioritize for improvement.

The aesthetic should also align with the property's location and target demographic. A beach cottage might lean towards a coastal, airy design with blues and whites, while a mountain cabin would suit a more rustic, cozy theme with natural wood and warmer tones. Understanding your ideal guest and tailoring the design to their expectations can significantly enhance their experience and, by extension, your property's appeal.

Ultimately, designing for guest experience and reviews is an ongoing process. It involves anticipating guest needs, providing comfort and convenience, and injecting personality and charm into the space. By focusing on quality furnishings, thoughtful amenities, effective lighting, and a cohesive design, you create an environment that not only meets but exceeds expectations, leading to those coveted positive reviews that are the lifeblood of a thriving short-term rental business. This investment in design is not merely cosmetic; it is a strategic business decision that directly impacts profitability and long-term success. The initial outlay for good design elements pays dividends in repeat bookings, higher occupancy rates, and the invaluable word-of-mouth marketing that comes from happy guests sharing their positive experiences. It's about crafting a narrative for your property, one that unfolds through the senses and leaves a lasting impression of comfort, quality, and care, encouraging guests to return and recommend your space to others.

The Day Transformation A Practical Setup Guide

The prospect of launching a short-term rental can feel overwhelming, especially when faced with the task of transforming a vacant property into a welcoming haven for guests. The urgency to begin generating income means that efficiency and a structured approach are not just desirable, they are essential. This is where the "14-Day Transformation" comes into play – a meticulously planned roadmap designed to guide you through every critical step, ensuring your property is not only ready for guests within a fortnight but is also set up for success from the very first booking. This isn't about rushing; it's about strategic execution, focusing on the highest impact activities to achieve a fully functional, appealing, and profitable short-term rental space in a concentrated timeframe. By breaking down the process into manageable daily tasks, you can systematically tackle everything from the foundational deep clean to the final, delightful touches that elevate a house into a home-away-from-home.

Day 1-3: The Deep Dive - Cleaning and Repairs

The initial phase of the 14-day transformation is dedicated to the foundational elements: immaculate cleanliness and structural integrity. Think of these first three days as building the bedrock upon which all subsequent design and furnishing choices will rest.

Day 1: The Ultimate Deep Clean. This is not your typical weekend spruce-up. We are talking about a forensic-level clean. Begin with a top-down approach. Start in the highest points of each room – ceiling fans, light fixtures, and the tops of cabinets and door frames. Dust and grime accumulate here and will fall downwards, so cleaning them first ensures you don't have to re-clean surfaces below. Move to walls, paying close attention to baseboards, which can accumulate significant dust and scuff marks. Use a damp microfiber cloth or a vacuum cleaner with a brush attachment. For tougher scuffs, a magic eraser or a gentle all-purpose cleaner can work wonders. Windows and window frames deserve attention; clean both the interior and exterior glass for maximum light and visual appeal. Don't forget to deep clean curtains or blinds; if they are washable, launder them. If not, a thorough vacuuming with an upholstery attachment is recommended.

Bathrooms require a special focus. This means scrubbing grout lines in tiles, deep cleaning showerheads to remove mineral deposits, ensuring the toilet is sanitized inside and out, and meticulously cleaning mirrors and surfaces. Pay attention to the ventilation fan; clean its cover to ensure proper air circulation. Kitchens are another critical zone. Cabinets, inside and out, should be wiped down, paying attention to handles and edges. The oven, stovetop, refrigerator (including the interior, door seals, and drip tray), and microwave must be thoroughly cleaned. Don't overlook the dishwasher – run a cleaning cycle if possible – and the sink and faucet, polishing them to a shine.

Flooring demands significant attention. Vacuum carpets with a powerful vacuum, ideally one with a beater bar, to lift embedded dirt. For a truly transformative clean, consider renting a carpet cleaner or hiring a professional for a deep steam clean, especially if the carpets are older or stained. For hard floors, sweep or vacuum thoroughly, then mop with an appropriate cleaner for the material (e.g., hardwood cleaner, tile cleaner). Ensure you get into corners and along edges.

Day 2: Minor Repairs and Preparation. With the deep clean under-way, dedicate day two to identifying and rectifying any minor repairs. This is the time to address the small issues that, while perhaps not immediately obvious, detract from the overall impression of care and quality. Walk through each room, making a comprehensive list. This might include:

Patching and Painting: Fill any small holes from picture nails or minor drywall damage with spackle. Once dry, sand smooth and touch up with matching paint. It's advisable to have leftover paint from the original application, but if not, obtaining a sample or a quart of a closely matching shade is usually sufficient for touch-ups. Focus on high-traffic areas or visible spots.

Loose Fixtures: Tighten any loose doorknobs, cabinet handles, light switch plates, or drawer pulls.

Leaky Faucets or Running Toilets: Address any plumbing issues promptly. Even a minor drip can be an annoyance and a waste of resources.

Damaged Grout or Caulk: Re-caulk around tubs, showers, and sinks where old caulk is cracked or discolored. Re-grout any areas where grout is missing or crumbling. This significantly improves the appearance and hygiene of bathrooms.

Light Bulbs: Replace any burnt-out light bulbs. It's also a good opportunity to standardize the type and color temperature of bulbs for a consistent ambiance. Consider brighter, cooler bulbs for task areas and warmer, softer bulbs for relaxation spaces.

Door Hinges and Squeaks: Lubricate squeaky door hinges with WD-40 or a silicone spray.

Test all Appliances: Ensure the oven, stove, dishwasher, washing machine, dryer, refrigerator, and any other appliances are functioning correctly. Check the water pressure and hot water supply.

Smoke and Carbon Monoxide Detectors: Test all detectors and replace batteries if necessary. Ensure they are within their expiry dates.

Day 3: Deep Cleaning Continuation and Final Touches. This day is about completing the intensive cleaning and making final preparations for the next stages. Revisit any areas that may have been missed or require a second pass. If you hired professional carpet cleaners, this is likely when they would finish. Ensure all floors are dry and clean. Thoroughly clean the interior of all cabinets and drawers. Wipe down all surfaces one last time with a disinfectant cleaner. Clean light fixtures and ceiling fans again if any dust settled during repairs. Ensure all vents are clean and free of dust. The goal by the end of day three is a property that is impeccably clean, functional, and free of obvious disrepair. This sets a pristine canvas for decorating and furnishing.

Day 4-7: Furnishing and Decorating - Creating the Ambiance

With the cleaning and repairs complete, the focus shifts to bringing the property to life. These days are about strategic furnishing and thoughtful decor to create a space that is both attractive and functional for guests. The key here is to balance aesthetics with durability and ease of maintenance, always keeping the target guest in mind.

Day 4: The Living Area Foundation. Start with the primary living space. Position the sofa and any armchairs to create a conversational grouping. Consider the flow of traffic – ensure pathways are clear and unimpeded. Place a coffee table within easy reach of the seating and side tables next to armchairs for convenience. Ensure there are accessible power outlets for charging devices, perhaps by incorporating tables with built-in outlets or using power strips discreetly. If you haven't already, place a rug to anchor the seating area and add warmth.

Day 5: Bedrooms – Comfort is King. The bed is the most critical piece of furniture in a bedroom. Ensure your mattress is comfortable and in good condition; a mattress topper can revitalize an older mattress. Invest in good quality sheets, pillowcases, and a duvet or comforter. Provide a variety of pillows, including firm and soft options, to cater to different preferences. Bedside tables on both sides of the bed are essential, each with a functional lamp for reading. Ensure easy access to power outlets for charging phones and other devices. If space allows, a dresser or wardrobe with sufficient hangers is a must for guests staying more than a night or two.

Day 6: Kitchen and Dining Functionality. Equip the kitchen with essential cookware, utensils, dinnerware, and glassware. Think about what a guest would need to prepare a simple meal. This includes pots, pans, baking sheets, mixing bowls, knives, cutting boards, spatulas, whisks, and a can opener. Ensure there are enough place settings for the maximum occupancy of the property. The dining area, whether a dedicated table or a breakfast bar, should be functional. Ensure there are enough chairs and adequate lighting overhead.

Day 7: Bathroom Essentials and Final Decor Touches. Stock the bathrooms with plush, clean towels – at least two sets per guest capacity (bath towel, hand towel, washcloth). Provide hand soap by the sink and toilet paper. A hairdryer is a highly appreciated amenity. Consider a small selection of travel-sized toiletries like shampoo, conditioner, and body wash, especially for the initial setup. Beyond the essentials, begin layering in decorative elements. This includes artwork that complements the overall color scheme and adds personality. Plants, whether real or high-quality faux, can bring life and color to a space. Throw pillows and blankets on sofas and beds add comfort and visual appeal. Ensure all decorative items are securely placed and not fragile if children might be present.

Day 8-10: Stocking and Systems – The Practicalities

This phase focuses on ensuring the property is fully equipped with all necessary supplies and that essential systems are in place and clearly communicated to guests. These practical elements are crucial for a smooth and enjoyable stay.

Day 8: Linens, Towels, and Bedding. This is a critical area where quality matters. Ensure you have enough sets of sheets and pillowcases for each bed to allow for frequent changes between guests. Aim for at least three sets per bed to manage laundry cycles effectively. High thread count cotton or breathable linen blends are excellent choices for guest comfort. The same applies to towels – having multiple sets means you won't be caught short if a guest needs an extra. Launder all linens and towels before the first guest arrives, ensuring they are fresh and clean. Store them neatly in linen closets or designated storage areas.

Day 9: Kitchen and Cleaning Supplies. Beyond the cookware, stock the kitchen with everyday consumables. This includes coffee, tea, sugar, salt, and pepper. A small starter supply of olive oil or cooking spray can be a thoughtful addition. For cleaning, provide dish soap, dishwasher detergent, sponges, dish towels, and all-purpose cleaner. Ensure guests know where these are located. For laundry facilities (if applicable), provide laundry detergent and dryer sheets. A basic vacuum cleaner, mop, and bucket should also be readily available for any minor spills guests might need to address during their stay, along with clear instructions on their use and where to store them.

Day 10: The Tech and Welcome Pack. This day is dedicated to connectivity and guest information.

Wi-Fi: Ensure your Wi-Fi is set up, tested for speed and reliability, and that you have a clear, easy-to-find card or sign with the network name and password. Consider a mesh network if you have dead spots in the property.

Entertainment: Set up any smart TVs with access to popular streaming services (Netflix, Hulu, etc.). Ensure they are logged out of any personal accounts and provide instructions on how to use them. Cable TV is also an option, but streaming is often preferred by modern travelers.

Welcome Book/Guide: Create a comprehensive guide for your guests. This should include:

Welcome message.

Wi-Fi details.

Instructions for operating appliances (TV, coffee maker, oven, HVAC system, etc.).

Local recommendations: restaurants, attractions, grocery stores, pharmacies.

Emergency contact information (host contact, local emergency numbers).

House rules (smoking policy, pet policy, quiet hours, check-out procedures).

Information about trash and recycling disposal.

Any specific quirks of the property (e.g., how to lock a specific window, how the shower works).

A map of the local area.

Day 11-13: The Final Polish and Review

These days are about fine-tuning, staging, and preparing for the very first guest's arrival. It's the final sweep to ensure everything is perfect.

Day 11: Staging and Visual Appeal. Now that the property is furnished and stocked, it's time for staging. This involves arranging items to make the space look its best.

Table Settings: Set a few places at the dining table with placemats and cutlery.

Bed Making: Make all beds immaculately with crisp linens, a neatly folded duvet, and perfectly placed pillows.

Decorative Flourishes: Place fresh flowers or a bowl of fruit on the kitchen counter or coffee table for an immediate welcoming touch. Arrange throw pillows and blankets on sofas and beds to make them look inviting.

Lighting: Ensure all lamps are working and positioned to create a warm and inviting ambiance. Consider smart bulbs that can be controlled remotely or set on timers.

Decluttering: Do a final sweep for any personal items or clutter that may have been left behind during the setup process. Ensure all storage areas are neat and organized.

Day 12: The Guest Experience Walkthrough. Put yourself in the guest's shoes. Imagine arriving at the property.

Entry: Is the lockbox easy to find and operate? Is the key readily accessible? If using a smart lock, have you sent the code in advance? Is the entrance clean and welcoming?

Inside: Is the temperature comfortable upon arrival? Is the lighting appropriate? Are there any unusual smells? Is the welcome book clearly visible and easy to understand?

Functionality Check: Test every light switch, faucet, appliance, and remote control again. Ensure there are enough toilet paper rolls, soap, and towels. Check that the Wi-Fi is working and accessible.

Safety Check: Confirm smoke detectors and carbon monoxide detectors are functional. Ensure fire extinguishers (if provided) are accessible and charged.

Cleanliness Audit: Do a final, thorough inspection of every surface, corner, and crevice. Look for dust, smudges, or streaks that might have been missed. Ensure bathrooms and kitchens are spotless.

Day 13: Final Stocking and Contingency Planning.

Replenish Consumables: Top up coffee, tea, sugar, and any other provided consumables. Ensure there are enough trash bags and that the trash cans are empty and clean.

Check Supplies: Double-check that you have enough toilet paper, hand soap, dish soap, and cleaning supplies.

Contingency Items: Prepare a small emergency kit. This could include extra light bulbs, basic first-aid supplies (band-aids, antiseptic wipes), a multi-tool, and perhaps some extra batteries. Have a plan for how guests can reach you if something goes wrong outside of your working hours. This might involve a secondary contact or a dedicated emergency line.

Prepare Welcome Basket (Optional but Recommended): A small welcome basket with local snacks, a bottle of wine, or a thoughtful local souvenir can create a memorable first impression.

Day 14: Ready for Launch!

The 14th day marks the culmination of this intensive setup process. The property should now be thoroughly cleaned, repaired, furnished, decorated, stocked, and thoroughly inspected. All essential systems, from Wi-Fi to heating and cooling, should be operational and clearly explained to guests. Your comprehensive welcome guide should be in place, ready to orient your first visitors. The property is now transformed from a vacant space into a fully functional, inviting, and guest-ready short-term rental. This meticulous, day-by-day approach ensures that no critical detail has been overlooked, minimizing the risk of negative guest experiences and maximizing the potential for positive reviews and repeat bookings right from the start. This structured method not only saves time and reduces stress but also lays a strong foundation for a profitable and sustainable short-term rental business, proving that a focused, two-week transformation can indeed unlock immediate earning potential. The investment in this structured setup phase will pay dividends in guest satisfaction and operational efficiency for the lifetime of your rental.

Essential Amenities That Drive Bookings

The true differentiator in the competitive short-term rental market isn't just a clean space; it's a thoughtfully equipped one. Guests arrive with expectations, and meeting, then exceeding, those expectations through essential amenities is the bedrock of securing bookings and fostering glowing reviews. Think of these amenities not as mere add-ons, but as strategic investments that directly impact guest satisfaction and, consequently, your occupancy rates and revenue. While aesthetics and location are primary drivers, the tangible comforts and conveniences provided within the property are what transform a good stay into a memorable one, prompting guests to return and recommend your listing to others.

Let's delve into the categories of amenities that consistently receive positive guest feedback and are actively sought after. At the forefront is the kitchen. While not every guest plans to cook elaborate meals, a well-equipped kitchen is a significant draw. This goes beyond just having pots and pans. It means providing a comprehensive set of quality cookware, including a variety of skillet sizes, saucepans, and a Dutch oven. Essential utensils such as spatulas, whisks, ladles, tongs, and a sharp set of knives with a cutting board are non-negotiable. A can opener, bottle opener, corkscrew, and basic measuring cups and spoons are also vital. For the coffee or tea aficionado, offering a coffee maker (drip, Keurig, or French press – consider your target demographic) with a starter supply of coffee and tea, along with sugar and sweetener, is a thoughtful touch. Don't forget basic pantry staples like salt, pepper, and perhaps a small bottle of cooking oil or spray. Providing enough dinnerware and cutlery for your maximum occupancy is crucial, as is having a good selection of glassware, including wine glasses and tumblers. Even for guests who primarily dine out, having these provisions offers flexibility and a sense of being well-catered for, reducing the need for last-minute trips to the store for basic cooking needs.

Moving to the bathrooms, the standard of cleanliness established in the earlier stages must be maintained through consistent stocking. High-quality, plush towels are a must. Aim for at least two sets per guest – a bath towel, hand towel, and washcloth. Fresh, clean towels signal hygiene and comfort. Essential toiletries include hand soap by every sink and an ample supply of toilet paper, with extra rolls easily accessible. A hairdryer is a highly appreciated amenity that many guests don't think to pack. For an elevated experience, consider providing travel-sized, good-quality shampoo, conditioner, and body wash. Ensuring the showerhead is clean and offers good water pressure significantly impacts guest satisfaction. A well-functioning exhaust fan is also important for comfort and preventing moisture buildup.

In today's connected world, high-speed, reliable Wi-Fi is no longer a luxury; it's an absolute necessity. Guests rely on it for work, entertainment, and staying in touch. Ensure your Wi-Fi network is robust enough to handle multiple devices simultaneously without lagging. Clearly communicate the network name and password in an easily accessible location, such as your welcome book or a framed sign. Consider investing in a mesh Wi-Fi system if your property is large or has known dead spots, guaranteeing consistent connectivity throughout the entire space. The speed should be sufficient for streaming high-definition video and supporting video calls without interruption.

Entertainment options are also key drivers of bookings. Smart TVs are now the standard, offering access to a wide range of streaming services. Ensure your TVs are connected to the internet and provide clear instructions on how to use them, including how to access popular platforms like Netflix, Hulu, or Disney+. If offering cable TV, ensure it's a comprehensive package that appeals to a broad audience. Beyond televisions, consider other entertainment amenities. For families, a selection of board games or puzzles can be a huge draw. For adults, a curated collection of books or magazines related to the local area can add a nice touch. Good quality Bluetooth speakers for music listening also enhance the guest experience.

Beyond the expected, certain thoughtful touches can significantly elevate a property's appeal and lead to exceptional reviews. A well-prepared welcome basket or amenity kit is a fantastic way to create a positive first impression. This can range from a simple arrangement of local snacks, a bottle of wine, or artisanal coffee to a more comprehensive collection of local goods. Including a locally sourced item, such as honey, jam, or handcrafted soap, not only provides a delightful surprise but also supports the local economy and gives guests a taste of the region.

A comprehensive and well-organized welcome book or guest guide is indispensable. This document should serve as a central resource for all guest needs. Beyond the Wi-Fi details and appliance instructions, it should include a curated list of local recommendations. Think beyond just restaurants; include nearby grocery stores, pharmacies, laundromats, popular tourist attractions, hidden local gems, and public transportation information. Emergency contact numbers, including your own and local emergency services, are crucial for guest peace of mind. Clearly outlining house rules – such as smoking policies, pet policies, quiet hours, and check-out procedures – in a friendly and informative manner helps to prevent misunderstandings. Details on trash and recycling disposal are also important for operational efficiency and environmental responsibility. If your property has any unique quirks, like a particular way to operate a shower or lock a specific window, explain these clearly. A local area map, perhaps marked with key points of interest, can be incredibly helpful.

For longer stays or guests who plan to do laundry, providing a functional washer and dryer with a starter supply of detergent and dryer sheets is a significant convenience. This amenity is particularly attractive to families and those on extended trips. Ensure all laundry appliances are clean, well-maintained, and have clear operating instructions.

Comfortable and functional workspaces are increasingly important, especially with the rise of remote work. If your property has the space, a dedicated desk with a comfortable chair and adequate lighting can be a major selling point for business travelers or digital nomads. Ensure there are conveniently located power outlets near the workspace for charging laptops and other devices.

For properties catering to families, child-friendly amenities can make a huge difference. This might include a crib or bassinet, a high chair, and a selection of age-appropriate toys or books. Safety items like outlet covers and stair gates can also provide peace of mind for parents.

Outdoor spaces, if available, should also be equipped to enhance guest enjoyment. This could mean comfortable seating on a patio or balcony, a barbecue grill with necessary tools, or even simple amenities like outdoor lighting for evening ambiance. If you have a garden or yard, ensure it's well-maintained and inviting.

Consider the climate and season when stocking certain amenities. For colder months, providing extra blankets and ensuring the heating system is reliable is paramount. In warmer climates, ceiling fans, portable fans, or air conditioning are essential. A well-functioning thermostat that guests can easily control is also important for comfort.

The details in the bathroom extend to the practicalities of grooming and personal care. Providing a few spare toilet paper rolls, extra hand soap, and ensuring that any soap dispensers are full is a basic but critical check. A clean, accessible trash bin in the bathroom is also a must.

In the kitchen, beyond the cookware, think about the small appliances that add significant convenience. A toaster, microwave, blender, and perhaps even an electric kettle can be highly valued. Ensure these are clean, in good working order, and accompanied by their instruction manuals if they have complex features. The presence of basic cleaning supplies like dish soap, sponges, dish towels, and a multi-purpose cleaner is vital for guests to maintain tidiness during their stay.

The importance of comfortable bedding cannot be overstated. While the mattress quality is key, the linens themselves play a huge role. Opt for good quality sheets with a comfortable thread count. Providing at least two sets of sheets per bed allows for easy turnover and ensures guests always have fresh linens available. A selection of pillows – firm, soft, and perhaps hypoallergenic options – caters to a wider range of preferences. A duvet or comforter, appropriate for the season, adds a layer of cozy comfort.

In essence, the amenities you provide are a direct reflection of the value you place on your guests' experience. By anticipating their needs and offering a well-equipped, comfortable, and convenient environment, you not only meet expectations but create opportunities for positive feedback, repeat bookings, and strong word-of-mouth referrals. Each amenity, from high-speed Wi-Fi to a thoughtfully assembled welcome basket, contributes to the overall impression your property leaves, transforming a simple stay into a delightful and memorable experience that guests will want to repeat. This strategic approach to amenity provision is a cornerstone of building a successful and profitable short-term rental business.

Cost Effective Furnishing Strategies

Furnishing a short-term rental property is a critical juncture where aesthetics meet practicality, and budget considerations are paramount. The goal is to create a space that is not only inviting and stylish but also durable enough to withstand the constant use of various guests. Striking this balance requires a strategic approach to sourcing furniture and decor, focusing on value, longevity, and guest appeal. This isn't about acquiring the most expensive pieces; it's about making smart, cost-effective choices that contribute to a positive guest experience and a healthy bottom line.

One of the most impactful strategies for cost-effective furnishing is to leverage wholesale suppliers and discount retailers. Many manufacturers and distributors offer furniture at significantly reduced prices when purchased in bulk, which can be ideal for outfitting an entire property. Look for online wholesale marketplaces or local furniture distributors that cater to businesses. These suppliers often have a wider selection of durable, contract-grade furniture designed for commercial use, meaning it's built to last in high-traffic environments. While you might not find the exact designer pieces you see in high-end magazines, you can discover well-made, stylish options that fit within your budget. For instance, purchasing sofas, dining sets, and beds from a wholesale supplier can yield substantial savings compared to buying individual pieces from a retail store. Pay close attention to the materials used; opting for solid wood frames over particleboard, durable upholstery fabrics like microfiber or tightly woven polyester, and sturdy metal components will pay dividends in the long run.

Discount retailers and outlet stores also present significant opportunities. These stores often carry overstock, floor models, or items with minor imperfections at a fraction of their original price. Think of large home goods stores with dedicated clearance sections, furniture outlets, or even specialized discount chains. The key here is to be patient and persistent, as inventory can vary widely. Inspect each item carefully for any damage that might compromise its durability or guest appeal. A small scratch on a coffee table might be easily repaired or overlooked, but a wobbly leg on a dining chair or a ripped seam on a sofa is a red flag. Many of these retailers offer solid, well-constructed pieces that, with a little careful selection, can form the backbone of your furnishing plan. Furthermore, keeping an eye out for seasonal sales and promotions can further reduce costs. Purchasing during holiday weekends, end-of-season clearances, or special store events can unlock even deeper discounts.

The second-hand market is another treasure trove for budget-conscious hosts. Websites like Craigslist, Facebook Marketplace, and local online classifieds are excellent resources for finding used furniture. You can often find quality pieces from individuals who are moving, downsizing, or redecorating. This approach requires a keen eye and a willingness to put in some effort. Inspecting items in person is crucial to assess their condition, smell for any musty odors, and test for structural integrity. Often, gently used furniture can be cleaned, reupholstered, or given a fresh coat of paint to look almost new. This is particularly effective for items that are less prone to heavy wear and tear, such as decorative accents, side tables, or even solid wood dressers. For instance, a vintage dresser found at a flea market, sanded and refinished, can add unique character to a bedroom at a fraction of the cost of a new piece. Remember to factor in transportation costs if you're buying larger items, and be prepared to collect them yourself.

When furnishing, it's crucial to prioritize durability for high-traffic items that guests will interact with most frequently. These include sofas, dining chairs, beds, and tables. Investing slightly more in these core pieces can prevent costly replacements down the line. For sofas and armchairs, look for frames made of kiln-dried hardwood and upholstery that is stain-resistant and easy to clean. Performance fabrics like Crypton or Sunbrella are excellent choices, though they can be more expensive initially. Alternatively, tightly woven polyester or microfiber can offer good durability and affordability. Dining chairs should have robust construction; metal or solid wood frames are generally more resilient than those made from cheaper composite materials. Bed frames should be sturdy, and it's often worthwhile to invest in a good quality mattress and box spring, as this directly impacts guest comfort and reviews. Even if the frame is a simpler metal or wood design, ensure it's stable and won't creak or wobble.

For less critical items or decorative pieces, you can afford to be more budget-friendly. Think about accessories like throw pillows, blankets, wall art, and lamps. These are where you can inject personality and style without a huge financial commitment. Discount home decor stores, online marketplaces like Amazon or Wayfair, and even dollar stores can provide great options for these items. Consider sourcing items that are easily replaceable or that won't cause significant loss if damaged. For instance, a decorative vase or a set of picture frames can be acquired affordably, allowing you to update your decor periodically without breaking the bank.

The concept of "rental-grade" furniture is also worth exploring. Many companies specialize in selling furniture specifically designed for short-term rentals, which tends to be more durable and cost-effective than typical residential furniture. These pieces are often designed with ease of cleaning and maintenance in mind, and some suppliers even offer package deals for furnishing entire properties. While these might not be the absolute cheapest options, they represent a good balance of quality, durability, and price for the rental market.

When it comes to flooring, think about resilience. While you might be tempted by beautiful hardwood, consider durable alternatives that are easier to clean and maintain in a rental setting. Luxury vinyl plank (LVP) flooring, for example, offers the aesthetic appeal of wood or tile but is highly resistant to scratches, water, and stains, making it an excellent choice for kitchens, bathrooms, and high-traffic living areas. It's also generally more affordable than natural stone or real hardwood. Similarly, for bedrooms, a good quality, low-pile carpet can be comfortable and quiet, but ensure it's treated for stain resistance and opt for a neutral color that hides minor soiling.

Paint colors are one of the most cost-effective ways to transform a space. Opt for durable, washable paint finishes like eggshell or satin for walls, as they can be easily wiped clean. Neutral color palettes are generally best, as they appeal to a wider range of guests and provide a versatile backdrop for decor. White, beige, gray, and soft blues or greens are popular choices that create a sense of calm and spaciousness. When selecting paint, consider purchasing larger quantities during sales at hardware stores, which can lead to significant savings.

For lighting, while stylish fixtures can enhance a property's appeal, prioritize functionality and energy efficiency. LED bulbs are a must for both cost savings and longevity. Consider the type of lighting needed in each space. Task lighting in the kitchen and bathroom, ambient lighting in living areas, and reading lamps in bedrooms are all important. You can find attractive and affordable lighting options at big-box home improvement stores, online retailers, and even discount furniture stores. Sometimes, a simple lampshade replacement or a coat of spray paint on an older lamp base can give it a fresh, updated look.

When sourcing decor, think about layering and accessorizing strategically. A few well-chosen pieces can make a significant impact. Consider buying items in sets or bundles when possible, as this can sometimes offer a better price point. For artwork, explore options like canvas prints from online retailers, downloadable art prints that you can have framed yourself, or even local artists who may offer more affordable pieces.

The kitchen, being a central hub, requires particularly durable and functional items. Stainless steel appliances, while often more expensive upfront, are generally durable and easy to clean. If a full stainless steel suite is out of budget, consider focusing on key pieces like the refrigerator or range. For smaller appliances like toasters, microwaves, and coffee makers, look for reputable brands known for reliability. Purchasing these from discount retailers or during sales can save money. For cookware and dinnerware, prioritize items that are dishwasher safe and microwave safe. Investing in a good set of non-stick pans and a basic but complete set of dinnerware and cutlery will serve you well. You don't need the most expensive brands; focus on function and ease of cleaning.

In bathrooms, durable and easy-to-clean materials are key. For fixtures like faucets and showerheads, look for finishes like brushed nickel or chrome, which are more resistant to water spots and fingerprints than polished chrome. When it comes to accessories like towel racks and toilet paper holders, opt for sturdy metal constructions over plastic. Even inexpensive items can look high-end if they are well-made and installed correctly.

When furnishing, always consider the "cost per use" or "cost per night." A slightly more expensive, but significantly more durable, item that lasts for years will ultimately be more cost-effective than a cheaper item that needs frequent replacement. This means scrutinizing the construction of furniture: check for solid wood where possible, sturdy joinery (like dovetail drawers rather than stapled ones), and robust upholstery. For instance, a sofa that costs twice as much but lasts twice as long, while also providing a more comfortable guest experience, is a better investment.

It's also wise to create a comprehensive inventory list before you start shopping. This list should detail every item needed for each room, from furniture to kitchenware to linens. Having a detailed plan prevents impulse purchases and ensures you're buying exactly what you need, allowing you to compare prices more effectively across different suppliers.

Consider the long-term maintenance and replacement costs. If a piece of furniture is known to be difficult to clean or repair, it might be worth investing in a more resilient alternative, even if it costs a little more upfront. For example, choosing furniture with removable, washable slipcovers can save a lot of money on professional cleaning and extend the life of the piece.

The overall aesthetic should be cohesive, but this doesn't necessitate buying everything from the same store or collection. Mixing and matching pieces from different sources can create a more unique and curated look. A stylish sofa from a discount retailer can be complemented by a unique side table found at an antique market and artwork from an online print shop. This approach not only saves money but also contributes to a more visually interesting and welcoming space.

Finally, remember that furnishing is an ongoing process. As you gain experience and receive guest feedback, you may identify opportunities to upgrade or replace certain items. Start with the essentials and focus on quality and durability for high-use items, and then gradually refine your furnishing choices based on what works best for your property and your guests. The aim is to create a comfortable, stylish, and resilient space that maximizes guest satisfaction and minimizes your expenses. This strategic approach ensures that your investment in furnishings contributes directly to the profitability and longevity of your short-term rental business, proving that quality and cost-effectiveness can indeed go hand-in-hand.

Professional Photography Capturing Your Property's Appeal

In the competitive landscape of short-term rentals, your property's listing photos are arguably the most critical element in attracting potential guests. They serve as your virtual storefront, offering the first impression and often dictating whether a traveler clicks through to learn more or scrolls past. High-quality photography is not merely a recommendation; it is an absolute necessity for a successful Airbnb business. Think of it as the visual handshake that invites guests into your world, conveying the essence of their potential stay before they even read a single word of your description. Investing in professional real estate photography is, without question, one of the most impactful and financially rewarding steps you can take to elevate your listing, attract a higher volume of bookings, and crucially, command premium nightly rates.

The power of compelling imagery cannot be overstated. In a digital-first world, potential guests make split-second decisions based on what they see. A professionally captured image can transform a functional space into a desirable destination, highlighting its unique features, ambiance, and overall appeal. Conversely, amateurish, poorly lit, or cluttered photos can inadvertently communicate neglect, a lack of attention to detail, or simply fail to showcase the true value of your property. This can lead to fewer inquiries, lower booking rates, and ultimately, a diminished return on your investment. Therefore, approaching your listing photography with the seriousness it deserves is paramount.

When embarking on the journey of professional photography for your short-term rental, it's crucial to understand what makes a photograph truly effective in this context. It goes beyond simply documenting the space; it's about creating an emotional connection and painting a picture of the experience a guest will have. This involves meticulous attention to detail, understanding the psychological impact of light and composition, and knowing precisely which aspects of your property will resonate most with potential bookers. The aim is to showcase your property not just as a place to sleep, but as an inviting and memorable escape.

One of the foundational pillars of exceptional property photography is optimal lighting. Natural light is your most powerful ally. Professional photographers are adept at harnessing daylight, understanding how it interacts with a space to create warmth, depth, and a sense of openness. They will schedule shoots during hours when the sun provides the most flattering illumination, often mid-morning or late afternoon, avoiding harsh midday glare. Large windows, skylights, and well-placed mirrors can all be leveraged to maximize the natural light flooding into each room. This not only makes the space appear brighter and more inviting but also conveys a sense of airiness and spaciousness. Think about how sunlight streaming into a living room can highlight the textures of furniture and create inviting shadows, adding visual interest.

Beyond natural light, artificial lighting plays a crucial role. A professional photographer will ensure that all interior lights are turned on, including ambient lighting, task lighting, and accent lighting. This creates a warm and welcoming atmosphere, especially for twilight or evening shots. They will strategically use lamps to add pools of warm light, making spaces feel cozier and more inviting. The goal is to avoid dark corners and create a consistent, pleasant illumination throughout the property. The careful use of lighting can dramatically influence how a space is perceived, transforming a functional room into a comfortable and appealing living area. For example, a well-lit kitchen feels more usable and enjoyable, while softly lit bedrooms evoke a sense of relaxation and tranquility.

Staging is another critical element that professional photographers expertly employ. This involves preparing the property to look its absolute best for the camera. It's about decluttering, arranging furniture to create visually appealing compositions, and adding thoughtful touches that enhance the overall aesthetic. Before the photographer arrives, ensure every surface is spotless, all personal items are removed, and the space is immaculately clean. Think of it as preparing a stage for a theatrical performance; every prop, every piece of furniture, and every decorative element should be intentionally placed to tell a story.

During the staging process, the photographer will often advise on or even assist with the arrangement of furniture to maximize visual appeal and flow. This might involve repositioning a sofa to better frame a view, arranging decorative pillows to add color and comfort, or placing fresh flowers or a bowl of fruit to add life and vibrancy. The aim is to create a sense of lived-in comfort without making the space look cluttered. For instance, arranging throw pillows artfully on a sofa, placing a neatly folded throw blanket over an armchair, or setting a coffee table with a few curated items like a book and a candle can all contribute to a more inviting and aspirational image.

Every room should tell a story and highlight its purpose and key features. In a living room, this might mean showcasing comfortable seating arrangements, entertainment options, or a striking architectural feature. In a bedroom, the focus will be on comfort, serenity, and the quality of the bedding. The kitchen should appear functional and well-equipped, while bathrooms should exude cleanliness and a spa-like atmosphere. The photographer will expertly frame shots to emphasize these aspects, ensuring that each photograph communicates the intended experience to the potential guest.

When it comes to the essential shots that potential guests want and need to see, a comprehensive set of images is crucial. This typically includes a wide shot of the exterior, showcasing the property's curb appeal and surrounding environment. This first image sets the tone and provides context. Following this, a strong "hero shot" of the main living area is essential. This is often the most important image in your listing, so it needs to be exceptional, capturing the overall ambiance and primary appeal of the property.

The kitchen, being a focal point for many travelers, requires detailed shots. This includes a general view of the kitchen space, but also close-ups of key amenities like the oven, stovetop, refrigerator, and any special features such as a coffee maker or a well-stocked pantry. Guests want to see that the kitchen is modern, clean, and equipped for their needs. Similarly, bathrooms should be presented with clarity, highlighting cleanliness, the quality of fixtures, and any luxury amenities like rainfall showerheads or spacious vanities.

Bedrooms are where guests will rest and recharge, so their presentation is vital. Each bedroom should have at least one dedicated photograph, showcasing the bed made with crisp linens, ample space around the bed, and any notable features like a bedside table, lamp, or view. If there are multiple bedrooms, it's important to show each one distinctly.

Beyond these core areas, it's beneficial to include photographs of any unique selling propositions your property offers. This could include a dining area, a dedicated workspace, a laundry room, outdoor living spaces like a patio or balcony, or any recreational facilities such as a pool or hot tub. If your property is in a desirable location with access to amenities or views, capture these aspects as well. For instance, a shot of a cozy reading nook, a well-appointed dining table ready for a meal, or a balcony with a city skyline view can significantly enhance a listing's appeal.

The photographer will also consider different angles and perspectives to provide a comprehensive view of the space. This includes eye-level shots, slightly elevated shots that offer a broader perspective, and detail shots that highlight specific design elements or high-quality finishes. A well-rounded set of photos will give potential guests a clear and accurate understanding of the property's layout and features, building trust and confidence.

The selection of a professional real estate photographer is a decision that warrants careful consideration. Look for photographers who specialize in interior and architectural photography. Review their portfolios to assess their style, quality of work, and ability to capture the essence of a space. Do their photos look bright, sharp, and inviting? Do they effectively use natural light? Do they showcase the property in a way that makes you want to book a stay?

When you engage a professional, communicate your vision and highlight your property's unique selling points. Discuss which features are most important to showcase and what kind of mood or ambiance you wish to convey. A good photographer will often offer suggestions based on their expertise, guiding you on staging and the best times to shoot. It's also wise to ask about their experience with short-term rental photography specifically, as they may have insights into what guests typically look for.

The investment in professional photography is a strategic one that pays dividends over the lifetime of your rental business. While it might seem like an upfront cost, consider it an investment in marketing that directly influences your revenue. A well-photographed listing can lead to a higher occupancy rate, allow you to charge more per night, and ultimately, generate significantly more income than a property with subpar images. For example, a difference of $10-$20 per night in pricing, coupled with a higher booking frequency due to attractive photos, can easily recoup the photography costs within a few bookings and continue to drive profits thereafter.

Furthermore, professional photos contribute to a higher perceived value of your property. Guests are more likely to book a place that looks well-maintained, stylish, and professionally managed, even if it means paying a premium. This can help you attract a more discerning clientele, who are often willing to pay more for a quality experience. It also helps manage guest expectations; when the reality of your property matches the high-quality images, it leads to positive reviews and repeat bookings. Conversely, a mismatch between photos and reality can result in disappointment and negative feedback, which can be detrimental to your listing's reputation.

In essence, your listing photos are the silent salespeople for your short-term rental. They are the first point of contact and often the deciding factor in a guest's booking decision. By investing in professional real estate photography, you are not just capturing images; you are crafting a compelling narrative, showcasing the unique charm and potential of your property, and ultimately, setting yourself up for greater success in the short-term rental market. This commitment to visual excellence is a foundational step in building a profitable and thriving rental business.

Chapter Three

Optimizing Your Listing for Maximum Bookings

Crafting Compelling Listing Descriptions

In the competitive arena of short-term rentals, while captivating photographs serve as the initial hook, it is the meticulously crafted listing description that solidifies a potential guest's decision to book. This written narrative acts as your digital ambassador, weaving a compelling story that translates the visual appeal of your property into a tangible experience. It's where you bridge the gap between a browsing traveler and a confirmed reservation, transforming curiosity into commitment. A well-written description is not merely a recitation of facts; it's an invitation, a promise, and a crucial element in differentiating your offering in a crowded marketplace.

The foundation of a compelling listing description lies in understanding your target audience and what they are seeking. Are you catering to budget-conscious families, business travelers needing a convenient workspace, couples looking for a romantic getaway, or adventurers seeking proximity to outdoor activities? Each demographic has distinct priorities and desires. By identifying your ideal guest, you can tailor your language, highlight relevant amenities, and emphasize the unique aspects of your property that will resonate most strongly with them. Consider the keywords your target audience might use when searching for accommodation. For instance, if you're targeting families, terms like "kid-friendly," "crib available," "spacious," and "close to attractions" are essential. For business travelers, "fast Wi-Fi," "desk space," "quiet neighborhood," and "easy commute" will be more impactful.

Your description's opening lines are paramount. They serve as the headline, the hook that compels a reader to delve deeper. Aim for an opening that is both informative and enticing, immediately communicating the essence of your property and its prime selling points. Instead of a generic "This is a nice house," try something like, "Escape to a tranquil oasis just minutes from downtown, where modern comfort meets charming character." Or, for a different property, "Experience the vibrant energy of the city from this stylish, centrally located apartment, perfect for urban explorers." This initial statement should encapsulate the overall vibe and primary benefit of staying at your property.

Once you have their attention, it's time to paint a vivid picture of the space. Go beyond simply listing features; describe the experience those features provide. Instead of saying, "The living room has a sofa and TV," try, "Unwind after a day of exploration in the cozy living room, featuring plush seating and a smart TV for your evening entertainment, creating the perfect ambiance for relaxation." For a kitchen, don't just list appliances; evoke the joy of cooking or preparing a morning coffee. "Whip up culinary delights in the fully equipped, gourmet kitchen, complete with stainless steel appliances and ample counter space, making meal preparation a pleasure."

Highlight your unique selling propositions (USPs) with clarity and enthusiasm. What makes your property stand out from the rest? Is it a breathtaking view, a unique architectural feature, a private back-yard oasis, an exceptionally well-equipped kitchen, or proximity to a sought-after attraction? These are the details that guests will re-member and that can sway their booking decision. If your property boasts a stunning ocean view, make that a prominent feature. Describe the experience: "Savor your morning coffee on the private balcony as you gaze out at the shimmering turquoise waters and enjoy the gentle sea breeze." If you have a particularly stylish and comfortable interior design, highlight that: "Step into a meticulously designed space where contemporary elegance meets cozy comfort, with curated artwork and high-quality furnishings creating an atmosphere of sophisticated re-laxation."

Structure is key to readability. Long, unbroken blocks of text can be daunting. Utilize paragraphs to break up information logically. Start with an engaging summary, then delve into specific areas of the property, followed by details about amenities, and finally, information about the local area. Bullet points are incredibly effective for listing amenities, house rules, or key features. This allows guests to quick-ly scan and find the information they need without having to sift through lengthy prose. For example, under a heading like "What this place offers," you might use bullet points for:

High-speed Wi-Fi

Fully equipped kitchen

Comfortable queen-sized bed

Smart TV with streaming services

Free parking on premises

Washer and dryer access

When describing amenities, be specific and honest. If you offer a "fully equipped kitchen," detail what that includes – coffee maker (and type, e.g., Keurig, Nespresso), toaster, blender, microwave, oven, dishwasher, essential cookware, dishes, and cutlery. If you mention a "workspace," describe it – is it a dedicated desk with an ergonomic chair, or a simple table? Transparency builds trust and manages expectations, which is crucial for positive reviews.

The local area and attractions are often as important as the property itself. Don't assume guests know what your neighborhood offers. Act as their local guide. Briefly mention nearby points of interest, restaurants, transportation hubs, or natural attractions. Instead of just saying "Close to downtown," specify what downtown offers: "Just a 10-minute walk to the vibrant downtown core, you'll find a plethora of acclaimed restaurants, trendy cafes, boutique shops, and lively entertainment venues." If you're near a national park, mention it and the activities available: "Nestled a short drive from the entrance to [National Park Name], your gateway to breathtaking hiking trails, scenic vistas, and unforgettable outdoor adventures."

Leverage keywords that potential guests are actively searching for. Think about terms related to location, property type, amenities, and the experience you offer. Integrating these naturally into your description can significantly improve your listing's visibility in search results.

If your property is ideal for remote workers, ensure "remote work," "work from home," "digital nomad," and "fast Wi-Fi" are present. If it's a family-friendly option, include "family vacation," "kid-friendly," "children welcome," and "baby gear" if applicable. Analyze what terms other successful listings in your area are using.

Tone of voice is crucial. It should align with the experience you aim to provide. A luxury villa might use sophisticated and elegant language, while a rustic cabin would adopt a more down-to-earth, cozy tone. Consistency in your tone across your photos, description, and communication is vital for creating a cohesive brand for your rental. Be enthusiastic, inviting, and professional.

Remember the importance of proofreading. Typos, grammatical errors, and awkward phrasing can detract from your professionalism and create a negative impression. Read your description aloud to catch errors and ensure it flows well. Consider having a friend or colleague review it before you publish.

To truly maximize the impact of your written description, consider a narrative approach. Tell the story of a perfect day at your property. Start with waking up to the gentle morning light, enjoying a cup of coffee on the patio overlooking a serene garden, followed by exploring local attractions, and returning for a cozy evening by the fireplace. This creates an emotional connection and allows potential guests to envision themselves enjoying the experience.

Let's delve deeper into specific techniques for crafting persuasive and informative descriptions.

Crafting the Opening Hook:

The initial sentences of your description are your digital handshake. They need to be warm, inviting, and immediately convey value. Think about the most compelling aspect of your property or its location.

Location-centric: "Discover your perfect urban escape in the heart of [Neighborhood Name], steps away from acclaimed dining and vibrant nightlife."

Experience-centric: "Imagine waking up to the sound of waves and stepping onto your private balcony with panoramic ocean views – welcome to paradise."

Amenity-centric: "Experience ultimate relaxation in our newly renovated home, featuring a luxurious hot tub, a fully equipped chef's kitchen, and ultra-fast Wi-Fi."

Benefit-centric: "Seeking a peaceful retreat? Our charming cottage offers a tranquil setting and easy access to hiking trails, perfect for nature lovers and those needing to recharge."

Avoid clichés and overused phrases. Instead of "cozy," try "inviting," "snug," or "intimate." Instead of "beautiful," describe

why it's beautiful – "sun-drenched," "elegantly appointed," "bursting with natural light."

Detailing the Space: Room by Room:

Walk potential guests through your property, room by room, highlighting key features and the atmosphere of each space.

Living Area: Describe the seating arrangements, entertainment options (smart TV, streaming services, sound system), and the overall ambiance. Is it a space for lively gatherings or quiet relaxation? "Sink into the plush sectional sofa in the spacious living room, perfect for movie nights with the family or engaging conversations with friends, all while enjoying the warmth of the electric fireplace."

Kitchen: Emphasize its functionality and appeal. What appliances are present? Is there ample counter space? What cookware and utensils are provided? "The heart of the home is our modern, fully-equipped kitchen, boasting granite countertops, stainless steel appliances including a professional-grade oven and a Keurig coffee maker. It's a joy to prepare meals here, and the adjacent dining area comfortably seats six for shared meals."

Bedrooms: Focus on comfort and tranquility. Describe the bed size and quality, the linens, storage space, and any special features like en-suite bathrooms or private balconies. "Retreat to the master bedroom sanctuary, featuring a king-sized bed dressed in crisp, high-thread-count linens, a spacious walk-in closet, and an en-suite bathroom for your ultimate privacy and comfort." For other bedrooms, specify their features: "The second bedroom offers a comfortable queen bed and ample storage, while the third bedroom is perfect for children, equipped with two twin beds and playful decor."

Bathrooms: Highlight cleanliness, modern fixtures, and any luxury touches. "Freshen up in our sparkling clean bathrooms, featuring walk-in showers with rainfall showerheads, modern vanities, and complimentary high-quality toiletries for a spa-like experience."

Showcasing Amenities and Unique Selling Points (USPs):

This is where you shine and differentiate yourself. Make a dedicated section or integrate these features seamlessly.

Outdoor Spaces: Patios, balconies, gardens, decks, yards, pools, hot tubs. Describe the experience: "Sip your morning coffee on the private balcony overlooking the bustling city skyline, or unwind in the evening in the soothing hot tub under the stars."

Workspaces: If you cater to remote workers, this is crucial: "Stay productive in our dedicated home office space, complete with a comfortable ergonomic chair, a large desk, and exceptionally fast, reliable Wi-Fi – perfect for video conferencing and focused work."

Entertainment: Game rooms, home theaters, high-quality sound systems, board games, books. "Challenge your travel companions to a friendly game in the dedicated game room, complete with a pool table and a selection of classic board games for endless entertainment."

Convenience: Washer/dryer, ample parking, keyless entry, pet-friendliness. "Enjoy the convenience of an in-unit washer and dryer, ensuring you always have fresh clothes, and a hassle-free check-in experience with our smart lock system."

Special Touches: Welcome baskets, local coffee, high-quality toiletries, curated decor. "We've added thoughtful touches to make your stay exceptional, including locally sourced coffee, premium organic toiletries, and a curated selection of books and games."

Describing the Local Area and Attractions:

Become your guests' personal concierge. Help them discover the best of your location.

Proximity to key sites: "Just a 5-minute walk to the famous [Landmark Name], and within easy reach of world-class museums and art galleries."

Dining and nightlife: "Explore a vibrant culinary scene with award-winning restaurants, cozy cafes, and lively bars all within a short stroll from your doorstep."

Nature and recreation: "Nature enthusiasts will love our proximity to [Park/Trail Name], offering miles of scenic hiking and biking trails, or try your hand at kayaking on the nearby [River/Lake Name]."

Transportation: "Conveniently located near public transport links, including the subway and bus routes, making it easy to explore the entire city."

Optimizing for Search Engines (SEO) and Readability:

Keywords: Naturally weave in relevant keywords that people use when searching for accommodations. Think about what your ideal guest would type into the search bar. Examples: "beachfront condo," "family-friendly cabin," "pet-friendly apartment," "downtown loft," "historic district stay," "quiet neighborhood," "secluded getaway."

Structure: Use short paragraphs, bullet points, and bold text for emphasis on key features. This breaks up the text and makes it scannable.

Conciseness: While you want to be descriptive, avoid unnecessary jargon or overly long sentences. Get to the point effectively.

Positive Language: Frame everything positively. Instead of "No smoking allowed," try "This is a smoke-free property to ensure a comfortable stay for all guests."

Storytelling and Emotional Appeal:

People book experiences, not just places to sleep. Tell a story that evokes emotion and allows guests to envision their stay.

A Day in the Life: "Wake up to the gentle sunlight streaming through the large windows, brew a fresh pot of coffee, and step out onto the balcony to greet the day with breathtaking views of the mountains. Spend your afternoon exploring the charming local boutiques or hiking scenic trails, then return to the comfort of your cozy retreat for a home-cooked meal, perhaps enjoyed al fresco on the patio as the sun sets."

Call to Action (Implicit):

While you don't directly say "Book now" in the description itself (that's handled by the platform), your compelling description should naturally lead to that action. By highlighting benefits, addressing needs, and creating desire, you prompt guests to click the booking button.

Examples of Vivid Descriptions:

Instead of: "Nice kitchen with appliances."

Try: "Our gourmet kitchen is a chef's delight, featuring high-end stainless steel appliances, including a professional-grade gas range, a spacious French-door refrigerator, and a quiet dishwasher. Fully stocked with all the essentials, from premium cookware and utensils to artisanal coffee and teas, it's the perfect place to create memorable meals for your loved ones."

Instead of: "Bedroom with a bed."

Try: "The master suite is your private oasis of tranquility, boasting a luxurious king-sized bed adorned with sumptuously soft, high-thread-count linens. Wake up feeling refreshed and energized, ready to embrace the day ahead. A spacious walk-in closet provides ample room for your belongings, and the en-suite bathroom offers a spa-like experience with a deep soaking tub and a separate rainfall shower."

Instead of: "Close to restaurants."

Try: "Immerse yourself in the vibrant culinary scene just steps from your door. Explore a curated selection of acclaimed restaurants, from innovative farm-to-table eateries to authentic international bistros, all within a leisurely stroll. Discover cozy cafes perfect for morning coffee and charming pubs for evening relaxation."

Maintaining and Updating Your Description:

Your listing description is not a static document. As you gather feedback from guests or make improvements to your property, update your description accordingly. If guests consistently rave about a particular amenity or feature, highlight it more prominently. If a nearby attraction changes or a new one opens, update your local recommendations. Regularly reviewing and refining your description ensures it remains accurate, appealing, and optimized.

By investing time and thought into crafting a compelling listing description, you are not just filling out a form; you are building a narrative that sells the experience of staying at your property. This attention to detail, combined with high-quality photography, forms the bedrock of a successful short-term rental business, attracting more bookings and paving the way for positive reviews and long-term profitability.

It's your opportunity to make an unforgettable first impression and persuade potential guests that your property is the perfect choice for their next adventure.

Strategic Title and Headline Optimization

The digital storefront of your short-term rental is your listing, and within that, the title and headline are the primary billboards. They are the initial point of contact, the very first impression a potential guest has of your property before they even glimpse a photograph or read a single word of the description. In the highly competitive landscape of online travel agencies (OTAs) and direct booking platforms, a powerful and strategic title is not just beneficial; it's essential for cutting through the noise and capturing the attention of your target audience. Think of it as the headline of a compelling newspaper article – it needs to be informative, engaging, and pique curiosity to encourage further reading.

Crafting an effective title requires a nuanced understanding of what guests are searching for and what makes your property unique. It's a delicate balance between being descriptive and being captivating. The goal is to clearly communicate the core offering of your rental while simultaneously highlighting its most attractive features or the overall experience it provides. This means moving beyond generic placeholders and investing thought into words that resonate and differentiate. Your title is, in essence, your initial sales pitch, condensed into a few potent phrases.

One of the most powerful strategies for optimizing your listing title is the intelligent incorporation of relevant keywords. Potential guests often start their search with specific terms related to location, property type, amenities, or the purpose of their trip. By understanding these search queries, you can strategically embed keywords that will help your listing appear prominently in search results. For example, if your property is located in a popular tourist destination known for its beaches, including terms like "beachfront," "ocean view," or "steps to the sand" can significantly improve your visibility to travelers specifically seeking coastal accommodations. Similarly, for a property catering to families, incorporating "family-friendly," "kid-friendly," or "near theme park" can attract the right demographic.

Consider the location as a primary keyword. Guests are often looking for a specific city, neighborhood, or even proximity to a particular landmark or attraction. If your property is situated in a desirable area, make it known. For instance, "Charming Bungalow in Historic Downtown Savannah" immediately tells potential guests where you are and hints at the character of the neighborhood. If you're near a major airport or convention center, that can be a valuable keyword for business travelers: "Modern Apartment Near Convention Center with Fast Wi-Fi."

Beyond location, property type is another crucial keyword. Are you offering a "Luxury Villa," a "Cozy Cabin," a "Stylish Loft," a "Beachfront Condo," or a "Secluded Treehouse"? Clearly stating the property type helps guests quickly identify if your offering matches their preferences. For instance, "Rustic Woodland Cabin with Hot Tub" paints a clear picture and appeals to a specific segment of travelers looking for a nature-focused escape.

Highlighting unique selling propositions (USPs) within your title can be a significant differentiator. What makes your rental stand out from the hundreds, if not thousands, of others in the area? Is it a breathtaking view, a private pool, a pet-friendly environment, a dedicated workspace, or an exceptionally well-equipped kitchen? These distinctive features are powerful hooks. Instead of a simple "Apartment in City Center," consider "Penthouse City Views with Rooftop Pool" or "Pet-Friendly Oasis with Private Garden Oasis." These titles don't just state facts; they evoke an aspirational experience.

The experience and ambiance you offer are equally important for title optimization. Are you selling a romantic getaway, a family adventure, a peaceful retreat, or a convenient business stay? Conveying this emotional aspect can attract guests looking for a specific type of vacation. Phrases like "Romantic Beachfront Escape," "Family Fun Lakeside Retreat," or "Tranquil Mountain Hideaway" communicate the intended atmosphere and help guests self-select. For those seeking relaxation, "Serene Garden Apartment with Spa Access" or "Peaceful Countryside Cottage with Fireplace" can be highly effective.

The length of your title is also a consideration. While you want to be descriptive, most platforms have character limits for titles, and longer titles can sometimes be truncated in search results. The key is to be concise and impactful, packing the most important information and appeal into the available space. Prioritize keywords and USPs that are most likely to attract your ideal guest. A title like "Spacious 4-Bedroom Family Home with Pool, Near Disney, Free Wi-Fi" is effective because it hits on space, guest type, location, a major draw (Disney), and a key amenity (Wi-Fi), all within a reasonable length.

A/B testing your titles can provide invaluable insights into what resonates best with potential guests. Many hosting platforms allow you to experiment with different titles and track which ones lead to more clicks and bookings. This data-driven approach can help you refine your strategy and continuously improve your listing's performance. For example, you might test a title that emphasizes location against one that highlights a specific amenity to see which garners more engagement.

Another aspect of effective headline creation is understanding the nuances of different platforms. While a core set of keywords and USPs should remain consistent, the way they are presented might need slight adjustments depending on whether you are listing on Airbnb, Vrbo, Booking.com, or your own direct booking website. Some platforms might favor shorter, punchier titles, while others may allow for more descriptive phrasing. Researching the top-performing listings in your area on each platform can provide a good benchmark.

Let's explore some concrete examples of how to strategically optimize titles. Imagine you have a charming cottage near a national park.

Generic Title: "Cottage in Park City"

Improved Title (Location + Property Type): "Cozy Cottage Near Zion National Park"

Further Improved Title (Location + Property Type + USP): "Charming Woodland Cottage Steps from Zion National Park Entrance"

Even Better Title (Location + Property Type + USP + Experience): "Secluded Woodland Cottage: Romantic Getaway Near Zion NP, Hot Tub & Stargazing"

In this progression, each iteration adds more value and appeal, making the listing more likely to stand out. The final version clearly communicates the location, property type, target audience (romantic getaway), and key amenities (hot tub, stargazing), providing a strong incentive for a potential guest to click.

Consider another scenario: a modern apartment in a bustling city.

Generic Title: "Apartment in Downtown"

Improved Title (Location + Property Type): "Modern Downtown Apartment"

Further Improved Title (Location + Property Type + USP): "Stylish Downtown Loft with City Views and Fast Wi-Fi"

Even Better Title (Location + Property Type + USP + Experience): "Vibrant City Loft: Modern Design, Panoramic Views, Perfect for Urban Explorers"

Here, "Vibrant City Loft" and "Urban Explorers" convey the energy and target audience. "Panoramic Views" is a strong visual selling point.

The phrasing of your title also matters. Using evocative adjectives can create a stronger emotional connection. Instead of just "Big House," try "Spacious Family Estate" or "Expansive Holiday Home." Words like "breathtaking," "stunning," "luxurious," "charming," "serene," and "vibrant" can all add personality and appeal.

It's also crucial to ensure your title is entirely truthful and accurate. Misleading titles will lead to disappointed guests, negative reviews, and a damaged reputation, which is far more detrimental than a slightly less clickable title. Always under-promise and over-deliver. If your property has a "partial ocean view," calling it a "stunning oceanfront property" is dishonest. Stick to factual descriptions that accurately represent the reality of your rental.

Think about the common questions guests might have and see if you can address them in the title. For instance, if parking is a common concern in your area, and you offer it, including "Free Parking" or "Dedicated Parking" can be a significant draw. If you cater to remote workers, "High-Speed Wi-Fi Included" or "Work-Friendly Space" can be essential keywords.

The evolution of short-term rental platforms also means that search algorithms are constantly being refined. Staying updated on best practices and observing what works for successful listings in your niche and location is a continuous process. Regularly reviewing your title and making small adjustments based on performance data and market trends can lead to significant improvements in booking volume over time.

In conclusion, your listing title is far more than just a label; it is a powerful marketing tool. By strategically employing keywords, highlighting your unique selling propositions, conveying the guest experience, being concise yet descriptive, and maintaining accuracy, you can create a title that not only grabs attention but also resonates with your ideal guests, driving more traffic to your listing and ultimately increasing your booking potential. It's the first step in weaving the narrative of your property and inviting guests to discover the magic of their potential stay. Investing time and effort into crafting the perfect title is a fundamental step towards maximizing your short-term rental's success. It's the digital handshake that opens the door to further engagement and, ultimately, to reservations.

The headline, often integrated with or closely following the title, serves to expand on the initial hook and provide a slightly more detailed glimpse into the property's appeal. While the title might offer a broad strokes overview, the headline can zero in on a key benefit or a more specific characteristic. Think of it as a sub-headline in a magazine article, designed to entice the reader to dive into the main content. This secondary line of text is another prime opportunity to attract attention and convey value.

Many platforms offer a dedicated field for a headline or a descriptive tagline, allowing for a bit more flexibility than the primary title. This is where you can get more creative and really paint a picture. For instance, if your title is "Modern Apartment in Historic District," your headline could be "Experience the Charm of Old Town with Contemporary Comfort." This adds a layer of intrigue and promises a blend of experiences. Alternatively, if the title is "Beachfront Villa," the headline could emphasize a specific amenity or feeling: "Wake Up to Ocean Breezes in Your Private Tropical Paradise."

The art of crafting effective headlines involves using strong verbs and evocative adjectives that resonate with the desired guest experience. Instead of simply stating features, aim to describe the

feeling those features provide. For example, "Enjoy the sunset from the balcony" is good, but "Savor breathtaking sunset views from your private balcony with a glass of local wine" is far more compelling. It appeals to the senses and creates a vivid mental image.

Consider the "why" behind a guest's booking. Are they looking for adventure, relaxation, romance, family time, or a productive work trip? Your headline should ideally tap into these underlying motivations. For a family trip, a headline like "Kid-Approved Fun: Steps from Parks & Playgrounds, Spacious for All" directly addresses parental needs and desires. For a romantic getaway, "Unwind Together: Secluded Cabin with Jacuzzi & Fireplace for Two" speaks to couples seeking intimacy and relaxation.

When incorporating keywords into your headline, remember the context. While the title might capture broader search terms, the headline can refine these with more specific or experiential language. If your title included "Downtown Condo," your headline could specify "Walk to Best Restaurants & Nightlife" or "Ultimate Urban Convenience for Business & Leisure." This provides more targeted information and can capture guests who are refining their search parameters.

The structure of your headline can also impact its effectiveness. Using a colon to separate a descriptive phrase from a benefit-driven clause is a common and effective technique. For example, "Central Location: Your Gateway to Exploring the City's Best Attractions." Or, "Luxury Retreat: Experience Tranquility and Style in this Designer Home."

It's also vital to ensure consistency between your title, headline, and the rest of your listing. The message conveyed by your headline should align with the photographs and the description. If your head-line promises a "serene escape," but the photos show a busy street, or the description details a lack of privacy, this dissonance will create distrust. Authenticity is key.

Furthermore, think about the emotional impact. Headlines that evoke positive emotions tend to perform better. Words associated with happiness, comfort, excitement, and peace can be very persuasive. For instance, "Discover Your Bliss: A Peaceful Haven with Stunning Mountain Vistas" aims for an emotional connection by using words like "bliss" and "peaceful."

When deciding on the most impactful features to highlight in your headline, consider what your past guests have consistently praised in reviews. If a particular amenity or aspect of your property receives consistent positive feedback, it's a strong candidate for prominent display in your headline. This social proof can be incredibly powerful in attracting new bookings.

The length of your headline is also a factor. Similar to titles, most platforms have limits. It's about being impactful and informative without being verbose. Aim for clarity and conciseness, ensuring the most crucial information is communicated effectively. A good rule of thumb is to keep it to one or two short, punchy sentences.

Consider the competitive landscape again. What are other suc-cessful hosts in your area using for their headlines? While you don't want to copy, observing popular phrasing and keywords can give you ideas. Identifying what makes other listings stand out can inform your own strategy. Are they highlighting amenities, location benefits, or a unique vibe?

Testing different headlines is as crucial as testing titles. What might seem like a winning headline to you may not resonate as strongly with potential guests. Experiment with variations that emphasize different aspects of your property or experience. Track which headlines lead to more clicks and inquiries. This iterative process of testing and refinement will help you optimize your listing for maximum visibility and engagement.

For example, if your property is a well-appointed home suitable for remote work, you might test headlines like:

"Work from Home Paradise: Ultra-Fast Wi-Fi & Dedicated Office Space"

"Productivity Meets Comfort: Stylish Apartment with Essential Workspace Amenities"

"Your Home Office Away From Home: Quiet Location, Reliable Internet & Desk Space"

Each of these targets the "remote work" segment but uses slightly different phrasing and highlights different supporting benefits.

Similarly, for a family-friendly rental, consider:

"Family Adventure Base: Spacious Home, Kid-Friendly Amenities, Near Major Attractions"

"Stress-Free Family Vacation: All the Essentials for Little Ones, Close to Parks"

"Room for Everyone: Perfect for Families, Featuring Backyard Play Area & High-Speed Internet"

The headline is your opportunity to provide that extra nudge, that compelling reason for a guest to click through and explore your listing further. It's a crucial element in the initial discovery phase, working in tandem with your title and photographs to create an irresistible first impression. By dedicating time to crafting an effective headline that is both informative and enticing, you significantly increase your chances of capturing your ideal guest's attention and setting your listing apart in a crowded marketplace. It's about more than just describing your property; it's about selling an experience and a solution to a traveler's needs.

In the competitive arena of short-term rentals, static pricing—setting a single rate and leaving it—is akin to leaving money on the table. The true key to unlocking maximum revenue lies in the implementation of dynamic pricing strategies. This approach is not merely about adjusting prices; it's about understanding the intricate ebb and flow of market demand and aligning your property's value with what travelers are willing to pay at any given moment. It's a sophisticated dance between supply, demand, seasonality, local events, competitor activity, and even day-of-the-week variations. By embracing dynamic pricing, you transform your rental from a fixed-price offering into a responsive revenue-generating asset that capitalizes on opportunities and mitigates potential losses during slower periods.

The foundation of dynamic pricing is a deep understanding of seasonality. Every location experiences predictable shifts in demand throughout the year. High seasons, often dictated by favorable weather, school holidays, or major cultural events, typically see an influx of travelers, driving up demand and allowing for premium pricing. Conversely, low seasons or shoulder seasons (the periods between peak and off-peak) may experience reduced demand, necessitating more competitive pricing to attract guests and maintain occupancy. A thorough analysis of historical booking data for your specific location, combined with an awareness of general travel trends, will help you identify these seasonal patterns. For example, a beachside property will likely see its highest demand and pricing in the summer months, while a ski resort cabin will command top dollar during the winter. Understanding these cycles allows you to proactively set your rates, ensuring you are charging the most when demand is high and offering attractive value when it is lower.

Beyond broad seasonal trends, the impact of local events on pricing cannot be overstated. Major festivals, sporting events, concerts, conferences, and even significant local gatherings can dramatically increase demand for accommodation in a specific area, often for a limited period. These events create a surge in travelers seeking places to stay, sometimes with little advance notice. Being aware of your local event calendar is crucial. Properties located near venues for these events can often command significantly higher nightly rates during these times. For instance, a rental near a major university might see a spike in bookings and pricing during homecoming weekends, graduation ceremonies, or major athletic competitions. Similarly, a city hosting a large international conference or a popular music festival can experience a demand surge that allows hosts to implement premium pricing. Identifying these events and strategically adjusting your rates upward in anticipation of them is a cornerstone of maximizing revenue. This often involves setting rates several months in advance for key dates, ensuring you capture the heightened demand.

Demand-based pricing is the engine that drives dynamic pricing. This involves continuously monitoring the level of interest in your property and the surrounding market. If your booking calendar is filling up quickly for a particular period, it signals high demand, and you may be able to increase your nightly rate. Conversely, if you have significant availability in the weeks leading up to a particular date, it might be an indicator to lower your rates slightly to encourage bookings. This constant recalibration is essential. Many pricing tools can help automate this process by analyzing booking velocity and occupancy rates in your market. The goal is to avoid being too cheap when demand is strong, thereby leaving money on the table, and also to avoid being too expensive when demand is weak, leading to prolonged vacancies.

Competitor pricing analysis is another vital component of a successful dynamic pricing strategy. Your property does not exist in a vacuum. Potential guests are likely comparing your offering with others in the same area. Therefore, it is imperative to understand what your direct competitors are charging. This involves regularly checking the rates of similar properties on booking platforms. Identify properties that are comparable in size, amenities, location, and quality. If your prices are consistently higher than comparable properties with similar occupancy levels, you may need to adjust downward. Conversely, if your property is consistently booked while similar properties remain empty, you might be able to increase your rates. Many dynamic pricing tools automate this by pulling competitor data and suggesting optimal rates based on this information. This ongoing competitive intelligence ensures your pricing remains relevant and attractive in the market.

The day of the week also plays a significant role in pricing. Weekends, particularly Friday and Saturday nights, typically experience higher demand than weekdays, especially in leisure destinations. This is because most travelers have more flexibility for weekend trips. As a result, weekend nights are often priced higher than weekday nights. For business-oriented rentals or properties in cities with strong weekday business travel, you might see the opposite trend, with weekdays commanding higher rates. Implementing a tiered pricing structure based on the day of the week is a fundamental aspect of dynamic pricing. Many hosting platforms and pricing management software allow you to set different base rates for each day of the week, which can then be further adjusted by other dynamic factors.

Beyond these core elements, other factors can influence your pricing decisions. For instance, the length of stay can be a factor. While shorter stays might command higher nightly rates due to the increased turnover and cleaning costs associated with each booking, longer stays might offer a discount to ensure consistent occupancy. You might implement a minimum stay requirement, but offering a slight discount for stays of a week or more can be a good strategy to secure longer bookings. Furthermore, special booking conditions, such as last-minute deals for unfilled dates or early bird discounts for bookings made well in advance, can also be incorporated into your dynamic pricing strategy to optimize occupancy and revenue.

The advent of sophisticated pricing management software and tools has revolutionized the way hosts implement dynamic pricing. These platforms can automate much of the analysis and adjustment process, saving hosts significant time and effort. Tools like PriceLabs, Wheelhouse, and Beyond Pricing analyze vast amounts of data, including historical booking data, competitor pricing, local events, seasonality, and market demand, to recommend or automatically adjust your nightly rates. These tools often use algorithms to predict demand and set optimal prices to maximize revenue and occupancy. Integrating one of these tools into your hosting operation is highly recommended for any serious host looking to optimize their earnings. They provide data-driven insights that are often impossible to glean manually and can react to market changes much faster than a human operator.

When setting up your dynamic pricing, it's important to establish a floor price, or a minimum acceptable rate. This ensures that even during periods of exceptionally low demand or when using automated pricing tools, you don't inadvertently price your property so low that it becomes unprofitable. This floor price should account for all your costs, including mortgage payments, utilities, cleaning fees, maintenance, insurance, and platform fees, plus a desired profit margin. Knowing your absolute minimum allows you to set parameters for automated tools and make informed decisions when manually adjusting rates.

Conversely, you also need to understand your ceiling price. While dynamic pricing allows you to charge premium rates during peak demand, there's a point beyond which potential guests will simply not book, regardless of the event or season. This ceiling is influenced by the perceived value of your property, the quality of your amenities, and the overall guest experience you offer, as well as the pricing of other high-end alternatives in the market. Continuously assessing your property's market position and guest reviews will help you understand where your ceiling lies. Overpricing during peak demand can lead to vacancies, which defeats the purpose of dynamic pricing.

The implementation of dynamic pricing is not a set-it-and-forget-it strategy. It requires ongoing monitoring, analysis, and adaptation. Market conditions can change rapidly, and what worked last month might not work this month. Regularly reviewing your pricing performance, analyzing booking trends, and staying informed about new events or changes in the local market are essential. This iterative process of observation, adjustment, and re-evaluation is what will ultimately lead to sustained revenue maximization. It's about being agile and responsive to the ever-changing dynamics of the short-term rental market, ensuring your property remains competitive, attractive, and profitable year-round. By mastering dynamic pricing, you are not just managing a rental; you are strategically operating a business that adapts and thrives in a fluid economic landscape.

Mastering Airbnb Search Ranking Factors

The Airbnb search algorithm is a complex, constantly evolving system designed to connect travelers with the most relevant and appealing accommodations. For hosts, understanding how this algorithm works is not just beneficial; it's paramount to achieving consistent bookings and maximizing revenue. Think of it as the gatekeeper to visibility. Properties that rank higher in search results are seen by more potential guests, leading to a virtuous cycle of increased views, more inquiries, and ultimately, more bookings. Conversely, a lower ranking means fewer eyes on your listing, translating directly into lost opportunities.

At its core, Airbnb's algorithm aims to predict which listing a guest is most likely to book and enjoy. It achieves this by evaluating a multitude of factors, each contributing to a property's overall "ranking score." While Airbnb does not publicly disclose the exact weight of each factor, extensive host experience and data analysis have revealed the key components that consistently influence a listing's position. These can be broadly categorized into elements related to the listing itself, guest experience and satisfaction, and booking performance. By optimizing these areas, you can significantly influence how prominently your property appears when potential guests search for accommodations.

One of the most foundational aspects of your listing's search ranking is its completeness and quality. Airbnb rewards hosts who provide comprehensive and appealing information to potential guests. This starts with the basics: a clear, high-resolution profile picture of yourself (or your brand logo if applicable) and a compelling, well-written listing title and description. The title should be concise yet informative, highlighting key selling points like location, unique features, or proximity to attractions. For instance, a title like "Charming Beachfront Cottage with Ocean Views" is far more effective than a generic "Apartment for Rent."

The description is your digital storefront. It needs to be engaging, accurate, and persuasive. Detail the amenities offered, from Wi-Fi and kitchen facilities to special touches like a fireplace or a private balcony. Highlight the unique aspects of your property and the surrounding neighborhood. Are you close to public transport? Are there excellent restaurants nearby? Is it a quiet, residential area or a vibrant hub? Be honest and transparent. Misleading descriptions can lead to negative reviews, which directly harm your search ranking. Use formatting like bullet points to make key information easily digestible.

Photos are arguably the most critical element in attracting clicks. High-quality, professional photography is not an expense; it's an investment. Use a wide-angle lens to showcase the space, ensure good lighting, and capture the best features of your property. Include photos of every room, the exterior, and any appealing outdoor spaces. A potential guest often makes a decision within seconds of viewing photos. Blurry, dark, or insufficient images will deter clicks, regardless of how great your property actually is. Consider a professional photographer who specializes in real estate or hospitality photography. They understand how to best present a space.

Beyond the visual appeal, Airbnb also scrutinizes the completeness of your listing details. This includes accurately filling out all sections: the number of bedrooms and bathrooms, sleeping arrangements, house rules, check-in/check-out procedures, and any specific details about accessibility. A "100% complete" listing signals to Airbnb that you are a serious and organized host, which positively influences your ranking. This also helps guests filter searches effectively, ensuring they find properties that truly meet their needs, thus reducing the likelihood of cancellations or dissatisfactions.

Guest reviews are the lifeblood of Airbnb's trust system and a powerful ranking factor. Positive reviews not only build social proof but also directly signal to the algorithm that your property offers a great experience. Airbnb heavily weights the quantity and quality of your reviews. More reviews generally mean higher visibility, but the sentiment of those reviews is even more critical. Aim for a consistently high star rating across all categories: cleanliness, communication, check-in, accuracy, location, and value.

To encourage positive reviews, focus on delivering an exceptional guest experience. This means clear and prompt communication from the initial inquiry to post-stay follow-up. Respond to messages quickly, ideally within an hour, but certainly within 24 hours at the maximum. Airbnb tracks your response rate and response time, and these are significant ranking factors. A high response rate and fast response times indicate to Airbnb that you are an engaged and reliable host, which translates to better search placement.

When guests do leave reviews, acknowledge them. Thank guests for positive feedback and address any constructive criticism professionally and empathetically in your public response. This shows potential guests that you care about feedback and are committed to improvement. Never argue with a negative review publicly. Instead, address the concerns privately or offer a brief, professional response. A pattern of positive reviews builds trust and encourages bookings, pushing your listing higher in search results.

Booking conversion rate is another crucial, albeit less directly controllable, metric. This refers to the percentage of people who view your listing and then proceed to book it. While you can't force someone to book, you can significantly influence this by making your listing as attractive and competitive as possible. This ties back to all the factors discussed: compelling photos, an accurate and engaging description, competitive and dynamic pricing (as discussed in the previous section), excellent reviews, and a high response rate.

Properties that are frequently booked are seen as more desirable by the algorithm. This creates a positive feedback loop: higher booking rates lead to better search ranking, which in turn leads to more views and more bookings. To improve your conversion rate, ensure your calendar is up-to-date and that your pricing is competitive. Minimizing "blocked" dates unnecessarily can also help, as it signals availability. If you have a high number of inquiries but low bookings, analyze why. Is your pricing too high? Are your house rules too strict? Are your photos not compelling enough?

Another key performance indicator that impacts search ranking is the cancellation rate. Airbnb penalizes hosts who frequently cancel confirmed bookings, as this disrupts guest travel plans and damages the platform's reputation. Aim for a zero cancellation rate. If an unavoidable situation arises that forces a cancellation, communicate with Airbnb support immediately and be prepared for potential penalties, including a temporary suspension of your listing's visibility. Ensure your calendar is always accurate and that you don't overbook yourself.

The "listing quality score" is a holistic measure that Airbnb uses internally, encompassing many of the factors already mentioned. It's a broad assessment of how well your listing meets the platform's standards for desirability and reliability. Factors contributing to this score include:

Guest Experience Metrics: This covers your Superhost status (if applicable), your average guest review rating, and your response rate and time. Superhosts, who consistently provide excellent experiences, often receive a visibility boost.

Listing Appeal: This includes the quality and completeness of your photos, the accuracy and comprehensiveness of your description, and the overall attractiveness of your property and its amenities.

Booking History: Consistent bookings, a low cancellation rate, and a history of positive guest interactions all contribute to a higher listing quality score.

Think of the listing quality score as a grade Airbnb gives your entire operation. The higher the grade, the better your chances of appearing prominently in search results. Continually striving to improve each element of your hosting—from responding to messages promptly to ensuring your property is immaculate—will naturally improve your listing quality score over time.

Furthermore, Airbnb's algorithm is designed to favor listings that are readily bookable. This means keeping your calendar updated and ensuring your pricing is competitive. Listings that are frequently un-available or have irregular pricing patterns may be de-emphasized. Instant Book functionality can also play a role. While not mandatory, enabling Instant Book can signal to Airbnb that your property is easily bookable and that you are a responsive host, potentially giving you a slight edge in search rankings. However, ensure you are comfortable with this feature and have your house rules and booking settings clear-ly defined to avoid undesirable bookings.

The user's search behavior also influences what listings are dis-played. When a traveler searches for a specific location, dates, and number of guests, Airbnb's algorithm analyzes available properties and ranks them based on the factors discussed. It prioritizes listings that match the search criteria precisely and have a high likelihood of being booked. This means that if a traveler is looking for a specific amenity, like a pet-friendly property or a swimming pool, listings that prominently feature and deliver on these criteria will rank higher for that specific search.

Location, while not something you can change about your prop-erty, is an undeniable ranking factor that is heavily weighted by trav-elers. Airbnb considers the proximity of your listing to points of in-terest, public transport, and amenities that guests typically seek. If your property is in a highly desirable neighborhood or close to major attractions, this will inherently boost its ranking for relevant searches. However, even in less prime locations, you can still compete effectively by excelling in the other areas the algorithm prioritizes.

Finally, Airbnb periodically updates its algorithm. What works today might need slight adjustments tomorrow. Staying informed about Airbnb's best practices, participating in host forums, and continuously analyzing your own listing's performance are key to staying ahead. Regularly review your listing's performance metrics within your host dashboard. Pay attention to views, booking conversion rates, and how your ranking changes over time. This data-driven approach allows you to identify areas for improvement and adapt your strategy accordingly. By focusing on completeness, guest satisfaction, booking performance, and overall listing quality, you can significantly enhance your property's visibility on the Airbnb platform, attracting more guests and ultimately driving greater success for your short-term rental venture. Mastering these search ranking factors is an ongoing process of refinement and dedication to providing an exceptional guest experience.

Leveraging High Quality Photos in Search Results

In the bustling digital marketplace of Airbnb, where countless properties vie for the attention of weary travelers, your listing's visual appeal acts as your most potent first impression. While we've touched upon the foundational importance of imagery during the initial setup phase, this section delves deeper into the critical role high-quality photographs play specifically within the search results pages. Think of the search results page as a densely populated street, and your property's thumbnail image is the storefront window. It's the very first element a potential guest interacts with, often before they even read your title or description. This initial visual encounter can be the decisive factor in whether a traveler pauses their scrolling to explore your offering further, or swiftly moves on to a competitor's listing.

The Airbnb algorithm, in its relentless pursuit of connecting guests with their ideal stays, recognizes the power of a compelling visual. When users conduct a search, whether it's for a "beachfront villa in Bali" or a "cozy cabin near Yosemite," the results page typically displays a grid of properties. Each property is represented by a single, primary thumbnail image. This image is not merely decorative; it's a functional component of the search experience, designed to convey the essence and appeal of your property at a glance. A well-chosen, professionally captured photograph can instantly communicate key selling points – perhaps a stunning view, a luxurious amenity, or a unique architectural feature – thereby capturing a guest's interest and prompting them to click for more details. Conversely, a mediocre or uninspired photo can fail to convey the true value of your property, leading to missed opportunities and lost bookings.

The sheer volume of listings on Airbnb means that standing out is a constant challenge. Users are presented with numerous options, and their decision-making process is often rapid. In this fast-paced environment, professional, high-resolution photographs are not just a suggestion; they are a necessity. They serve as a powerful differentiator, immediately elevating your listing above those that rely on amateur snapshots or outdated images. Consider the impact of a well-lit, artfully composed photograph of your living space, showcasing comfortable seating, elegant decor, and ample natural light. This image, even as a small thumbnail, can convey a sense of warmth, comfort, and style that is far more enticing than a dimly lit, cluttered shot of the same space.

This initial visual engagement directly influences your click-through rate (CTR), a crucial metric that the Airbnb algorithm monitors. A higher CTR indicates to Airbnb that your listing is resonating with potential guests who are actively searching. When your thumbnail image effectively grabs attention and accurately represents the quality of your offering, travelers are more likely to click on your listing to learn more. This increased engagement signals to the algorithm that your property is desirable and relevant, which can, in turn, lead to a boost in your search ranking. It's a virtuous cycle: exceptional photos lead to more clicks, more clicks can lead to better visibility, and better visibility leads to more bookings.

The quality of your photos extends beyond mere aesthetics; it also speaks to your professionalism as a host. Guests instinctively associate high-quality imagery with a well-maintained, thoughtfully presented property and a host who pays attention to detail. If your photos look amateurish, blurry, or fail to showcase the best aspects of your property, potential guests might infer that the property itself is similarly neglected. This can create a subconscious barrier, even if your property is objectively excellent. Therefore, investing in professional photography is not an unnecessary expense, but rather a strategic investment in your listing's perceived value and your overall booking potential.

When thinking about the selection of your primary thumbnail image, consider what single aspect of your property is most likely to make a guest stop and think, "This is the place for me!" This could be an inviting exterior shot that highlights curb appeal, a beautifully styled bedroom that promises restful sleep, or a captivating view from a balcony or window that offers a unique selling proposition. It's essential that this primary photo is not only visually appealing but also accurately represents the overall experience a guest can expect. Misleading or overly edited "trick" photos can lead to disappointment and negative reviews, which will ultimately harm your search ranking far more than a less-than-stellar thumbnail. Honesty and appeal must go hand-in-hand.

Furthermore, the algorithm favors listings that are complete and well-populated with information. High-quality photos contribute significantly to this completeness. Airbnb encourages hosts to upload a minimum number of photos to adequately showcase their property, and a robust gallery of excellent images signals to the algorithm that you have invested time and effort into your listing. This attention to detail is rewarded. When guests are browsing search results, they often quickly scan the photos accompanying each listing. A property with a comprehensive and attractive photo gallery is more likely to capture their attention and encourage them to delve deeper into the listing's details.

It's also worth noting that the algorithm may consider user engagement with your photos. If guests who click on your listing spend more time looking through your photo gallery, this can be interpreted as a positive signal. This prolonged engagement suggests that the images are captivating and informative, reinforcing the desirability of your property. Therefore, not only the quality but also the selection and organization of your entire photo album matter. Each photo should tell a part of the story of staying at your property, from the welcoming entrance to the functional kitchen, the comfortable sleeping areas, and any unique amenities or neighborhood attractions.

In essence, leveraging high-quality photos in search results is about making an immediate and powerful connection with potential guests. It's about using the visual language of your property to convey its unique charm, comfort, and value before a single word is read. By investing in professional photography and strategically selecting your primary thumbnail, you are not just decorating your listing; you are actively optimizing it for visibility and bookings within the competitive Airbnb search landscape. This visual first impression is your golden ticket to attracting more eyes, generating more interest, and ultimately, driving more reservations for your short-term rental business.

Chapter Four

Seamless Operations and Stellar Guest Experiences

Developing Efficient Guest Communication Flows

The initial contact a potential guest makes with your property, beyond the captivating photographs we've discussed, often centers around their inquiry and subsequent booking. This is where the foundation for a stellar guest experience is truly laid, and it hinges critically on the efficiency and clarity of your communication. In the dynamic world of short-term rentals, where expectations can range from a simple overnight stay to a meticulously planned vacation, a well-defined communication flow is not just helpful; it's an absolute necessity for success. Think of your communication strategy as the invisible thread that connects you to your guests, ensuring their journey with your property is smooth, reassuring, and ultimately, memorable for all the right reasons. This involves establishing a system that is both proactive and responsive, anticipating guest needs while remaining readily available to address any questions or concerns that may arise.

One of the most impactful ways to streamline your guest communication is through the strategic use of automated messaging. Once a booking is confirmed, a series of automated messages can be triggered to provide essential information and set clear expectations. The first of these should ideally be sent shortly after booking confirmation. This initial message serves as a digital handshake, a warm welcome that solidifies the guest's decision. It's an opportunity to reiterate the booking details, perhaps include a brief overview of what makes your property special, and most importantly, to outline the next steps. For instance, you might inform them that they will receive further information regarding check-in procedures closer to their arrival date. This reassures them that they are in good hands and that details are being managed efficiently.

Crucially, this initial automated message should also include your primary communication channel. While Airbnb's messaging platform is convenient, some hosts prefer to guide guests towards direct email or even a dedicated messaging app for more complex communications or to build a more direct relationship. Clearly stating your preferred method, along with your typical response time, helps manage guest expectations from the outset. For example, you might state, "We typically respond to all messages within 24 hours." This transparency is vital. The tone of these automated messages should be welcoming, professional, and reflective of the hospitality you aim to provide.

Avoid overly robotic language; infuse a touch of personality that aligns with your property's brand and ambiance.

As the check-in date approaches, typically within 24 to 48 hours, a second automated message becomes invaluable. This is where you deliver the crucial check-in instructions. This message needs to be crystal clear and comprehensive. If you provide self-check-in via a smart lock or a lockbox, detail the exact process: the code, the location of the lockbox or smart lock, and any specific steps to follow. If a manual check-in is required, clearly state the meeting time and location, or the process for arranging access. Include essential details such as parking instructions, Wi-Fi network name and password, and any immediate points of contact for issues upon arrival. This proactive approach minimizes the chances of guests arriving confused or facing difficulties, which can cast a shadow over their entire stay.

Beyond the practicalities of check-in, these automated messages can also serve as gentle reminders about house rules, or perhaps highlight unique features of the property that guests might appreciate. For example, if your property has a particularly stunning view that is best enjoyed at a certain time of day, or a hidden local gem nearby that you recommend, this is the perfect opportunity to mention it. This adds value to the guest's experience even before they step through the door. Remember, the goal is to make the arrival process as seamless and stress-free as possible. A well-crafted check-in message can significantly reduce pre-arrival anxiety for guests and minimize last-minute inquiries for you.

The post-check-in communication is equally important for maintaining momentum and ensuring guest satisfaction throughout their stay. While direct intervention should be reserved for issues that arise, a subtle automated check-in message a few hours or a day after their confirmed arrival can be highly effective. This message can be framed as a simple "How's everything going?" or "Just wanted to check in and make sure you've settled in comfortably." It's a non-intrusive way to signal your availability and willingness to assist without hovering. This simple gesture can make guests feel valued and supported, encouraging them to reach out if anything is amiss rather than letting a minor issue fester and potentially lead to a negative review.

For guests who haven't responded to the initial check-in message, a follow-up message can be beneficial. However, be mindful of the timing and tone. You don't want to appear pushy, but a gentle nudge can ensure they've received the critical information. If a guest is unresponsive to multiple automated messages, it might be an indicator that they are experiencing technical difficulties, are traveling without reliable internet access, or perhaps have missed the messages entirely. In such scenarios, consider a more direct approach through the primary booking platform, especially if check-in is imminent.

The departure day presents another opportunity for thoughtful communication. An automated message can be sent the evening before or the morning of check-out. This message should clearly reiterate the check-out time and any specific instructions, such as where to leave keys, how to secure the property, or if there are any post-stay cleaning protocols guests need to follow. Again, clarity is paramount. Providing these details in advance reduces confusion and ensures a smooth departure. You might also use this message to express your gratitude for their stay and to subtly encourage them to leave a review.

Following their departure, a thank-you message is a critical component of the communication flow. This message should be sent within 24 hours of their scheduled check-out. It's a chance to express your appreciation for their patronage and to reinforce the positive aspects of their stay. You can say something like, "Thank you for choosing to stay with us! We hope you had a wonderful time and enjoyed your visit." This message should also include a polite request for a review. For example, "We would be grateful if you could take a moment to share your experience by leaving a review. Your feedback helps us improve and assists other travelers in making their booking decisions."

The act of requesting a review should be handled with grace and sincerity, not as a demand. The tone should be appreciative, acknowledging that leaving a review takes time and effort. It's also an opportune moment to gently remind them of any specific amenities or experiences they might have particularly enjoyed, subtly prompting them to include these in their feedback. For instance, if your property is known for its comfortable beds or its proximity to a popular attraction, a subtle mention can encourage guests to highlight these positive aspects in their review.

It is crucial to maintain consistency in your communication style across all messages, whether automated or manual. This consistency helps build a professional image and reinforces the overall guest experience. If your property is marketed as luxurious and serene, your messages should reflect that tone. Conversely, if it's a fun, quirky getaway, your communication can be more playful. The key is authenticity and alignment with your property's brand.

Furthermore, while automation is a powerful tool, it should not entirely replace personalized interaction. Be prepared to monitor guest communications and interject with personal messages when appropriate. If a guest sends a specific question or a compliment through the platform, a prompt, personal response is far more impactful than a generic automated reply. Building rapport through personalized touches can transform a satisfactory stay into an exceptional one and significantly increase the likelihood of repeat bookings and positive word-of-mouth referrals.

For instance, if a guest messages you prior to arrival asking for recommendations on local restaurants, a well-researched, personalized response with a few tailored suggestions based on their stated preferences is far more valuable than a pre-written list of popular eateries. This level of engagement demonstrates genuine care and a commitment to ensuring their trip is memorable. Similarly, if a guest encounters a minor issue during their stay, such as a Wi-Fi outage or a problem with an appliance, a swift, empathetic, and effective resolution delivered through clear communication is paramount. A prompt personal message acknowledging the issue and outlining the steps being taken to resolve it can significantly mitigate any negative impact on their experience.

It's also essential to have a clear system for handling guest inquiries that are not covered by automated messages. This means designating specific times to check your messages and respond promptly. Delays in responding to guest questions, especially those related to logistics or immediate needs, can lead to frustration and dissatisfaction. Aim to respond to all manual inquiries within a few hours, if not sooner, particularly if they pertain to issues that are currently impacting the guest's stay. Consider setting up notifications on your phone or computer to alert you to new messages, ensuring you never miss an important communication.

The communication flow should also anticipate potential issues. For example, if you know that local events or holidays might affect traffic or availability of services, you can proactively inform guests of this in your pre-arrival messages. This forethought demonstrates your commitment to guest comfort and can help them plan accordingly, thereby preventing potential frustrations. Similarly, if weather conditions are expected to be challenging during their stay, a message with advice on how to prepare or alternative activities can be greatly appreciated.

Beyond managing the direct guest interactions, it's also wise to have a strategy for responding to reviews, both positive and negative. Positive reviews are an opportunity to express gratitude and reinforce the good experience. A simple, sincere "Thank you for your kind words! We're so glad you enjoyed your stay" can go a long way. For negative reviews, it's crucial to respond promptly and professionally. Acknowledge the guest's feedback, apologize for any shortcomings they experienced, and briefly explain any steps being taken to address the issue. This demonstrates to future guests that you are responsive and committed to improvement, even when faced with criticism. Avoid becoming defensive; focus on empathy and solutions.

The efficiency of your communication system is directly tied to the tools you employ. Leveraging the messaging features within the Airbnb platform is a good starting point, but for more robust automation and integration, consider using specialized short-term rental management software. These platforms often allow for advanced automation rules, personalized message templates, and the ability to manage communication across multiple booking channels. Exploring these tools can significantly enhance your ability to deliver consistent and timely communication, freeing up your time to focus on other aspects of your business.

For example, software like Guesty, Hostaway, or Smoobu can automate your entire guest communication lifecycle. You can set up triggers for specific events, such as booking confirmation, approaching check-in, mid-stay check-ins, and post-stay thank you messages. These platforms often allow for dynamic content within messages, meaning you can automatically insert the guest's name, check-in dates, or specific property details. This level of personalization, even within automated messages, greatly enhances the guest experience and makes them feel individually valued.

Furthermore, these platforms can help manage inquiries from various sources, consolidating them into a single inbox. This is particularly beneficial if you are managing listings on multiple platforms beyond Airbnb, such as Booking.com or Vrbo. By having a unified communication system, you ensure that no guest inquiry falls through the cracks and that you can maintain a consistent response time across all channels.

When crafting your automated messages, it's beneficial to create a library of templates that you can easily adapt. These templates should cover common scenarios, such as initial booking confirmation, pre-arrival instructions, mid-stay check-ins, check-out procedures, and post-stay thank you notes. By having these pre-written, you can significantly reduce the time spent on repetitive communication tasks. However, always remember to review and personalize these templates before sending them out. Adding the guest's name and referencing specific aspects of their stay can make the communication feel much more personal and impactful.

Consider the timing of your messages very carefully. Sending check-in instructions too early might result in guests forgetting them by the time they arrive. Sending them too late can cause anxiety and last-minute scrambling. A good rule of thumb is to send critical information like check-in details 24-48 hours before arrival. Similarly, a post-stay thank you message should be sent soon after check-out, while the guest's experience is still fresh in their mind.

The ultimate goal of developing efficient guest communication flows is to create a seamless and positive experience from the initial inquiry to the final review. By leveraging automation strategically, maintaining personalized interactions, and ensuring prompt and clear responses, you build trust, manage expectations, and significantly contribute to guest satisfaction. This, in turn, leads to higher ratings, more positive reviews, and a stronger reputation for your short-term rental business, ultimately driving more bookings and increasing your profitability. It transforms the transactional nature of a booking into a relational experience, fostering loyalty and encouraging repeat business.

Implementing a Robust Checkin Checkout Process

The transition from a guest's anticipation to their actual arrival marks a pivotal moment in their short-term rental experience. This is where the carefully crafted digital handshake of pre-arrival communication solidifies into tangible reality. A robust check-in process isn't merely about handing over keys; it's about creating a welcoming atmosphere, providing essential information, and ensuring the guest feels comfortable and confident from the very first moment they interact with your property. The goal here is to eliminate any potential friction, confusion, or uncertainty, thereby setting a positive trajectory for their entire stay.

The method of check-in will heavily depend on your property's setup and your operational model. For those who can offer a personal welcome, this is an invaluable opportunity. A friendly face greeting guests at the door, offering a warm smile and a sincere "Welcome!", immediately humanizes the experience. Beyond the pleasantries, a brief, guided tour can be incredibly beneficial. This isn't about micromanaging, but rather about highlighting key features and essential functions. Pointing out how to operate the thermostat, where the circuit breaker is located (just in case), how to use the television or any streaming services, and the location of extra amenities like extra blankets, towels, or even a first-aid kit, can preempt many common questions. It also allows you to subtly reinforce house rules, such as designated smoking areas or quiet hours, in a non-confrontational manner. The personal touch fosters a sense of connection and demonstrates a commitment to guest comfort that automated messages, however well-crafted, cannot fully replicate. This approach is particularly effective for unique properties or for hosts who genuinely enjoy interacting with their guests. However, it requires careful scheduling and flexibility to accommodate varying arrival times and potential travel delays.

For many hosts, however, the logistics of personal check-ins are challenging to manage, especially with multiple properties or irregular guest arrivals. This is where self-check-in solutions shine, offering unparalleled convenience and flexibility for both the host and the guest. Smart locks, which allow for keyless entry via a unique access code, are increasingly popular. The process begins with generating a unique, temporary code for each guest, which is typically programmed to be active only for the duration of their stay. This code should be communicated securely and clearly in your pre-arrival message, ideally a day or two before they arrive. It's crucial to include precise instructions on how to use the smart lock, including any specific button presses or sequences required. For example, "To unlock the door, please enter your code [XXXX] and press the " button." The location of the lock should also be clearly indicated, perhaps with a photo or a description such as, "The smart lock is on the main entrance door, to the right of the peephole."

Alongside smart locks, traditional lockboxes remain a viable and cost-effective self-check-in option. These are secure metal boxes, typically attached to a railing, doorknob, or a discreet location near the entrance, which contain the physical key. The process involves providing guests with a combination or a key to open the lockbox, retrieve the key, and then re-securing the empty lockbox. Clear, step-by-step instructions are paramount here too. Specify the exact location of the lockbox – "It's mounted on the black metal railing to the left of the front door." – and detail how to open it. For combination lockboxes, provide the specific sequence of numbers. For keyed lockboxes, you'll need to arrange for the guest to obtain the key, which might involve picking it up from a nearby designated location or arranging a specific pick-up time. In either self-check-in scenario, it's vital to emphasize what guests should do with the key once they are inside the property. Should they leave it in the lockbox? In a designated bowl inside? Should they lock the door with the key when they leave? Clarity here prevents confusion and ensures the security of your property.

Regardless of the check-in method, the information provided must be exceptionally clear and comprehensive. This includes not only how to access the property but also critical details such as parking. Are there designated parking spots? Is street parking available, and are there any restrictions or meter requirements? If there's a particular parking permit guests need to display, ensure this is clearly explained and that the permit is readily available. Wi-Fi information, including the network name and password, is another essential piece of information that guests will want to access immediately upon arrival. Providing this upfront in your check-in instructions saves them the effort of searching for it. Any specific instructions about appliances, such as setting a programmable thermostat or operating a particular oven, can also be included if they are not immediately intuitive.

A crucial element of a successful check-in, particularly with self-access, is a "welcome pack" or a detailed digital guide. This can be a beautifully designed PDF document, a dedicated guest app, or even a physical binder left at the property. This guide should consolidate all essential information: contact details for emergencies, Wi-Fi password, instructions for all major appliances, local recommendations (restaurants, attractions, transport), and a summary of house rules. Having this readily available empowers guests to find answers to their questions independently, reducing their reliance on immediate host communication and enhancing their sense of autonomy. For a digital guide, consider including links to local transport schedules, menus of nearby restaurants, or even short video tutorials on how to use specific amenities.

The transition from the initial check-in to the guest settling in requires a thoughtful follow-up. A brief, non-intrusive message a few hours after the designated check-in time can make a significant difference. Something as simple as, "Hi [Guest Name], just wanted to check in and make sure you found everything okay and settled in smoothly. Please don't hesitate to reach out if you need anything at all!" This proactive touch assures guests that you are attentive and available, fostering a sense of care and support. It also provides an early opportunity to address any minor issues that may have arisen, such as a lightbulb needing replacement or a question about a kitchen appliance. Addressing these small concerns promptly can prevent them from escalating into larger problems that might impact the guest's overall satisfaction.

The check-out process, while perhaps less outwardly critical than check-in, is the final impression a guest takes away from your property. A smooth and clear check-out experience ensures that their departure is as hassle-free as their arrival. The evening before or the morning of their departure, send a reminder message that clearly states the check-out time. This message should also reiterate any specific procedures you require. For instance, "Please ensure all windows are closed and locked, and all lights are turned off before you depart." If you have a preferred method for key return with a lockbox or smart lock, restate those instructions. For example, if using a lockbox, remind them, "Please return the key to the lockbox located on the front door railing and scramble the numbers to secure it." If you require guests to strip beds or place used towels in a specific location, include these instructions politely. "We would appreciate it if you could gather all used towels in the laundry basket in the bathroom."

It's also an opportune moment to gently prompt for a review. Once again, the tone should be appreciative. "Thank you for staying with us, [Guest Name]! We hope you had a wonderful and comfortable stay. If you have a moment, we would be grateful if you could share your experience by leaving a review on [Platform Name]. Your feedback helps us improve and assists future travelers." Providing the direct link to leave a review can also be helpful, reducing the effort required from the guest. This reinforces the positive experience and encourages them to share their satisfaction, which is invaluable for your business.

For those who offer personal check-outs, ensure you arrive at the agreed-upon time, or a few minutes early. Be prepared to assist guests with any last-minute questions or help them load luggage into their vehicles. A final, warm farewell reinforces the positive impression. "Thank you for being wonderful guests. We hope you have a safe journey home!"

The efficiency of your check-in and check-out processes can be significantly enhanced through the use of technology and well-prepared materials. For self-check-in, ensure your smart lock or lockbox is regularly maintained and tested. Batteries in smart locks should be replaced proactively, and lockbox combinations should be reset between guests. Clear signage near the entry can also be beneficial, perhaps a small, discreet sign with your property name or a friendly "Welcome" message, guiding guests to the correct entrance. If your property is part of a larger complex, providing a map or specific directions to your unit within the complex can prevent guests from getting lost.

Consider implementing a tiered system for providing check-in information. A concise summary of the essential access details can be sent immediately after booking confirmation, while the more comprehensive instructions and property guide can be sent 24-48 hours prior to arrival. This layered approach ensures that guests have the critical information when they need it without overwhelming them too early.

The post-check-out period is also important. Once the guest has departed, it's beneficial to have a quick process for checking the property. This initial inspection can identify any immediate issues or damage. If any problems are discovered that were not reported by the guest, you can then address them and, if necessary, communicate with the guest through the booking platform about their stay. This is also the time to prepare the property for the next guest, a process that leads into the operational flow of cleaning and maintenance, which we will cover in the next chapter.

Ultimately, the goal of perfecting your check-in and check-out procedures is to create a seamless, welcoming, and convenient experience that aligns with the expectations set by your listing. It's about anticipating guest needs, providing clarity, and offering flexibility where possible. Whether you're there to greet them with a smile or entrusting them with a code, these transition points are your prime opportunities to demonstrate exceptional hospitality, ensuring guests feel valued from arrival to departure, and ultimately, encouraging them to return and recommend your property to others. A well-executed check-in and check-out is not just a logistical necessity; it's a powerful tool for building guest loyalty and enhancing your reputation in the competitive short-term rental market. It's the bedrock upon which a truly stellar guest experience is built, transforming a simple transaction into a memorable stay.

Maintaining Impeccable Cleanliness Standards

The cornerstone of any successful short-term rental operation, and indeed the bedrock of exceptional guest satisfaction, is an unwavering commitment to cleanliness. In an industry where guest reviews are currency, and word-of-mouth (both digital and anecdotal) can make or break a business, maintaining impeccable hygiene standards is not merely a best practice; it is an absolute imperative. Guests arrive with expectations shaped by personal experiences, online photos, and the general reputation of hospitality services. When they walk into your rental, the very first sensory inputs—sight and smell—will largely dictate their initial impression. A sparkling clean environment, free from dust, grime, and any lingering odors, immediately signals professionalism, care, and attention to detail. Conversely, even minor oversights in cleanliness can lead to disappointment, negative reviews, and a diminished reputation that is incredibly difficult to repair. Therefore, establishing and consistently executing rigorous cleaning protocols between each guest turnover is a critical operational function that directly impacts guest satisfaction, repeat bookings, and overall profitability.

To achieve this level of consistent cleanliness, a systematic approach is essential. This begins with the development of detailed cleaning checklists. These aren't just simple to-do lists; they are comprehensive, step-by-step guides designed to ensure that every single area and every item within the property is addressed with meticulous care. For professional cleaning teams, or even for yourself if you are self-managing, these checklists serve as a standardized operational manual. They should be broken down by room or specific task categories, ensuring nothing is overlooked.

Consider a typical guest bathroom. The checklist for this space should go far beyond a quick wipe-down. It needs to include sanitizing and scrubbing the toilet bowl, both inside and out, paying particular attention to the base and behind the tank. The sink and countertop must be thoroughly cleaned and disinfected, ensuring no soap scum or water spots remain. Faucets and handles should be polished to a shine. The mirror should be cleaned to a streak-free finish. The shower or bathtub requires a deep clean, addressing grout lines, showerheads, and drain covers to remove any soap residue or mildew. The floor should be swept, mopped, and ideally disinfected, paying attention to corners and around the toilet base. Emptying the trash bin, wiping it down, and replacing the liner is a standard but crucial step. Furthermore, areas that guests might not immediately think of, but are still vital for hygiene, should be included. This encompasses cleaning the light switches, door handles, and cabinet knobs, as these are frequently touched surfaces. A check for hair in drains, along with their cleaning, is also critical. The checklist should also specify the replenishment of essential supplies: toilet paper rolls should be full, soap should be readily available, and fresh hand towels should be neatly folded or rolled.

Moving to the kitchen, the standards should be equally, if not more, stringent. The checklist must mandate the thorough cleaning and sanitizing of countertops, ensuring all food debris and stains are removed. The sink needs to be scrubbed and disinfected, and the faucet polished. Appliance exteriors—refrigerator, oven, microwave, dishwasher—should be wiped down and polished to remove fingerprints and smudges. Inside the microwave, any splatters must be cleaned. The stovetop and oven require a more intensive clean, removing grease

and food remnants. If the oven has a self-cleaning function, its availability and condition should be noted. The refrigerator should be
checked for cleanliness, with any spills or residues wiped up. It's also
a good practice to ensure it's empty and odor-free for the next guest.
Cabinet fronts and handles should be cleaned to remove smudges.
The kitchen floor must be swept and mopped, with particular attention to areas around appliances where crumbs and spills can accumulate. Dish racks should be clean, and if a dishwasher is provided,
it should be emptied and the interior wiped down, and the filter
checked and cleaned if necessary. The checklist should also confirm
the availability and cleanliness of kitchen linens, such as dish towels
and hand towels.

For living areas and bedrooms, the focus shifts to creating a comfortable and inviting atmosphere, underpinned by cleanliness. This
involves dusting all surfaces, including furniture, shelves, and decorative items, ensuring no visible dust layers. Floors—whether carpet-
ed or hard surface—require thorough vacuuming or sweeping and
mopping, respectively. Baseboards should be wiped down to remove
dust and scuff marks. Upholstered furniture should be vacuumed,
checking under cushions for dropped items or debris. If there are any
stains on furniture or carpets, a plan for spot cleaning should be in
place. Beds should be stripped, and mattresses and pillows should be
inspected for cleanliness and protected with clean mattress and pillow
protectors. Bedding must be replaced with fresh, clean linens. It's also
crucial to check under beds and behind furniture for any forgotten
items or dust bunnies. Windows should be cleaned inside and out, and
window sills wiped down. Light fixtures and ceiling fans should be
dusted to remove accumulated dust. All accessible surfaces, including
TV remotes, light switches, and door handles, should be disinfected.

The checklist should also incorporate a thorough inspection of each room to ensure that all amenities are functioning correctly and are in their proper place. This includes checking that all lights work, that the TV and any associated remotes are present and have fresh batteries if needed, and that any provided electronics are clean and operational. For a property with a balcony or patio, outdoor furniture should be wiped down, and the area swept clean.

A critical element in maintaining these high standards is the management of laundry. The sheer volume of linens and towels required for short-term rentals necessitates an efficient and effective laundry process. This typically involves separate washes for towels and bedding to prevent cross-contamination and ensure optimal cleaning. High-temperature washes are often necessary to kill germs and bacteria. All linens and towels must be dried completely to prevent mildew and must be ironed or neatly folded and stored. Any linens or towels that show signs of wear, staining, or damage should be immediately retired from service and replaced. This requires a robust inventory management system for linens, ensuring you always have enough clean stock on hand. Consider having multiple sets of bedding for each bed and multiple sets of towels per guest capacity. The process of collecting used linens and transporting them to the laundry area should also be organized to prevent the spread of dirt and potential allergens throughout the property. This might involve using designated laundry bags.

Beyond the physical cleaning, the "presentation" of the property is also intrinsically linked to its perceived cleanliness. This means ensuring that everything is in its correct place, neatly arranged, and aesthetically pleasing. This includes aligning pillows on beds, folding towels in an appealing manner, ensuring decorative items are dusted and positioned correctly, and that the overall ambiance of the space is welcoming and uncluttered. A clean property that is also well-presented leaves a lasting positive impression.

To enforce these standards, a robust inspection process is indispensable. This inspection should ideally be conducted by someone other than the cleaning team to provide an objective assessment. The inspector's role is to review the property against the established cleaning checklist, ensuring all tasks have been completed to the required standard. This involves a systematic walk-through of each room, looking for any missed spots, streaks, or areas that require further attention. The inspector should have a keen eye for detail, checking high-touch surfaces, bathrooms, kitchens, and bedrooms with a critical perspective. This might involve using a flashlight to reveal dust in corners or under furniture, or checking that mirrors are truly streak-free.

Any deficiencies identified during the inspection must be documented and immediately communicated back to the cleaning team for rectification. This feedback loop is vital for continuous improvement. If the same issues arise repeatedly with a particular cleaner or team, it may indicate a need for retraining or a reassessment of their performance. For self-managed properties, this inspection serves as a personal quality control step, ensuring you are confident in presenting the property to the next guest.

The frequency of cleaning is obviously between every guest stay. However, for longer stays, a mid-stay cleaning service can be offered as an optional add-on or included in the rate, depending on your pricing strategy and the property type. This provides an additional touchpoint for maintaining cleanliness and can enhance guest satisfaction for those staying for extended periods.

The investment in high-quality cleaning supplies and equipment also plays a significant role. Using effective disinfectants, microfiber cloths, efficient vacuums, and reliable mops contributes to a better cleaning outcome and can also increase the speed and efficiency of the cleaning process. Ensuring that cleaning teams are properly trained on the correct usage of these supplies and equipment is also paramount.

In a competitive market, going above and beyond basic cleanliness can differentiate your property. This could include small touches like providing individually wrapped sanitizing wipes for guests to use during their stay, or having a readily available supply of hand sanitizer. Offering a pleasant, subtle scent to the property upon arrival – through diffusers or natural air fresheners – can also contribute to a positive sensory experience, provided that strong artificial fragrances are avoided, which can be irritating for some guests.

Furthermore, the maintenance schedule for the property should be integrated with the cleaning protocols. Regular deep cleaning of carpets, upholstery, and ventilation systems, along with routine checks of plumbing and electrical fixtures, contributes to an overall sense of hygiene and well-being. If any maintenance issues are identified during the cleaning or inspection process, they should be addressed promptly to prevent them from impacting future guest stays.

Building a relationship with a reliable and professional cleaning service is a wise investment for any short-term rental operator. When selecting a cleaning partner, look for services that specialize in short-term rentals, as they will understand the unique demands and timelines involved. Requesting references and checking their insurance coverage are essential steps in this process. Clear communication regarding expectations, turnaround times, and specific cleaning requirements is vital for a successful partnership.

Ultimately, the commitment to cleanliness is a continuous process, not a one-time task. It requires ongoing vigilance, a willingness to invest in quality, and a dedication to exceeding guest expectations. By implementing rigorous cleaning checklists, managing laundry efficiently, conducting thorough inspections, and fostering a culture of high standards, you can ensure that your short-term rental property consistently offers a welcoming, hygienic, and memorable experience for every guest, thereby building a strong reputation and a thriving business. This dedication to detail in cleanliness is one of the most powerful levers you have to ensure positive guest reviews and encourage repeat bookings, solidifying your position as a host of choice.

Managing Bookings and Calendar Synchronization

The lifeblood of a successful short-term rental business, beyond impeccable cleanliness and a welcoming atmosphere, is the efficient and accurate management of bookings. In today's multi-channel booking landscape, where guests can discover your property on Airbnb, Booking.com, Vrbo, or even your own direct booking website, maintaining a synchronized and up-to-date calendar is not just beneficial; it's absolutely critical. A single double booking can lead to a cascade of negative consequences: disappointed guests, cancellation fees, damage to your host reputation, and lost revenue that can be difficult to recoup. This section delves into the essential strategies and tools that will empower you to master your booking calendar, ensuring every reservation is processed smoothly and every potential guest finds your availability accurately reflected.

The fundamental challenge lies in the fact that each booking channel operates independently unless explicitly linked. If you list your property on Airbnb and then receive a booking directly through your own website or another platform, and your Airbnb calendar isn't updated in real-time, you risk accepting a reservation for a date that is already occupied. This scenario is the bane of any short-term rental host. The solution lies in robust calendar synchronization. At its core, calendar synchronization involves establishing a reliable connection between all the platforms where your property is listed. When a booking is confirmed on one channel, the system automatically updates the availability on all other connected channels, effectively blocking out those dates. This automated process is the most effective way to prevent the dreaded double booking.

The primary method for achieving this synchronization is through the use of the iCalendar (or .ics) feed. Most major booking platforms provide an iCalendar feed that exports your booking data in a standardized format. You can then import this feed into other platforms. For instance, you can export your Airbnb calendar and import it into Booking.com, and vice-versa. This creates a basic level of synchronization. However, it's important to understand the limitations of this method. iCalendar feeds are typically updated periodically, not instantaneously. This means there can be a delay, often several hours, between a booking being confirmed on one platform and the calendar being updated on another. During this delay window, the risk of a double booking still exists. Therefore, while iCalendar synchronization is a necessary step, it is often not sufficient for highly active properties or for hosts who are highly risk-averse.

To overcome the limitations of iCalendar feeds, many hosts graduate to using specialized Vacation Rental Management Software (VRMS) or Channel Managers. These powerful tools are designed specifically for the short-term rental industry and offer a far more sophisticated approach to calendar management. A channel manager acts as a central hub for all your booking channels. You connect all your listing sites (Airbnb, Booking.com, Vrbo, etc.) and any direct booking channels to the channel manager. The channel manager then pulls in all bookings and availability information from each source and pushes out your updated availability to all connected channels in near real-time. This sophisticated two-way synchronization significantly reduces, and in most cases, virtually eliminates the risk of double bookings.

When selecting a channel manager or VRMS, several features are paramount for effective calendar management. Firstly, the breadth of integrations is crucial. Ensure the software supports all the platforms you use or plan to use. Secondly, the speed of synchronization is key. Look for systems that offer real-time or near real-time updates. Thirdly, user-friendliness is important. You'll be interacting with this system daily, so an intuitive interface will save you time and frustration. Finally, consider the additional features offered. Many VRMS platforms also offer tools for automated guest communication, pricing optimization, task management for cleaning and maintenance, and direct booking website creation, all of which contribute to a more streamlined and profitable operation.

The implementation of a channel manager is a pivotal step in professionalizing your short-term rental business. It transforms a potentially chaotic system of manual updates and potential errors into an automated, efficient engine. For example, imagine a scenario where a guest books your property on Airbnb for a specific weekend. The channel manager receives this booking information, automatically updates your availability on Booking.com and Vrbo to block those dates, and simultaneously removes those dates from your direct booking website. This entire process happens seamlessly in the background, freeing you from the constant worry of manual calendar checks and updates across multiple interfaces.

Beyond avoiding double bookings, accurate calendar management is essential for maximizing revenue. By having a clear and up-to-date view of your availability, you can strategically price your property. Tools within VRMS can often suggest dynamic pricing based on demand, seasonality, local events, and competitor pricing. Without an accurate calendar, you might miss opportunities to adjust your rates during peak demand periods, or conversely, be forced to lower prices to fill dates that were incorrectly shown as unavailable elsewhere. A synchronized calendar ensures you are always presenting your most accurate availability to the widest possible audience, thereby increasing your visibility and booking potential.

Furthermore, maintaining an accurate calendar directly impacts your guest experience before they even arrive. When guests browse listings, they rely on the displayed availability. If they find your property and see it's available, they expect to be able to book it. If they go through the booking process only to be told the dates are no longer available due to a synchronization error on your end, it creates a negative first impression. This can lead to frustration, lost interest in your property, and potentially a negative review. Conversely, a consistently accurate display of availability builds trust and confidence with potential guests, making them more likely to choose your property.

The process of setting up calendar synchronization requires careful attention to detail. Once you've chosen your VRMS or channel manager, you'll need to connect each of your listing channels. This typically involves authorizing the channel manager to access your account on each platform. You'll also need to ensure that your property details, amenities, and photos are consistent across all platforms to avoid any discrepancies that might confuse guests. The initial setup can take some time, but the long-term benefits in terms of saved time, reduced stress, and increased bookings are substantial.

It's also important to regularly audit your synchronization to ensure it's working correctly. While channel managers are highly reliable, occasional glitches or connection issues can occur. Periodically, cross-reference your calendars on different platforms. Check if a recent booking on one platform has been correctly reflected on others. Many channel managers provide reporting tools that can help you track synchronization status and identify any errors. Proactive monitoring will catch any issues before they lead to a double booking.

For those who are just starting out or manage only one or two properties with limited listings on a few platforms, iCalendar synchronization might suffice initially. However, it's crucial to be aware of its limitations and to implement a robust system for manually updating calendars if you are relying on this method. This might involve setting calendar alerts for yourself or having a clear protocol for when and how you will manually update each platform after a booking is confirmed. As your business grows and you aim to maximize occupancy across multiple channels, investing in a reliable channel manager becomes an indispensable part of your operational toolkit. It's an investment that pays for itself by preventing lost revenue and enhancing your professional image in the competitive short-term rental market. The peace of mind that comes from knowing your calendars are reliably synchronized is invaluable, allowing you to focus on providing exceptional guest experiences rather than constantly worrying about booking conflicts.

Handling Guest Issues and Complaints Effectively

Even with the most meticulous planning and robust systems in place, the dynamic nature of short-term rentals means that unforeseen issues and guest complaints are an inevitable part of the hosting journey. Your ability to navigate these challenges effectively will be a defining factor in the success of your business, significantly impacting guest satisfaction, online reputation, and ultimately, your profitability. This section is dedicated to equipping you with the essential strategies and mindset to handle guest issues and complaints with professionalism, empathy, and a commitment to finding optimal solutions. The goal is not merely to resolve problems, but to transform potentially negative experiences into demonstrations of exceptional customer service, thereby strengthening guest loyalty and safeguarding your hard-earned reputation.

The first and perhaps most critical principle when faced with a guest complaint is to remain calm and composed. It can be tempting to become defensive, especially if you feel the complaint is unfounded or exaggerated. However, allowing frustration or anger to dictate your response will only escalate the situation. Take a deep breath. Remember that from the guest's perspective, their issue is real and impacting their stay. Your immediate reaction sets the tone for the entire interaction. Approach the situation with a calm demeanor and a genuine willingness to listen. This initial step of emotional regulation is paramount to de-escalating any potential conflict and creating an environment conducive to resolution.

Empathy is your most powerful tool in handling guest complaints. Put yourself in the guest's shoes. Imagine arriving at a property only to discover an issue that is causing inconvenience or discomfort. How would you want to be treated? Acknowledging their feelings and validating their experience is crucial. Phrases like "I understand how frustrating that must be," or "I'm so sorry to hear you're experiencing this," can go a long way in making the guest feel heard and understood. This doesn't necessarily mean admitting fault immediately, but rather demonstrating that you appreciate the impact the issue is having on their stay. This empathetic approach builds rapport and creates a foundation of trust, making the guest more receptive to your proposed solutions.

Once you've listened and shown empathy, it's time to gather all the necessary information about the issue. Ask clarifying questions to fully understand the nature and scope of the problem. Is it a minor inconvenience or a significant disruption? Are there specific details about the malfunction, the cleanliness issue, or the amenity that isn't working as expected? The more clearly you understand the problem, the better equipped you will be to offer an appropriate and effective solution. Avoid making assumptions. Sometimes, what seems obvious to you might be different from the guest's perception.

The key to effective problem-solving is to be solution-oriented. Once you have a clear understanding of the issue, focus your energy on finding a resolution rather than dwelling on blame. Present the guest with clear, actionable options for addressing the problem. This might involve offering a repair, a replacement, a partial refund, a discount on a future stay, or an alternative amenity. The best solution will often depend on the nature of the complaint, its severity, and the impact it has on the guest's experience. Empower the guest by allowing them to choose from a few viable solutions, if appropriate. This sense of agency can significantly improve their perception of how the issue was handled.

For instance, if a guest reports that the Wi-Fi is not working, your immediate response should be to troubleshoot. This could involve guiding them through a simple router reset, checking if other guests are experiencing the same issue, or contacting your internet service provider. If the problem persists and cannot be resolved quickly, you might offer a credit for a portion of their stay, a voucher for a local cafe or attraction, or even offer to relocate them to another comparable property if one is available. The specific remedy should be proportionate to the inconvenience caused. The aim is to restore their satisfaction with their stay, or at least mitigate the negative impact.

Consider a scenario where a guest reports an issue with cleanliness, such as finding hair in the bathroom or crumbs on a surface. Your initial response must be one of sincere apology. This is a critical failure in the basic expectation of a short-term rental. Immediately offer to send your cleaning team back to re-clean the affected area, or if possible, the entire property. If it's late at night or early in the morning, and immediate re-cleaning isn't feasible, you might offer a complimentary service for their next stay or a partial refund to compensate for the lapse in quality. Providing them with fresh towels or toiletries can also be a small gesture that shows you are actively addressing the issue.

When dealing with noise complaints, either from the guest or about the guest, your approach needs to be diplomatic and swift. If a guest is complaining about noise from neighbors or other guests, you need to investigate the source and address it promptly. If the complaint is about your guest making too much noise, you will need to contact them directly. Your communication should be polite but firm, reminding them of the house rules regarding quiet hours. Offering to check in with them later to ensure the issue has been resolved is a good practice. If the noise continues despite a warning, you may need to take further action as outlined in your booking agreement, such as issuing a warning that further disturbances could lead to eviction.

In situations involving malfunctioning amenities, such as a broken air conditioner in the summer or a faulty heating system in the winter, prompt action is crucial. These are not minor inconveniences; they can significantly impact a guest's comfort and health. If the repair can be made within a few hours, and you have a reliable handyman available, that should be your first course of action. If a repair will take longer, or if the amenity is essential for comfort, you may need to offer alternative solutions. This could include providing portable fans or heaters, offering a discount on their stay, or in extreme cases, arranging for them to stay at a comparable property until the issue is resolved. Documenting your attempts to fix the problem is essential, as is communicating your efforts clearly to the guest.

It's also important to establish clear communication channels for guests to report issues. Provide them with your contact number, email address, or a dedicated messaging app. Let them know the best times to reach you and what to expect in terms of response times. The quicker a guest can report a problem, the quicker you can address it. This proactive communication strategy can prevent minor issues from escalating into major complaints. Transparency about your availability and your process for handling issues builds confidence and manages guest expectations.

Turning a negative situation into a positive one is an art form in customer service. While you aim to prevent complaints, when they do arise, your response can significantly influence the guest's overall perception of their stay and your professionalism. If you handle a complaint swiftly, empathetically, and effectively, guests are often more impressed by your problem-solving skills than they would have been if everything had gone perfectly. This can lead to glowing reviews specifically praising your responsiveness and willingness to go the extra mile. For example, a guest who initially booked a property and encountered a minor issue that you resolved to their complete satisfaction might leave a review stating, "The Wi-Fi went out briefly, but the host was incredibly responsive and had it fixed within an hour. They even offered a complimentary bottle of wine for the inconvenience. Excellent service!"

Always follow up with the guest after an issue has been resolved. A quick message or a call to ensure they are now satisfied and that no further problems have arisen demonstrates your continued commitment to their comfort. This follow-up can be the final touch that solidifies a positive resolution and reinforces their positive impression of your hosting. It also provides a final opportunity to address any lingering concerns before they have a chance to post a review.

Furthermore, use guest feedback and complaints as valuable learning opportunities. Analyze recurring issues. Is there a pattern in the complaints you are receiving? For example, if multiple guests have complained about the lack of clear instructions for the smart TV, you can create a more detailed guide. If there are consistent comments about difficult check-in procedures, you can refine your instructions or explore alternative check-in methods. This continuous improvement cycle is vital for evolving your service and preempting future problems. Keep a log of all complaints, the issues, your responses, and the resolution. This not only helps in identifying trends but also serves as a record should any disputes arise later.

It is also wise to have a protocol in place for various types of complaints. This might include a tiered response system, where minor issues are handled directly by you, while more complex or safety-related issues require the involvement of specific service providers or even authorities. Having a clear understanding of when to delegate or seek external help is crucial for efficient and appropriate resolution. For instance, if a guest reports a plumbing emergency that you cannot fix immediately, having a trusted local plumber on speed dial is essential.

When a guest complains, actively listen and apologize sincerely for the inconvenience caused. Avoid making excuses. Focus on what you can do to rectify the situation. Offer concrete solutions, such as sending a repair person, offering a partial refund, or providing a discount on a future stay. It's important to have the authority to offer these resolutions or to have a system in place to get approval quickly. Delays in offering solutions can exacerbate a guest's frustration.

Documenting every interaction and resolution is also a crucial aspect of handling complaints. This record-keeping can be invaluable if a dispute arises or if the guest leaves a review that misrepresents the situation. Ensure your communication with the guest is clear, concise, and professional at all times. Keep a record of all messages, emails, and phone call summaries. This documentation serves as evidence of your efforts to resolve the issue and maintain a high standard of service.

Consider the impact of online reviews. A poorly handled complaint can lead to a scathing review that deters future bookings. Conversely, a guest who experiences a problem but sees it resolved professionally and empathetically might leave a positive review that highlights your excellent customer service. For example, a guest might write, "We had an issue with the hot water on our first night, but [Host Name] responded immediately, sent a plumber, and even offered us a complimentary breakfast voucher at a nearby cafe. They turned a potential disaster into a testament to their commitment to guest satisfaction." Such reviews are invaluable marketing assets.

Never underestimate the power of a well-written apology and a tangible gesture of goodwill. A sincere apology validates the guest's feelings, and a small compensation, whether it's a discount, a free amenity, or a local gift, shows that you value their business and are willing to make amends. The key is to offer something that is perceived as fair and proportionate to the inconvenience experienced.

Finally, remember that your response to issues is a direct reflection of your brand and your commitment to providing a superior guest experience. By approaching every complaint with a problem-solving mindset, empathy, and a dedication to excellence, you can not only mitigate negative outcomes but also create loyal guests who will return and recommend your property to others. Mastering the art of handling guest issues is not just about damage control; it's about opportunity creation. It's about demonstrating your professionalism, resilience, and unwavering dedication to ensuring every guest has a memorable and positive stay, even when things don't go exactly as planned. This proactive and empathetic approach to problem resolution is what separates good hosts from exceptional ones in the competitive landscape of short-term rentals.

Chapter Five

Scaling Your Portfolio: Beyond the First Property

Developing a Scalable Operational System

The transition from managing a single property to overseeing a portfolio of short-term rentals marks a significant inflection point in your entrepreneurial journey. While the thrill of expansion is palpable, the inherent complexity of managing multiple distinct locations, each with its own unique set of guests, operational demands, and potential challenges, can quickly become a bottleneck if not approached strategically. This is where the concept of developing a scalable operational system truly comes into play. It's not merely about acquiring more properties; it's about building a robust framework that allows you to manage this growth efficiently, consistently, and without sacrificing the quality of guest experience that forms the bedrock of your success. Without a well-defined and repeatable operational structure, scaling your portfolio can lead to a rapid descent into chaos, burnout, and ultimately, diminished returns. The aim is to create a business that runs

for you, not one that you are constantly running in.

At its core, a scalable operational system is a meticulously documented set of procedures and protocols designed to handle every facet of property management in a consistent and efficient manner. This involves moving beyond ad-hoc problem-solving and embracing a proactive, system-driven approach. Think of it as building the internal machinery of your business. Each machine—each process—must be designed for optimal performance and repeatability. This foundation is critical because as you add more properties, the sheer volume of tasks multiplies, and without standardization, each new property becomes a fresh set of unique challenges to be solved, draining your time and resources. The goal is to standardize the mundane, so you have more capacity to handle the exceptions and to strategize for future growth.

One of the foundational pillars of any scalable operational system is comprehensive documentation. This isn't just about creating a simple to-do list; it's about creating an operational bible for your business. Every process, from the initial guest inquiry to the final post-stay review, needs to be broken down into its constituent steps and clearly documented. This documentation serves multiple purposes. Firstly, it ensures consistency. When you have multiple cleaners, maintenance staff, or even co-hosts involved, having documented procedures guarantees that tasks are performed to the same high standard every time, regardless of who is performing them. For instance, the "check-in procedure" document should detail every single step: from confirming the guest's arrival time, sending the access code with clear instructions, performing a final walk-through of the property before their arrival, to a designated time for checking in with the guest shortly after their arrival to ensure everything is in order. Similarly, a cleaning checklist should be exhaustive, detailing the specific tasks for each room—from sanitizing light switches and doorknobs to ensuring linens are changed according to specific standards and that all amenities are stocked.

This documentation should also include visual aids where appropriate. For a cleaning checklist, this might mean having photos of what a perfectly clean bathroom or kitchen should look like. For a maintenance task like resetting a smart lock, a step-by-step guide with screenshots or short video clips can be invaluable, especially for remote teams. The level of detail should be such that someone with no prior experience could, in theory, follow the instructions and achieve the desired outcome. This meticulous documentation is what enables you to delegate tasks effectively and confidently, knowing that the quality of service will not suffer. As your portfolio grows and you bring on staff or outsource services, this documented system becomes your primary training manual and quality control mechanism. It's the blueprint for success, ensuring that each guest experience aligns with the high standards you've established, no matter which property they are staying in.

Standardized procedures are the lifeblood of operational efficiency and consistency. These procedures should cover all critical aspects of your short-term rental business. Let's delve deeper into some of these key areas:

Cleaning Protocols: This is arguably the most critical operational area for short-term rentals. Guests expect pristine cleanliness, and any lapse here can lead to immediate negative reviews. Your standardized cleaning protocol needs to be incredibly detailed. It should start with a clear checklist that every cleaner must follow. This checklist should go beyond the obvious; it needs to include often-overlooked areas such as:

Sanitization: Every high-touch surface (light switches, doorknobs, remote controls, appliance handles, faucet handles, toilet flush handles) must be disinfected.

Bedding and Linens: Specify the exact procedure for stripping beds, washing linens (temperature, detergent type), drying, and making beds with fresh linens. Include protocols for pillow protectors and mattress encasements.

Kitchen: Detail cleaning for countertops, sink, stovetop, oven (interior and exterior), microwave (interior and exterior), refrigerator (interior and exterior), coffee maker, toaster, and all kitchen utensils and cookware. Emphasize ensuring all items are returned to their designated places.

Bathrooms: Rigorous cleaning of toilets, showers/bathtubs, sinks, mirrors, and floors is essential. Specify the use of specific cleaning agents for grout and mold if necessary. Check for and replace any used toiletries, soaps, and toilet paper.

Floors: Protocols for vacuuming carpets and rugs, and mopping hard floors, ensuring baseboards are also wiped down.

Trash and Recycling: Ensuring bins are emptied, liners are replaced, and bins themselves are wiped down if necessary.

Final Inspection: A final walk-through by the cleaner or a designated supervisor to ensure all checklist items are completed and the property is immaculate. This might include a photo submission of key areas upon completion.

Beyond the checklist, your documentation should include guidelines on the preferred cleaning products and equipment. This ensures not only consistency but also safety and cost-effectiveness. For example, specifying eco-friendly or hypoallergenic cleaning supplies can be a selling point and cater to a broader range of guests. Training for cleaning staff is paramount. This isn't just a written document; it needs to be a hands-on training process, perhaps involving shadowing experienced cleaners, until proficiency is demonstrated. Regular quality checks, perhaps through random spot-inspections or guest feedback analysis related to cleanliness, are vital to maintain these standards.

Maintenance and Repair Management: A proactive approach to maintenance can prevent many guest complaints. Your system should include:

Preventative Maintenance Schedule: For appliances like HVAC systems, water heaters, dishwashers, and refrigerators, establish a schedule for regular servicing and filter changes. Document when these services are due and who is responsible for scheduling and performing them.

Routine Checks: Implement a schedule for routine checks of minor items that can cause issues, such as smoke detector batteries, CO detector functionality, Wi-Fi connectivity, and general wear and tear on furniture or fixtures.

Reporting System: Create a clear system for reporting any maintenance issues that arise. This could be a digital form that staff or even guests can use, or a dedicated email address. The system should track the issue, its urgency, assigned technician, repair status, and completion.

Vendor Management: Develop relationships with reliable and responsive local service providers (plumbers, electricians, handymen, appliance repair specialists). Have their contact information readily available and pre-negotiate rates if possible. Your documentation should include preferred vendors for different types of repairs, with clear instructions on how to engage them.

Emergency Procedures: Define protocols for handling urgent maintenance issues, such as a burst pipe or a heating failure during winter. This includes having emergency contact numbers for your vendors and a clear escalation path if the primary contact is unavailable.

Guest Communication Standards: Consistent and professional communication is key to a positive guest experience. Your system should outline:

Response Times: Set clear targets for responding to guest inquiries, booking requests, and messages during their stay. For instance, aiming for a response within one hour during active booking times and within 24 hours for less urgent matters.

Standardized Messaging: Develop templated messages for common communications, such as booking confirmations, pre-arrival information (check-in instructions, Wi-Fi details, local recommendations), mid-stay check-ins, and post-stay thank-you messages. These templates should be professional, friendly, and informative, but also allow for personalization.

Issue Resolution Flow: As discussed in the previous section, have a documented process for handling guest complaints or issues, emphasizing empathy, promptness, and a solution-oriented approach. This flow should guide how messages are logged, escalated, and resolved.

Check-in/Check-out Procedures: Standardize the information provided for check-in and check-out, ensuring all necessary details (access codes, Wi-Fi passwords, house rules, departure instructions) are communicated clearly and in advance. Consider automated messaging systems to send these reminders.

The strategic implementation of technology can significantly amplify the scalability of your operations. Many repetitive and time-consuming tasks can be automated, freeing up your time and reducing the potential for human error.

Property Management Software (PMS): Investing in a robust PMS is one of the most impactful steps you can take. These platforms are designed to centralize and streamline various aspects of short-term rental management. Key features to look for include:

Channel Management: The ability to sync your listings across multiple booking platforms (Airbnb, Vrbo, Booking.com, etc.) from a single dashboard. This ensures your calendar is always up-to-date, preventing double bookings, and optimizes your pricing across channels.

Direct Booking Website Integration: Many PMS systems allow you to build and manage your own direct booking website, which can significantly reduce commission fees.

Automated Messaging: Set up automated communication sequences for guest inquiries, booking confirmations, pre-arrival instructions, check-in/check-out reminders, and post-stay follow-ups.

Task Management and Scheduling: Assign tasks to team members (cleaners, maintenance staff) and track their completion. Schedule recurring maintenance tasks.

Payment Processing: Securely process guest payments and manage payouts.

Reporting and Analytics: Generate reports on occupancy rates, revenue, expenses, and guest feedback, providing valuable insights for decision-making.

Examples of popular PMS platforms include Hostaway, Guesty, Smoobu, and OwnerRez. The choice of PMS will depend on the size of your portfolio, your budget, and the specific features you prioritize. It's crucial to select a system that can grow with you.

Smart Home Technology: Integrating smart home devices can enhance guest experience and improve operational efficiency.

Smart Locks: These allow for keyless entry, enabling you to provide unique access codes to guests for specific check-in and check-out times. This eliminates the need for physical key handovers, which can be logistically challenging with multiple properties, and provides an audit trail of who accessed the property and when. Many smart locks can be controlled remotely via a smartphone app, allowing you to grant or revoke access instantly.

Smart Thermostats: These can be programmed to adjust temperatures based on occupancy or time of day, saving energy when the property is vacant and ensuring comfort for guests. Some can be controlled remotely, allowing you to adjust the temperature before a guest arrives or address issues if a guest reports it's too hot or cold.

Smart Security Cameras (Exterior Only): For security and to monitor for unauthorized parties or extra guests, exterior cameras can be invaluable. Ensure these comply with privacy regulations and are clearly disclosed to guests.

Noise Monitoring Devices: These devices, like NoiseAware, can alert you to excessive noise levels within a property without recording conversations, helping you proactively address potential disturbances from guests without infringing on their privacy.

Automation for Specific Tasks: Beyond a full PMS, consider other automation tools:

Dynamic Pricing Software: Tools like PriceLabs or Wheelhouse can analyze market data, competitor pricing, and local events to automatically adjust your nightly rates, maximizing occupancy and revenue.

Digital Signature Tools: For rental agreements or addendums that may be required for certain bookings, using services like DocuSign can streamline the process.

Cloud Storage and Document Management: Utilize services like Google Drive, Dropbox, or OneDrive to store all your important documents (leases, insurance policies, vendor contracts, training materials) securely and make them accessible to your team from anywhere.

The transition to managing a portfolio necessitates a shift in your own role from hands-on operator to strategic manager. This is where delegation and team building become critical. You cannot personally oversee every cleaning, every check-in, and every maintenance request across multiple properties without sacrificing your strategic focus.

Building a Reliable Team: As you scale, you'll need to build a team of trusted individuals or outsource specific functions. This could include:

Cleaning Staff: Hiring professional cleaning companies or building your own in-house cleaning team. Clearly define roles, responsibilities, pay structures, and performance expectations. Provide them with the documented cleaning protocols and training.

Maintenance Technicians: Establishing relationships with reliable handymen, plumbers, electricians, and appliance repair specialists. You might hire a dedicated maintenance person if your portfolio is large enough.

Guest Support/Virtual Assistant: For handling inquiries, managing bookings, and communicating with guests, a virtual assistant can be invaluable. They can be trained on your communication standards and PMS.

Property Managers (if outsourcing): In some cases, especially if you are geographically distant from your properties or aiming for a truly passive investment, hiring a reputable short-term rental property management company might be the best approach. Understand their fee structure and the services they provide thoroughly.

The Art of Delegation: Effective delegation is more than just assigning tasks; it's about empowering your team.

Choose the Right Person for the Job: Match tasks to the skills and strengths of your team members.

Provide Clear Instructions and Context: Ensure they understand what needs to be done, why it's important, and what the desired outcome is. Refer back to your documented procedures.

Grant Authority: Give your team the authority to make decisions within defined parameters, especially when it comes to resolving guest issues. This empowers them and speeds up the resolution process.

Set Expectations and Deadlines: Clearly communicate what needs to be done and by when.

Provide Feedback and Recognition: Regularly review performance, offer constructive feedback, and acknowledge good work. This motivates your team and reinforces desired behaviors.

Creating a Feedback Loop: It's essential to have a system for gathering feedback from your team. Your cleaners might identify recurring maintenance issues that you aren't aware of, or your guest support might notice common guest questions that can be addressed proactively in your listing or pre-arrival messages. This internal feedback loop is crucial for continuous improvement and for identifying potential problems before they escalate. Encourage your team to report any issues they encounter or any suggestions they have for improving processes.

The ultimate goal of developing a scalable operational system is to build a business that is not only profitable but also resilient and sustainable. It's about creating predictability in a business that can often feel chaotic. By meticulously documenting processes, standardizing procedures, leveraging technology, and building a capable team, you can effectively manage a growing portfolio of short-term rental properties. This strategic approach allows you to maintain high standards of guest satisfaction, optimize your revenue, and, most importantly, free up your time to focus on the higher-level strategic decisions that will drive your business forward. It transforms your operation from a series of individual tasks into a cohesive, efficient, and scalable engine for wealth creation in the short-term rental market. Without this disciplined approach, scaling is often just a recipe for increased stress and diminished returns, rather than the expansion of a thriving business.

The Power of Automation Tools

The transition from managing a single property to overseeing a portfolio of short-term rentals marks a significant inflection point in your entrepreneurial journey. While the thrill of expansion is palpable, the inherent complexity of managing multiple distinct locations, each with its own unique set of guests, operational demands, and potential challenges, can quickly become a bottleneck if not approached strategically. This is where the concept of developing a scalable operational system truly comes into play. It's not merely about acquiring more properties; it's about building a robust framework that allows you to manage this growth efficiently, consistently, and without sacrificing the quality of guest experience that forms the bedrock of your success. Without a well-defined and repeatable operational structure, scaling your portfolio can lead to a rapid descent into chaos, burnout, and ultimately, diminished returns. The aim is to create a business that runs

for you, not one that you are constantly running in.

At its core, a scalable operational system is a meticulously documented set of procedures and protocols designed to handle every facet of property management in a consistent and efficient manner. This involves moving beyond ad-hoc problem-solving and embracing a proactive, system-driven approach. Think of it as building the internal machinery of your business. Each machine—each process—must be designed for optimal performance and repeatability. This foundation is critical because as you add more properties, the sheer volume of tasks multiplies, and without standardization, each new property becomes a fresh set of unique challenges to be solved, draining your time and resources. The goal is to standardize the mundane, so you have more capacity to handle the exceptions and to strategize for future growth.

One of the foundational pillars of any scalable operational system is comprehensive documentation. This isn't just about creating a simple to-do list; it's about creating an operational bible for your business. Every process, from the initial guest inquiry to the final post-stay review, needs to be broken down into its constituent steps and clearly documented. This documentation serves multiple purposes. Firstly, it ensures consistency. When you have multiple cleaners, maintenance staff, or even co-hosts involved, having documented procedures guarantees that tasks are performed to the same high standard every time, regardless of who is performing them. For instance, the "check-in procedure" document should detail every single step: from confirming the guest's arrival time, sending the access code with clear instructions, performing a final walk-through of the property before their arrival, to a designated time for checking in with the guest shortly after their arrival to ensure everything is in order. Similarly, a cleaning checklist should be exhaustive, detailing the specific tasks for each room—from sanitizing light switches and doorknobs to ensuring linens are changed according to specific standards and that all amenities are stocked.

This documentation should also include visual aids where appropriate. For a cleaning checklist, this might mean having photos of what a perfectly clean bathroom or kitchen should look like. For a maintenance task like resetting a smart lock, a step-by-step guide with screenshots or short video clips can be invaluable, especially for remote teams. The level of detail should be such that someone with no prior experience could, in theory, follow the instructions and achieve the desired outcome. This meticulous documentation is what enables you to delegate tasks effectively and confidently, knowing that the quality of service will not suffer. As your portfolio grows and you bring on staff or outsource services, this documented system becomes your primary training manual and quality control mechanism. It's the blueprint for success, ensuring that each guest experience aligns with the high standards you've established, no matter which property they are staying in.

Standardized procedures are the lifeblood of operational efficiency and consistency. These procedures should cover all critical aspects of your short-term rental business. Let's delve deeper into some of these key areas:

Cleaning Protocols: This is arguably the most critical operational area for short-term rentals. Guests expect pristine cleanliness, and any lapse here can lead to immediate negative reviews. Your standardized cleaning protocol needs to be incredibly detailed. It should start with a clear checklist that every cleaner must follow. This checklist should go beyond the obvious; it needs to include often-overlooked areas such as:

Sanitization: Every high-touch surface (light switches, doorknobs, remote controls, appliance handles, faucet handles, toilet flush handles) must be disinfected.

Bedding and Linens: Specify the exact procedure for stripping beds, washing linens (temperature, detergent type), drying, and making beds with fresh linens. Include protocols for pillow protectors and mattress encasements.

Kitchen: Detail cleaning for countertops, sink, stovetop, oven (interior and exterior), microwave (interior and exterior), refrigerator (interior and exterior), coffee maker, toaster, and all kitchen utensils and cookware. Emphasize ensuring all items are returned to their designated places.

Bathrooms: Rigorous cleaning of toilets, showers/bathtubs, sinks, mirrors, and floors is essential. Specify the use of specific cleaning agents for grout and mold if necessary. Check for and replace any used toiletries, soaps, and toilet paper.

Floors: Protocols for vacuuming carpets and rugs, and mopping hard floors, ensuring baseboards are also wiped down.

Trash and Recycling: Ensuring bins are emptied, liners are replaced, and bins themselves are wiped down if necessary.

Final Inspection: A final walk-through by the cleaner or a designated supervisor to ensure all checklist items are completed and the property is immaculate. This might include a photo submission of key areas upon completion.

Beyond the checklist, your documentation should include guidelines on the preferred cleaning products and equipment. This ensures not only consistency but also safety and cost-effectiveness. For example, specifying eco-friendly or hypoallergenic cleaning supplies can be a selling point and cater to a broader range of guests. Training for cleaning staff is paramount. This isn't just a written document; it needs to be a hands-on training process, perhaps involving shadowing experienced cleaners, until proficiency is demonstrated. Regular quality checks, perhaps through random spot-inspections or guest feedback analysis related to cleanliness, are vital to maintain these standards.

Maintenance and Repair Management: A proactive approach to maintenance can prevent many guest complaints. Your system should include:

Preventative Maintenance Schedule: For appliances like HVAC systems, water heaters, dishwashers, and refrigerators, establish a schedule for regular servicing and filter changes. Document when these services are due and who is responsible for scheduling and performing them.

Routine Checks: Implement a schedule for routine checks of minor items that can cause issues, such as smoke detector batteries, CO detector functionality, Wi-Fi connectivity, and general wear and tear on furniture or fixtures.

Reporting System: Create a clear system for reporting any maintenance issues that arise. This could be a digital form that staff or even guests can use, or a dedicated email address. The system should track the issue, its urgency, assigned technician, repair status, and completion.

Vendor Management: Develop relationships with reliable and responsive local service providers (plumbers, electricians, handymen, appliance repair specialists). Have their contact information readily available and pre-negotiate rates if possible. Your documentation should include preferred vendors for different types of repairs, with clear instructions on how to engage them.

Emergency Procedures: Define protocols for handling urgent maintenance issues, such as a burst pipe or a heating failure during winter. This includes having emergency contact numbers for your vendors and a clear escalation path if the primary contact is unavailable.

Guest Communication Standards: Consistent and professional communication is key to a positive guest experience. Your system should outline:

Response Times: Set clear targets for responding to guest inquiries, booking requests, and messages during their stay. For instance, aiming for a response within one hour during active booking times and within 24 hours for less urgent matters.

Standardized Messaging: Develop templated messages for common communications, such as booking confirmations, pre-arrival information (check-in instructions, Wi-Fi details, local recommendations), mid-stay check-ins, and post-stay thank-you messages. These templates should be professional, friendly, and informative, but also allow for personalization.

Issue Resolution Flow: As discussed in the previous section, have a documented process for handling guest complaints or issues, emphasizing empathy, promptness, and a solution-oriented approach. This flow should guide how messages are logged, escalated, and resolved.

Check-in/Check-out Procedures: Standardize the information provided for check-in and check-out, ensuring all necessary details (access codes, Wi-Fi passwords, house rules, departure instructions) are communicated clearly and in advance. Consider automated messaging systems to send these reminders.

The strategic implementation of technology can significantly amplify the scalability of your operations. Many repetitive and time-consuming tasks can be automated, freeing up your time and reducing the potential for human error. This is where technology transforms from a mere convenience into a powerful engine for growth. As your portfolio expands, the sheer volume of data entry, communication, and scheduling can become overwhelming if managed manually. By embracing automation, you can streamline these processes, allowing you to manage more properties with the same or even less effort.

Property Management Software (PMS): Investing in a robust PMS is one of the most impactful steps you can take. These platforms are designed to centralize and streamline various aspects of short-term rental management. Think of it as the central nervous system of your scaled operation. Key features to look for include:

Channel Management: The ability to sync your listings across multiple booking platforms (Airbnb, Vrbo, Booking.com, etc.) from a single dashboard. This ensures your calendar is always up-to-date, preventing double bookings – a major guest satisfaction killer and potential revenue loss. It also allows you to optimize your pricing and availability consistently across all channels, maximizing your visibility and bookings. Without this, manually updating each platform is a recipe for disaster and missed opportunities.

Direct Booking Website Integration: Many PMS systems allow you to build and manage your own direct booking website. This is a crucial step in reducing reliance on Online Travel Agencies (OTAs) and their associated commission fees. A well-integrated website, powered by your PMS, can offer a seamless booking experience for guests who prefer to book directly, significantly improving your profit margins over time.

Automated Messaging: This is a game-changer for guest communication. You can set up automated communication sequences for virtually every stage of the guest journey. This includes sending booking confirmations immediately after a reservation, pre-arrival instructions with check-in details, Wi-Fi passwords, and local recommendations a few days before arrival, mid-stay check-ins to ensure everything is satisfactory, and post-stay thank-you messages with requests for reviews. This ensures consistent, timely, and professional communication without you having to lift a finger for each individual guest. This also ensures that critical information, like check-in instructions, is never missed.

Task Management and Scheduling: As you scale, you'll have a team of cleaners, maintenance personnel, and perhaps even co-hosts. A

PMS can help you assign tasks (e.g., cleaning a specific property after check-out) to team members and track their completion. It can also schedule recurring maintenance tasks, ensuring your properties are always in top condition. This creates accountability and provides a clear overview of operational activities.

Payment Processing: Securely process guest payments and manage payouts through integrated systems. This centralizes financial transactions and reduces the risk of errors.

Reporting and Analytics: This is where you gain actionable insights. Generating reports on occupancy rates, revenue per property, expenses, guest feedback trends, and booking sources allows you to identify what's working, what's not, and where to focus your strategic efforts. Data-driven decision-making is essential for scaling effectively.

Examples of popular PMS platforms include Hostaway, Guesty, Smoobu, and OwnerRez. The choice of PMS will depend on the size of your portfolio, your budget, and the specific features you prioritize. It's crucial to select a system that can grow with you and integrate with other tools you might use. When selecting a PMS, consider its user-friendliness for your team, its integration capabilities with other software, and the quality of its customer support. A trial period is highly recommended to ensure it meets your needs.

Smart Home Technology: Integrating smart home devices can enhance guest experience and improve operational efficiency. These technologies offer convenience for guests and valuable data and control for you as the host.

Smart Locks: These allow for keyless entry, enabling you to provide unique, time-sensitive access codes to guests for specific check-in and check-out times. This eliminates the logistical headache of coordinating physical key handovers, especially across multiple properties and time zones. It also provides an audit trail of who accessed the property and when, enhancing security and accountability. Many smart locks can be controlled remotely via a smartphone app, allowing you to grant or revoke access instantly, which is invaluable for last-minute bookings or if a guest locks themselves out. For instance, you can program a code to expire automatically after check-out, ensuring security.

Smart Thermostats: These can be programmed to adjust temperatures based on occupancy or time of day, saving significant energy when the property is vacant and ensuring a comfortable arrival temperature for guests. Some models offer remote control capabilities, allowing you to adjust the temperature before a guest arrives or address issues if a guest reports it's too hot or too cold, often resolving the issue before it even becomes a complaint. This not only saves on utility bills but also contributes to a positive guest experience.

Smart Security Cameras (Exterior Only): For security purposes and to monitor for unauthorized parties or extra guests that violate house rules, exterior cameras can be invaluable. They can act as a deterrent and provide evidence if issues arise. However, it is crucial that these cameras comply with all privacy regulations and are clearly disclosed to guests in your listing and house rules. Indoor cameras are generally not recommended and can be a significant privacy concern for guests.

Noise Monitoring Devices: Devices like NoiseAware can alert you to excessive noise levels within a property without recording any conversations, helping you proactively address potential disturbances from guests without infringing on their privacy. This can be a lifesaver for preventing complaints from neighbors and ensuring a peaceful environment for all guests, especially in multi-unit buildings. When an alert is triggered, you can send a polite, automated message to the guest to remind them of the house rules regarding noise.

Automation for Specific Tasks: Beyond a comprehensive PMS, consider other specialized automation tools that can further optimize your operations:

Dynamic Pricing Software: Tools like PriceLabs or Wheelhouse can be a significant revenue booster. They analyze vast amounts of market data, including competitor pricing, local events, seasonality, demand, and historical booking patterns, to automatically adjust your nightly rates. This ensures you are always charging optimal prices, maximizing occupancy during high-demand periods and remaining competitive during slower times. This is a complex task to do manually and prone to error or missed opportunities.

Digital Signature Tools: For rental agreements or addendums that may be required for certain bookings, especially for direct bookings or longer stays, using services like DocuSign or HelloSign can streamline the process. This allows guests to sign documents electronically from anywhere, ensuring compliance and reducing administrative burden.

Cloud Storage and Document Management: Utilizing services like Google Drive, Dropbox, or OneDrive is essential for securely storing all your important business documents. This includes leases, insurance policies, vendor contracts, training materials, marketing assets, and financial records. The ability to access these documents from anywhere, securely, and to share them with your team or partners is critical for efficient operations, especially as your team might be distributed. Version control and easy retrieval of documents become paramount as your business grows.

Automated Review Requests: After a guest checks out, you can automate sending a polite request for them to leave a review. Positive reviews are crucial for attracting future bookings, and a consistent system ensures you are actively seeking feedback without it becoming a manual task for every single guest. Many PMS systems offer this functionality directly.

The transition to managing a portfolio necessitates a shift in your own role from hands-on operator to strategic manager. This is where delegation and team building become critical. You cannot personally oversee every cleaning, every check-in, and every maintenance request across multiple properties without sacrificing your strategic focus on growth, acquisition, and optimizing your business. Your time becomes your most valuable asset, and its allocation must be intentional.

Building a Reliable Team: As you scale, you'll need to build a team of trusted individuals or outsource specific functions to reliable third-party service providers. This could include:

Cleaning Staff: Hiring professional cleaning companies or building your own in-house cleaning team. Clearly define roles, responsibilities, pay structures, and performance expectations. Provide them with the documented cleaning protocols and comprehensive training to ensure consistency. For an in-house team, consider offering benefits and opportunities for growth to foster loyalty and reduce turnover. If outsourcing, carefully vet companies based on reviews, reliability, and their understanding of short-term rental specific cleaning needs.

Maintenance Technicians: Establishing relationships with reliable and responsive handymen, plumbers, electricians, and appliance repair specialists. You might hire a dedicated maintenance person if your portfolio is large enough and geographically concentrated, but often, building a strong network of trusted external contractors is more efficient initially. Ensure you have at least two trusted contacts for each trade to have backup options.

Guest Support/Virtual Assistant: For handling inquiries, managing bookings, coordinating with cleaners and maintenance, and communicating with guests, a virtual assistant (VA) can be invaluable. A

VA can be trained on your communication standards, your PMS, and your property specifics. This frees up a significant amount of your time and ensures guests receive prompt and professional responses, even when you are unavailable. Look for VAs with experience in hospitality or customer service.

Property Managers (if outsourcing): In some cases, especially if you are geographically distant from your properties, have a very large portfolio, or aim for a truly passive investment approach, hiring a reputable short-term rental property management company might be the best approach. These companies handle most, if not all, aspects of property management, from marketing and bookings to guest communication and on-the-ground operations. Understand their fee structure, the services they provide, their contract terms, and their performance metrics thoroughly. It's crucial to find a manager whose values and standards align with yours.

The Art of Delegation: Effective delegation is more than just assigning tasks; it's about empowering your team and building trust. When done correctly, it multiplies your capacity and allows you to focus on higher-value activities.

Choose the Right Person for the Job: Match tasks to the skills, experience, and strengths of your team members. A cleaner might not be the best person to handle complex guest complaints, for example.

Provide Clear Instructions and Context: Ensure they understand precisely what needs to be done, why it's important for the overall guest experience and business success, and what the desired outcome is. Refer back to your documented procedures and checklists. Clarity here prevents misinterpretation and rework.

Grant Authority: Give your team the authority to make decisions within defined parameters, especially when it comes to resolving guest issues. For example, empower your guest support to offer a small discount or amenity credit for minor inconveniences without needing your approval for every instance. This empowers them, builds their confidence, and significantly speeds up the resolution process, leading to happier guests.

Set Expectations and Deadlines: Clearly communicate what needs to be done and by when. For urgent tasks, be specific about turn-around times. For recurring tasks, ensure the cadence is understood.

Provide Feedback and Recognition: Regularly review performance, offer constructive feedback to help them improve, and acknowledge good work and exceptional performance. Public or private recognition (depending on the team member's preference) can be a powerful motivator and reinforce desired behaviors. This also creates a culture of continuous improvement.

Creating a Feedback Loop: It's essential to have a system for gathering feedback not only from guests but also from your team. Your cleaners might identify recurring maintenance issues that you aren't aware of, such as a frequently leaking faucet or a faulty appliance. Your guest support might notice common guest questions that can be proactively addressed in your listing description or pre-arrival messages, thereby reducing the volume of inquiries. This internal feedback loop is crucial for continuous improvement, operational efficiency, and for identifying potential problems before they escalate into significant issues or guest complaints. Encourage your team to report any issues they encounter or any suggestions they have for improving processes. Regular team meetings, even brief ones, can facilitate this open communication.

The ultimate goal of developing a scalable operational system, heavily augmented by technology and smart delegation, is to build a business that is not only profitable but also resilient and sustainable. It's about creating predictability in a business that can often feel chaotic due to the transient nature of guests and the physical presence required for property management. By meticulously documenting processes, standardizing procedures, leveraging automation tools, and building a capable and empowered team, you can effectively manage a growing portfolio of short-term rental properties. This strategic approach allows you to maintain consistently high standards of guest satisfaction, optimize your revenue through dynamic pricing and efficient operations, and, most importantly, free up your time to focus on the higher-level strategic decisions that will drive your business forward. This transformation moves you from being a busy operator to a strategic business owner. It transforms your operation from a series of individual, often time-consuming tasks, into a cohesive, efficient, and scalable engine for wealth creation in the short-term rental market. Without this disciplined approach, scaling is often just a recipe for increased stress, diminished returns, and personal burnout, rather than the expansion of a thriving, well-oiled business. The power of automation is not just about saving time; it's about building a business that can grow exponentially without a proportional increase in your personal workload, allowing you to achieve true scalability and financial freedom.

CoHosting and Management Agreement Strategies

The journey of scaling a short-term rental portfolio often leads entrepreneurs to explore avenues beyond the direct acquisition of additional properties. While purchasing more real estate is a direct path to expansion, it is also capital-intensive and can be time-consuming from a due diligence and financing perspective. Fortunately, there exist highly effective alternative growth models that allow you to leverage your established expertise, operational systems, and brand reputation to manage properties owned by others. These models effectively scale your business by multiplying the number of units under your management, without requiring you to deploy significant personal capital for each new property. This strategic pivot transforms your role from a property owner and operator to a service provider, capitalizing on the demand from other property owners who either lack the time, expertise, or desire to manage their own short-term rentals. The core principle here is recognizing that your accumulated knowledge in guest experience, operations, marketing, and revenue management is a valuable asset that can be monetized.

One of the primary and most accessible pathways for this type of scaling is through co-hosting agreements. A co-host on platforms like Airbnb is essentially an individual or entity authorized by the host to help manage their listing and bookings. While the platform's definition is somewhat basic, the real-world application of co-hosting can be far more comprehensive, evolving into a full-fledged property management service. In this model, you partner with property owners who retain ownership but delegate the day-to-day operational responsibilities to you. The revenue split or fee structure can be highly customized, often based on a percentage of the booking revenue generated by the property, a fixed monthly management fee, or a combination of both. This approach allows you to immediately add inventory to your portfolio by tapping into the existing assets of others, thereby accelerating your growth trajectory without the significant upfront costs associated with purchasing properties. It's a symbiotic relationship where you provide the expertise and operational bandwidth, and the owner benefits from the passive income generated by their asset, managed by a professional.

Structuring a co-hosting or property management agreement requires meticulous attention to detail to ensure clarity, protect your interests, and set realistic expectations for the property owner. The agreement should be a legally sound contract, ideally drafted or reviewed by a legal professional specializing in contract law or real estate. Key elements to include are:

1. Scope of Services: Clearly define precisely what services you will provide. This might include listing creation and optimization, dynamic pricing, guest screening and communication, booking management, coordinating cleaning and maintenance, handling guest issues, enforcing house rules, and providing monthly financial reports. It's equally important to define what is not included, such as major renovations, capital expenditures, or managing any long-term rental aspects if the property is used for mixed purposes. Transparency here is crucial to avoid misunderstandings later. For instance, explicitly stating that "guest support during their stay includes addressing issues related to property amenities and functionality but does not extend to resolving disputes with neighbors or local authorities" sets a clear boundary.

2. Term and Termination: Specify the initial duration of the agreement and the conditions under which either party can terminate the contract. Notice periods for termination are essential. Consider clauses that address what happens to existing bookings upon termination and how outstanding payments will be handled. A common approach is a 60- or 90-day notice period, allowing for an orderly transition of management. It's also wise to include provisions for early termination due to breach of contract, such as non-payment of fees or failure to maintain the property to agreed standards by the owner.

3. Compensation Structure: Detail how you will be compensated. This can be a percentage of gross booking revenue (e.g., 15-25%), a fixed monthly fee, or a hybrid model. If it's a percentage, clarify whether it's based on the booking subtotal, the total amount paid by

the guest, or the net revenue after platform fees. Consider tiered commission structures where higher revenue volumes might attract slightly lower percentages, incentivizing you to maximize performance. If there are additional services that incur costs (e.g., specialized deep cleaning, minor repairs you manage), how those costs are passed on or incorporated into your fee structure should also be clearly outlined. For example, you might agree on a 20% management fee on all booking revenue, with an additional fee for coordinating any repairs exceeding a certain threshold, say $200, with owner approval.

4. Financial Management and Reporting: Outline how funds will be handled. Will bookings be deposited into your account and then you remit the net amount to the owner, or will bookings go directly to the owner's account, and you invoice them for your fees? The latter requires greater trust and potentially more complex reconciliation. A more common and efficient model is for you to receive all funds, pay yourself your management fee, pay any direct operating expenses (like cleaning fees or minor repairs you authorize), and then remit the net proceeds to the owner on a regular basis (e.g., monthly). Specify the frequency and format of financial reporting. Owners will want to see statements detailing bookings, revenue, expenses, and net payout. Detailed, transparent reporting builds trust and a strong working relationship.

5. Owner Responsibilities: Clearly enumerate the responsibilities of the property owner. This typically includes maintaining the property in good condition, ensuring all utilities are functional and paid, covering the costs of utilities, property taxes, insurance, and any major repairs or upgrades. Defining these responsibilities upfront prevents disputes about who is responsible for what. For instance, the owner is responsible for ensuring the property meets safety codes and has adequate insurance coverage for short-term rentals. They are also respon-

sible for ensuring the property is staged appropriately for short-term stays, including furniture and essential amenities.

6. Insurance and Liability: Specify the insurance requirements. You will need your own business liability insurance. The property owner will need to maintain their own property insurance, and it's crucial that this policy covers short-term rental activity. You should require owners to provide proof of adequate insurance. The agreement should also address liability for damages caused by guests, specifying that while you manage the guest relationship, the ultimate responsibility for the physical property often rests with the owner, and your management is conducted with due care. Your service agreement should clarify that you are acting as an agent for the owner and that your liability is limited to the scope of services defined and performed with reasonable care.

7. Performance Metrics and KPIs: While not always legally mandated, including key performance indicators (KPIs) in the agreement can align expectations and provide a benchmark for success. This could include target occupancy rates, average daily rates (ADR), or guest review scores. While guaranteeing specific metrics is difficult, setting aspirational targets can serve as a mutual commitment to performance. You might agree that you will strive to achieve an average occupancy rate of 70% or higher, subject to market conditions.

8. Branding and Representation: Define how the properties will be presented to the market. Will they be listed under your brand, the owner's brand, or a co-branded approach? This impacts your marketing efforts and how guests perceive the service. Most often, you will manage these properties under your established brand, providing a consistent guest experience that benefits all your managed properties.

9. Legal Compliance: Ensure the agreement states that both parties will comply with all applicable local, state, and federal laws and reg-

ulations pertaining to short-term rentals, including licensing, zoning, and tax collection. This is a shared responsibility, but your expertise in navigating these often-complex regulations is a key part of your value proposition.

Managing client expectations is paramount to building long-term, successful co-hosting relationships. Property owners often have a range of experience with short-term rentals, from complete novices to those who have experimented with limited success. Your role is not only to manage their property but also to educate them on the realities of the short-term rental market.

Be Realistic About Returns: Avoid overpromising on revenue. While your goal is to maximize income, market fluctuations, seasonality, and unexpected events can impact performance. Provide data-backed projections based on comparable properties and market analysis, rather than guarantees. Explain the factors that influence pricing and occupancy.

Educate on Property Standards: Ensure owners understand the level of upkeep required for a successful short-term rental. This includes regular maintenance, professional cleaning to a high standard, and providing amenities that guests expect. If an owner is reluctant to invest in necessary upgrades or consistent maintenance, it can directly impact guest satisfaction and your ability to perform. The agreement should empower you to recommend or enforce certain standards.

Communicate Proactively and Transparently: Regular, clear communication is the cornerstone of trust. Provide owners with timely financial reports, updates on any significant issues, and summaries of guest feedback. A dedicated owner portal or regular email updates can be highly effective. Be honest about challenges encountered and the steps taken to resolve them.

Set Boundaries: While you are providing a service, it's important to maintain professional boundaries. Define your availability for owner communications and how you prefer to be contacted. This prevents your personal time from being consumed by owner inquiries outside of your operational scope.

Address Issues Swiftly: When problems arise, whether it's a guest complaint or a maintenance issue, communicate them to the owner promptly and outline your plan of action. Demonstrating that you are proactively managing and resolving issues instills confidence.

By mastering these contractual and relational strategies, you can effectively scale your short-term rental business by managing properties for others. This model allows for rapid portfolio growth, diversification of your income streams, and the establishment of a robust management company without the capital outlay of property acquisition. It leverages your core competencies and builds a reputation as a trusted manager in the short-term rental ecosystem. This approach is particularly powerful because it allows you to achieve economies of scale. As you manage more units, your fixed operational costs (e.g., software subscriptions, administrative staff) are spread over a larger revenue base, increasing your profit margins per unit. Furthermore, it enables you to build stronger relationships with vendors (cleaning companies, maintenance services) as you can offer them a consistent volume of work, potentially leading to better rates and prioritized service. This synergistic effect accelerates your growth and solidifies your position in the market. The ability to manage multiple properties under different owners also offers a degree of insulation from market downturns that might affect the value of your directly owned assets. If one market experiences a dip, your diversified portfolio of managed properties in various locations can continue to perform well, smoothing out your overall business performance and providing greater financial stability.

This strategic expansion into co-hosting and property management is often the key differentiator between a solo operator managing a few properties and a true scalable business owner in the short-term rental industry. It requires a shift in mindset, from simply being a host to becoming a professional service provider and business manager.

Building a Recognizable Brand Identity

In the burgeoning landscape of short-term rentals, where countless properties vie for attention, establishing a distinct and recognizable brand identity is no longer a mere luxury; it is a fundamental necessity for sustained growth and competitive advantage. As you transition from managing your first property to scaling your portfolio, particularly by taking on properties owned by others through co-hosting or full-fledged management agreements, your brand becomes the unifying thread that ties together disparate assets under a singular banner of quality and guest satisfaction. This brand identity is your promise to potential guests, a declaration of the experience they can expect, and a cornerstone upon which trust and loyalty are built. It's about creating a memorable impression that transcends the individual property and speaks to a consistent standard of excellence that guests can rely on, time and again.

The essence of building a strong brand identity lies in consistency, clarity, and a deep understanding of your target audience. It's a multi-faceted approach that begins with defining what your business stands for and then meticulously translating that vision into every touchpoint a guest has with your service. Think of it as crafting a personality for your business, one that is relatable, trustworthy, and aspirational. This isn't just about having a pretty logo; it's about cultivating a comprehensive brand experience that resonates with travelers and differentiates you from the competition.

At the very foundation of your brand identity is the visual representation. This typically starts with a professional logo. Your logo is often the first impression a potential guest has of your business. It needs to be memorable, scalable across various platforms (from a website and social media to a welcome book or even a subtle embroidered detail on linens), and reflective of the quality and style of the properties you manage. When designing your logo, consider what emotions or associations you want it to evoke. Are you aiming for luxury and sophistication, or perhaps a more rustic, cozy, and approachable vibe? The color palette, typography, and overall design should align with this overarching brand persona. For instance, a property management company focusing on high-end urban apartments might opt for a sleek, minimalist logo with a refined color scheme like charcoal grey and gold, conveying elegance and exclusivity. Conversely, a brand managing charming countryside cottages might choose a more organic logo featuring natural elements or softer, warmer colors, evoking feelings of comfort and tranquility. It's about creating a visual language that immediately communicates the essence of your offering.

Beyond the logo, the broader visual identity encompasses your choice of fonts, color schemes, and imagery used across all your marketing materials and online presence. Consistency in these elements creates a cohesive and professional look, reinforcing your brand's identity. Imagine seeing the same sophisticated serif font and deep emerald green accent color used consistently across a website, social media posts, email newsletters, and even the physical signage at a property. This visual repetition builds familiarity and strengthens brand recall. It signals that this is a business that pays attention to detail, which is a critical trait for a property manager.

Equally vital is your brand messaging and narrative. This is the story you tell about your business and the experience you provide. What makes you unique? What problem do you solve for property owners and guests? Your messaging should be authentic, compelling, and consistently communicated across all platforms. This includes your "About Us" page on your website, your property descriptions on booking platforms, your social media captions, and even the way you communicate with potential and current guests. If your brand promise is "seamless stays and unforgettable experiences," your messaging should consistently highlight guest comfort, ease of booking, and the unique local experiences your properties offer.

Crafting this narrative often involves identifying your unique selling proposition (USP). What do you do better than anyone else? Perhaps it's your exceptional guest communication, your hyper-local knowledge that enables you to curate curated neighborhood guides, or your commitment to eco-friendly practices. Whatever your USP, weave it into your brand story. For example, if you manage properties in a historic district, your brand narrative could focus on blending modern comfort with the charm of the past, highlighting the unique heritage of the locations. This narrative should be woven into your property descriptions, using evocative language that paints a picture for the guest and sets expectations for a distinctive experience.

The customer experience, from the initial booking inquiry to the post-stay follow-up, is arguably the most powerful manifestation of your brand. This is where your brand identity truly comes to life. Every interaction, every detail, should align with the promise your brand makes. This includes the ease of the booking process, the clarity and helpfulness of pre-arrival communication, the welcome experience at the property, the cleanliness and upkeep of the space, the responsiveness to any issues that arise during the stay, and the thoughtful follow-up after departure.

Consider the entire guest journey. How does a guest first discover your property? Is it through a visually appealing listing on Airbnb or Booking.com, with a captivating title and engaging description that hints at your brand's quality? When they inquire, is the response prompt, friendly, and informative, mirroring your brand's communication style? Upon arrival, is there a well-organized check-in process, a professionally prepared welcome packet or digital guide that reflects your brand's aesthetic, and a spotlessly clean and well-appointed space? Throughout their stay, if they need assistance, is your team responsive, empathetic, and efficient, embodying the brand's commitment to excellent service? And after they leave, does a personalized thank-you message or a request for feedback reinforce their positive experience and encourage future bookings?

To operationalize this, you need to establish clear brand standards for every aspect of the guest experience. This involves creating standardized procedures for cleaning, maintenance, guest communication, and problem resolution. These procedures ensure that the quality of service is consistent, regardless of which property the guest is staying in or which team member is assisting them. For example, a "welcome book" or digital guide should follow a uniform template across all your managed properties, containing essential information about the property, local attractions, house rules, and contact information, all presented with your brand's visual elements and tone of voice.

Furthermore, investing in professional photography and compelling copywriting for your listings is essential. High-quality images that showcase the best features of the property, illuminated with the right natural light and styled attractively, are crucial for attracting bookings. Similarly, well-written descriptions that highlight the unique aspects of the property and its location, infused with your brand's narrative, can significantly influence a guest's decision to book. Avoid generic descriptions; instead, tell a story. Describe the morning coffee enjoyed on the balcony with a view of the sunrise, or the cozy evenings spent by the fireplace, and use language that aligns with your brand's intended persona.

Building a recognizable brand also involves creating a sense of community and encouraging user-generated content. When guests have a positive experience, they are often eager to share it. Encourage them to tag your business on social media or leave reviews that mention specific aspects of your service or branding. You can even incentivize this by running contests for the best guest photos or testimonials. This organic promotion is invaluable, as it comes with the inherent trust of a personal recommendation. Feature these positive reviews and guest-generated content prominently on your website and social media channels, further solidifying your brand's reputation.

Another key element in developing a strong brand is understanding and catering to your target audience. Who are your ideal guests? Are they families looking for spacious, amenity-rich homes? Business travelers seeking convenient locations and reliable Wi-Fi? Couples looking for romantic getaways? Knowing your target demographic allows you to tailor your brand messaging, property selection (if you have influence over that), and overall guest experience to meet their specific needs and preferences. For example, if your target audience is families, your brand messaging might emphasize safety, convenience, and family-friendly amenities, and your visual identity might incorporate brighter colors and playful elements.

Consistency is paramount across all these touchpoints. A guest who experiences excellent service and a well-branded environment in one of your properties should expect the same level of quality when booking another property under your management. This consistency builds reliability and reduces perceived risk for guests, making them more inclined to choose your brand repeatedly. It transforms a transactional booking into a relationship based on trust and familiarity.

In essence, your brand identity is the sum of all these parts: your visual elements, your messaging, your operational standards, and your overall guest experience. It's about creating a memorable and positive impression that resonates with your target audience, fosters loyalty, and ultimately drives the growth of your short-term rental portfolio. As you scale, this cohesive brand becomes your most valuable asset, enabling you to attract more property owners who want their assets managed by a reputable and professional entity, and more guests who seek out the quality and experience your brand promises. It's the engine that drives repeat bookings, positive word-of-mouth referrals, and a sustainable, scalable business in the competitive short-term rental market. It's the difference between being just another listing and being a sought-after hospitality provider.

Financial Management for Multiple Properties

As your short-term rental portfolio expands beyond a single property, the complexity of managing your finances escalates significantly. What might have been a relatively straightforward bookkeeping task for one unit can quickly become a tangled web of revenue streams and expenditure categories when you're managing multiple distinct assets, each with its own operational nuances. Effective financial management is not merely about tracking money; it's about building a robust framework that ensures profitability, facilitates informed decision-making, and safeguards your business against potential pitfalls. This is where transitioning from a sole proprietor mindset to a business owner's approach becomes paramount, demanding a structured and disciplined strategy for handling the financial health of your growing venture.

The cornerstone of sound financial management for multiple properties is the establishment of distinct financial entities. This begins with setting up separate business bank accounts for your short-term rental operations, ideally even further segmented per property if your structure allows or necessitates it. Commingling personal and business funds is a surefire recipe for confusion, accounting errors, and potential legal or tax complications. By creating dedicated business accounts, you immediately bring clarity to your financial picture. These accounts serve as the central hubs for all income generated from bookings and all expenses incurred in operating and maintaining each property. This segregation not only simplifies bookkeeping but also provides a clear audit trail, which is invaluable for tax purposes and for understanding the true profitability of each individual asset within your portfolio. Think of each bank account as a distinct ledger for each of your business units, allowing you to see precisely where money is coming from and going to for every single property.

Meticulously tracking income and expenses for each property is the next critical step. This requires a systematic approach, utilizing accounting software or sophisticated spreadsheets that allow for granular categorization. For each property, you need to record every dollar of revenue received, noting the source (e.g., Airbnb, Booking.com, direct bookings) and the dates of stay. Simultaneously, every expense must be diligently logged and attributed to the correct property. This includes a broad spectrum of costs: mortgage payments, property taxes, insurance premiums, utilities (electricity, gas, water, internet), cleaning fees, maintenance and repair costs (plumbing, electrical, appliance repairs), supplies (toiletries, linens, cleaning products), management fees (if applicable), marketing and advertising expenses, and any initial furnishing or renovation costs. Furthermore, it's crucial to differentiate between capital expenditures (significant improvements that add value, like a new roof or HVAC system) and operating expenses (recurring costs necessary for day-to-day operations). Proper categorization ensures you can accurately calculate the net operating income (NOI) for each property, a key metric for assessing performance.

Understanding the tax implications of owning and operating multiple short-term rental properties is an area that cannot be overstated. This is where professional advice becomes indispensable. Depending on your location and business structure, you will be subject to various taxes, including income tax, occupancy taxes (lodging taxes), sales tax (in some jurisdictions), and potentially others. You'll need to understand which of your expenses are tax-deductible. Common deductions for short-term rental owners include mortgage interest, property taxes, insurance, repairs and maintenance, utilities, cleaning fees, supplies, travel expenses related to managing the properties, depreciation of the property and its furnishings, and professional fees (accountants, lawyers). Keeping meticulous records for all income and expenses is vital for accurate tax filing and maximizing eligible deductions. Furthermore, the IRS has specific rules regarding the deductibility of expenses for rental properties, particularly concerning personal use of the property and the "passive activity loss" rules. It's advisable to consult with a tax professional who specializes in real estate or short-term rentals to ensure you are compliant and taking advantage of all legitimate tax benefits. This expertise can save you a significant amount of money and prevent costly errors.

Implementing sound financial controls is not a one-time setup; it's an ongoing process. This involves establishing clear procedures for authorizing expenses, processing payments, and reconciling bank accounts regularly. For instance, you might implement a system where all invoices over a certain threshold require a second level of approval. Regular reconciliation of your bank statements against your accounting records is crucial to catch any discrepancies or unauthorized transactions promptly. Furthermore, consider implementing budgeting for each property. By forecasting anticipated income and expenses, you can set financial targets and monitor your progress against them. This proactive approach allows you to identify potential shortfalls or overspending early on, enabling you to take corrective action before they significantly impact your profitability.

Regular performance analysis is the engine that drives informed strategic decisions in a multi-property portfolio. This means moving beyond simply looking at monthly bank statements to conducting in-depth reviews of your financial data. Key performance indicators (KPIs) to track include:

Occupancy Rate: The percentage of days your property is booked and generating revenue.

Average Daily Rate (ADR): The total revenue divided by the total number of occupied days.

Revenue Per Available Room (RevPAR): ADR multiplied by occupancy rate. This is a critical metric for comparing property performance.

Net Operating Income (NOI): Gross rental income minus all operating expenses (excluding debt service and depreciation).

Cash Flow: The actual cash generated after all expenses, including mortgage payments, are accounted for.

Return on Investment (ROI): The net profit divided by the total investment in the property. This is a crucial metric for understanding the profitability of your capital outlay.

Guest Acquisition Cost (GAC): The total marketing and sales costs divided by the number of new guests acquired. Understanding this helps optimize marketing spend.

Guest Lifetime Value (GLV): The total revenue a guest is expected to generate over their relationship with your business.

Analyzing these KPIs for each property on a monthly or quarterly basis will reveal which properties are excelling, which are underperforming, and why. For example, if one property consistently has a lower occupancy rate despite a competitive ADR, you might investigate its listing quality, marketing efforts, or guest reviews. If another property's expenses are consistently higher than anticipated, it might be time to review utility consumption, maintenance contracts, or supplier costs. This data-driven approach allows you to identify trends, make objective decisions about property management strategies, pricing adjustments, marketing focus, and even potential property acquisitions or divestitures.

When managing multiple properties, the choice of accounting software becomes even more critical. While simple spreadsheets might suffice for a single property, scaling necessitates a more robust solution. Popular options include QuickBooks, Xero, or specialized property management software that often includes integrated accounting features. These platforms allow for multi-entity accounting, detailed expense tracking, automated invoicing, and seamless integration with bank feeds and booking platforms. Some property management systems can even automate expense allocation to individual properties, further streamlining the process. The key is to select a system that can grow with your portfolio and provides the level of detail and reporting you need to effectively manage your business.

Furthermore, consider setting up a holding company or a Limited Liability Company (LLC) structure. This can offer liability protection, separating your personal assets from your business liabilities. The financial management for such structures often involves inter-company transactions and consolidated financial statements, adding another layer of complexity that requires expert accounting guidance. However, for a growing portfolio, the legal and financial protections offered by a separate business entity are often well worth the additional administrative effort. The financial reporting for these structures will need to account for all subsidiary properties and provide a clear overview of the entire portfolio's financial health.

The concept of "cash reserves" or an emergency fund also takes on greater importance with multiple properties. Each property can experience unexpected vacancies, major repair needs, or seasonal dips in demand. Having readily accessible funds to cover these eventualities without dipping into operational cash flow is vital for maintaining financial stability and avoiding debt. A good rule of thumb is to maintain a reserve equivalent to three to six months of operating expenses for each property, or a consolidated fund that can cover a significant unexpected cost across the portfolio. This financial cushion provides peace of mind and ensures that your business can weather unforeseen storms.

As your portfolio expands, you might also explore financing options for future acquisitions. Lenders will require detailed financial statements and a clear understanding of your portfolio's performance. Having well-organized financial records and demonstrating consistent profitability and strong cash flow will be crucial for securing favorable loan terms. This underscores the importance of robust financial management not just for current operations but also for future growth and capital raising. Being able to present a professional and transparent financial picture to potential investors or lenders can be a significant competitive advantage.

In essence, financial management for a multi-property short-term rental portfolio is about establishing order, clarity, and accountability. It involves a commitment to meticulous record-keeping, a proactive approach to tax compliance, the implementation of strong internal controls, and a data-driven strategy for performance analysis. By treating your short-term rental business as a serious enterprise with dedicated financial systems, you lay the groundwork for sustained profitability, informed expansion, and long-term success. This disciplined approach to finances is not just about managing money; it's about building a resilient and valuable business that can continue to grow and thrive.

Chapter Six

Advanced Strategies for Revenue Enhancement

Off Platform Booking Channels and Direct Bookings

Diversifying your booking channels beyond the dominant online travel agencies (OTAs) like Airbnb and Vrbo is a critical evolutionary step for any short-term rental operator aiming for sustained growth and enhanced profitability. While these platforms offer unparalleled initial reach and access to a vast pool of travelers, an over-reliance on them can create several significant vulnerabilities. The most immediate concern is the commission structure. Each booking facilitated by an OTA comes with a fee, typically ranging from 3% to 15% of the booking total, depending on the platform and the host's tier. When managing a single property, these fees might be an acceptable cost of doing business, offset by the convenience and marketing power of the platform. However, as your portfolio expands, these fees compound, significantly eroding your net profit margins. For a multi-property owner, these platform fees can amount to tens, if not hundreds, of thousands of dollars annually, representing a substantial portion of potential revenue that is essentially being siphoned away. Reducing or eliminating these fees through direct bookings directly translates to a tangible increase in your bottom line.

Beyond the financial aspect, dependence on OTAs also means a lack of direct control over your brand and customer relationships. While OTAs provide a framework for guest interaction, the communication, branding, and data collection are largely dictated by the platform's policies. This limits your ability to build a loyal customer base, encourage repeat bookings directly, and gather valuable guest insights that could inform future marketing and service improvements. Furthermore, algorithm changes, policy shifts, or even account suspension on these platforms can have an immediate and devastating impact on your bookings and revenue, exposing your business to external forces beyond your control. Building off-platform booking channels is not just about saving money; it's about building a more resilient, independent, and ultimately, more valuable business.

The first and perhaps most impactful strategy for achieving direct bookings is the development of your own branded website. This serves as your digital storefront, a central hub where potential guests can learn about your properties, view availability, and make reservations directly. The investment in a professional website is an investment in your brand identity and your business's long-term sustainability. A well-designed website should showcase your properties with high-quality photography and compelling descriptions that highlight unique selling propositions. Essential features include an integrated booking engine, a clear display of rates and availability, and a secure payment gateway. Many website builders and specialized property management software solutions offer integrated booking engines that can be seamlessly embedded into your site. These engines allow guests to check real-time availability, select dates, choose specific properties if you manage multiple units in close proximity, and complete the booking process securely. The key is to make the booking experience as intuitive and user-friendly as possible, mirroring the convenience offered by major OTAs.

The content on your website is crucial for attracting and converting visitors. Go beyond basic property descriptions. Share the story behind your rentals, highlight local attractions, provide detailed neighborhood guides, and showcase guest testimonials. This content not only enhances your search engine optimization (SEO) but also builds trust and encourages guests to book directly. Consider incorporating a blog section where you can share travel tips, local events, or behind-the-scenes glimpses of your properties. This not only provides value to potential guests but also keeps your website fresh and improves its ranking in search engine results.

Driving traffic to your direct booking website is the next critical step. Organic search engine optimization (SEO) is paramount. This involves optimizing your website content with relevant keywords that potential guests might use when searching for accommodations in your area. Think about terms like "luxury cabin rentals [your location]," "pet-friendly vacation home [your location]," or "boutique hotel [your city]." Regularly updating your website with fresh content, such as blog posts and new property listings, also signals to search engines that your site is active and relevant. Building high-quality backlinks from reputable travel blogs or local tourism sites can further boost your website's authority and search engine ranking.

Paid advertising, such as Google Ads or social media advertising, can also be an effective way to drive targeted traffic to your website. By using precise targeting options, you can reach individuals who have shown interest in travel to your specific location or who fit the demographic profile of your ideal guest. For instance, you can target users based on their search history, location, interests, and even their past booking behavior. The key is to track the performance of your ad campaigns meticulously, focusing on cost per acquisition (CPA) and return on ad spend (ROAS) to ensure your marketing budget is being used efficiently. Directing these paid campaigns to your own website, rather than an OTA listing, allows you to capture bookings without paying the hefty OTA commissions.

Social media platforms offer a powerful and cost-effective avenue for driving direct bookings, especially if you have a visually appealing product like a short-term rental. Platforms like Instagram, Facebook, Pinterest, and even TikTok can be leveraged to showcase your properties and engage with potential guests. High-quality photography and videography are essential. Think about creating visually stunning content that highlights the unique features of your rentals and the surrounding area. This could include professional photos of the interiors and exteriors, drone footage showcasing the location, short video tours, and lifestyle content that depicts guests enjoying their stay.

On platforms like Instagram and Facebook, you can create dedicated business pages for your rental portfolio. Regularly post captivating images and videos, share guest testimonials, announce special offers or last-minute availability, and engage with your followers by responding to comments and messages promptly. Utilizing relevant hashtags can increase the visibility of your posts to a wider audience. Paid social media advertising allows for highly targeted campaigns, enabling you to reach specific demographics and interests. You can run campaigns to drive traffic directly to your booking website, promote special packages, or even retarget individuals who have previously visited your website but did not book.

For visually oriented platforms like Pinterest, creating boards featuring your property, local attractions, and travel inspiration can attract users in the planning stages of their trips. Similarly, short-form video content on TikTok or Instagram Reels can capture attention and drive curiosity, leading users to seek out more information about your properties. Building an engaged community on social media can foster brand loyalty and encourage direct bookings from followers who feel a connection to your brand. Consider running contests or giveaways to increase engagement and brand awareness.

Email marketing is another foundational element of a robust direct booking strategy. Once you have a website and social media presence, you need to capture leads and nurture them into bookings. Implementing a system to collect email addresses is crucial. This can be done through a website pop-up offering a discount for signing up, a lead magnet such as a local guide, or by collecting emails from past guests. A well-managed email list allows you to communicate directly with potential and past guests.

Your email marketing strategy should include several types of campaigns:

Welcome Series: For new subscribers, a series of emails introducing your brand, highlighting your properties, and offering an incentive for their first direct booking.

Promotional Campaigns: Announcing special offers, seasonal discounts, or last-minute availability to encourage bookings.

Content Marketing: Sharing valuable content like local event guides, travel tips, or new property updates to keep your audience engaged.

Post-Stay Emails: Following up with guests after their stay to thank them, encourage reviews, and invite them to book directly for their next visit. This is also an excellent opportunity to request referrals.

Re-engagement Campaigns: For subscribers who haven't booked in a while, sending targeted offers or updates to entice them back.

The key to successful email marketing is personalization and segmentation. Sending relevant content to specific segments of your audience (e.g., families, couples, business travelers) will significantly increase open and conversion rates. Ensure your emails are mobile-friendly, visually appealing, and contain clear calls to action (e.g., "Book Now," "View Availability").

Leveraging online reviews and testimonials is also a powerful way to build trust and encourage direct bookings. While OTAs are a primary source of reviews, you should actively encourage guests to leave reviews on multiple platforms, including your own website, Google My Business, and other relevant review sites. Positive reviews act as social proof, assuring potential guests of the quality and reliability of your offerings. Displaying curated testimonials prominently on your direct booking website can significantly boost conversion rates. Consider creating short video testimonials from satisfied guests, which can be highly engaging and persuasive.

Furthermore, actively managing your online reputation is essential. Respond professionally and promptly to all reviews, both positive and negative. Addressing negative feedback constructively shows that you are committed to guest satisfaction and continuous improvement. This proactive approach can turn potentially damaging reviews into opportunities to demonstrate your customer service excellence. For guests who have had exceptional experiences, don't hesitate to politely ask them to share their positive feedback through a direct booking channel, perhaps by offering a small discount on their next direct booking as a thank you.

Building a direct booking engine often involves integrating with channel managers or property management systems (PMS) that can sync availability and pricing across all your booking channels, including your direct website and OTAs. This ensures that you avoid over-bookings and maintain consistent information across all platforms. A good PMS will also often include a built-in direct booking website and payment processing capabilities, simplifying the entire process. When selecting a PMS, look for features like automated guest communication, task management for cleaning and maintenance, and robust reporting and analytics. These tools are vital for efficiently managing a multi-property portfolio and scaling your direct booking efforts.

Consider offering incentives for guests to book directly. This could include a slightly lower price than OTA rates, complimentary amenities such as a welcome basket or local wine, late check-out options, or exclusive access to special packages. Clearly communicate these benefits on your website and in your marketing materials. For instance, a sign on your property's welcome book or a note included with the check-in instructions could say, "Enjoyed your stay? Book your next visit directly through our website at [YourWebsite.com] and receive a 10% discount!" or "Book directly with us for exclusive access to our premium services." These small gestures can significantly influence guest booking behavior.

Another effective strategy for generating direct bookings involves building relationships with local businesses and tourism boards. Partnering with nearby restaurants, tour operators, or activity providers can create mutually beneficial referral systems. You can offer special packages that include accommodation and local experiences, promoting these through your website and marketing efforts. In return, these local businesses can recommend your properties to their customers. Engaging with local tourism boards and destination marketing organizations (DMOs) can also provide valuable exposure through their websites, visitor guides, and marketing campaigns. Ensure your properties are listed and promoted through these official channels, driving interested travelers to your direct booking platforms.

For larger portfolios, creating a distinct brand identity separate from the individual property names can be beneficial. This allows you to build a recognizable brand that can encompass multiple properties, each potentially having its own unique charm and target audience. A strong brand narrative and consistent visual identity across your direct booking website, social media, and marketing materials will foster recognition and trust. This brand can then become synonymous with quality and exceptional guest experiences, encouraging repeat business and direct bookings across your entire portfolio. Think of it as building a mini-hotel chain with a consistent quality promise.

The journey to maximizing direct bookings is an ongoing process of optimization and adaptation. Regularly analyze your data: which marketing channels are driving the most direct bookings? Which incentives are most effective? What are your website conversion rates? By understanding these metrics, you can refine your strategies, allocate your marketing budget more effectively, and continually improve the guest experience to encourage loyalty and repeat direct bookings. The ability to capture guest data from direct bookings also provides invaluable insights into guest preferences, booking patterns, and demographics, enabling even more targeted and effective marketing efforts in the future. This direct line of communication and data ownership is the essence of building a sustainable and profitable short-term rental business, independent of the fluctuations and costs associated with third-party platforms. It's about owning your customer, owning your brand, and ultimately, owning your revenue.

Cross Selling Additional Services and Packages

Beyond the core offering of comfortable accommodation, the short-term rental landscape presents a fertile ground for diversifying revenue streams through the strategic cross-selling of additional services and packages. This approach not only enhances the overall guest experience by providing convenience and enriching their stay but also opens up significant avenues for increased profitability, transforming your property from a simple lodging option into a comprehensive travel solution. The key lies in identifying guest needs and desires that extend beyond the basic provision of a place to sleep, and then leveraging partnerships or developing in-house capabilities to meet those needs.

Consider the journey of a typical guest. Upon booking, they are often in the planning phase, eager to make the most of their visit to your location. This is the opportune moment to introduce them to curated local experiences. Partnering with reputable local tour operators is a prime example. This could range from historical walking tours that delve into the unique character of your neighborhood, to adventure excursions like hiking or kayaking in nearby natural attractions, or even culinary tours that showcase the best local food and drink establishments. When establishing these partnerships, prioritize reliability, quality of service, and a genuine connection to the local culture. Negotiate wholesale rates or commission structures that ensure profitability for you while offering competitive pricing to your guests. This requires thorough vetting of potential partners. Request their service brochures, check online reviews, and if possible, experience their tours firsthand to ensure they align with the standards you've set for your own property. Clearly communicate the benefits of booking through you – convenience, potentially bundled discounts, and the assurance that you've pre-vetted the service.

Beyond organized tours, think about individual activities and experiences that cater to a variety of interests. For the food enthusiast, this might involve arranging private cooking classes focusing on regional cuisine or securing reservations at highly sought-after local restaurants, especially if walk-in availability is scarce. For the family, consider partnerships with local attractions like theme parks, museums, or interactive exhibits, potentially offering bundled ticket packages. Even something as simple as recommending and facilitating the booking of popular local events, such as concerts, festivals, or sporting matches, can be a valuable add-on service. The aim is to become a concierge, anticipating and fulfilling the desires of your guests to explore and engage with the destination.

Airport transfers represent another significant convenience that guests highly value, particularly those arriving on longer journeys or unfamiliar with local transportation options. Establishing relationships with reliable local taxi services or private car hire companies can allow you to offer pre-booked airport pick-up and drop-off services. This not only provides a seamless transition for your guests but also generates a commission or a markup on the service. Ensure that the drivers are professional, punctual, and aware of your property's location and check-in procedures. For an enhanced touch, you could even arrange for a small welcome amenity to be placed in the vehicle, such as bottled water or a local snack.

The concept of curated local product packages offers a unique way to enhance the guest experience while supporting local artisans and businesses. Imagine assembling welcome baskets featuring arti-sanal cheeses, locally roasted coffee, handcrafted chocolates, or re-gional wines. These can be offered as optional upgrades at the time of booking or as a surprise amenity for guests who book direct or opt for a premium package. Clearly showcase these packages on your booking platform or website, highlighting the origin and quality of the products. This not only adds a delightful touch to the arrival experience but also provides a tangible taste of the local culture. You could even extend this to include locally made soaps, candles, or small decorative items that guests can purchase as souvenirs. These packages can be themed – for instance, a "Romantic Getaway Package" might include local wine, gourmet chocolates, and scented candles, while a "Family Fun Package" could feature local treats and vouchers for a nearby ice cream parlor.

When implementing these cross-selling strategies, a phased ap-proach is often most effective. Begin by identifying one or two high-demand services that align well with your property's location and target demographic. For example, if your property is situated near a popular hiking trail, partnering with a local outfitter for bicycle rentals or guided nature walks would be a natural fit. If you cater to business travelers, offering early check-in, late check-out, or secretarial services might be more relevant. Start small, test the market, and gather feedback from your guests. This iterative process will help you refine your offerings and identify the most lucrative opportunities.

Effective communication is paramount to the success of any cross-selling initiative. Integrate these offerings seamlessly into your booking process. On your direct booking website, dedicate a section to "Enhance Your Stay" or "Local Experiences." During the booking confirmation, provide guests with a link or a brochure detailing the available add-on services and packages, along with clear instructions on how to book them. This can be automated through your property management system (PMS). Post-booking, a personalized email a week or so before arrival is an excellent time to remind guests of these options and assist them in making selections. For guests who booked via OTAs, you can still reach out post-booking (within platform guidelines) or send a pre-arrival email from your own system, offering these additional conveniences.

The pricing strategy for these additional services is crucial. For services outsourced to partners, you'll typically negotiate a commission or a wholesale rate. When setting your prices, aim for a balance between offering value to the guest and ensuring a healthy profit margin for yourself. Avoid simply marking up the partner's price significantly; instead, consider the added value you provide through convenience, curation, and assurance. For instance, if a local tour costs $50 per person, you might offer it to your guests for $55, with $5 going to you. If you are developing in-house offerings, such as welcome baskets, meticulously calculate the cost of goods and add a reasonable margin for your labor and overhead.

Consider creating tiered packages that combine accommodation with several of these services. A "Standard Stay" might just be the accommodation, while a "Deluxe Experience" could include a welcome basket, airport transfer, and a guided local tour. A "Premium Getaway" might bundle a fine dining experience reservation, a spa treatment voucher, and a private guided excursion. These packages can offer a perceived discount to the guest compared to booking each element individually, encouraging them to spend more and enhancing their overall experience. Clearly outline what is included in each package and the value proposition.

The operational aspect of managing these cross-sold services also requires attention. If you are partnering with external providers, clear communication channels and booking confirmations are essential to ensure smooth execution. For example, when a guest books an airport transfer through you, you must relay the booking details promptly and accurately to the transport company. Similarly, if you are assembling welcome baskets, you'll need a system for inventory management, assembly, and placement in the guest's room before arrival. Your housekeeping or guest services team will need to be trained on these procedures. Integrating these services into your PMS can greatly streamline operations by centralizing bookings and communications.

Data analysis plays a vital role in optimizing your cross-selling strategies. Track which services are most popular, which packages are selling best, and which marketing messages are most effective in driving uptake. Use your booking data and guest feedback to identify new opportunities. Are guests frequently asking for recommendations for babysitters? Consider partnering with a reputable local childcare service. Are many of your guests booking ski passes? Investigate partnerships with ski rental shops or lift ticket vendors. The goal is to continuously evolve your offerings based on genuine guest demand.

Furthermore, these additional services can serve as a powerful tool for encouraging direct bookings. Guests who book ancillary services through you are more likely to see the value you provide beyond just accommodation. This can make them more receptive to booking directly with you in the future to access these convenient, curated options and potentially better rates or exclusive package deals. Highlight this synergy: "Book direct and enjoy seamless integration with our premium local experiences."

By strategically identifying and offering complementary services and packages, you transform your short-term rental into a holistic travel experience. This not only taps into new revenue streams, significantly boosting your property's overall profitability, but also elevates the guest experience, fostering loyalty and positive word-of-mouth referrals. It's about providing value, convenience, and a deeper connection to the destination, all while building a more robust and resilient business. The investment in building these relationships and streamlining these processes will yield significant returns, both financially and in terms of guest satisfaction. This proactive approach to revenue enhancement moves you beyond simply being a landlord to becoming a true hospitality provider.

Upselling Premium Amenities and Experiences

The previous discussion focused on the foundational strategies for diversifying revenue streams, primarily through cross-selling services that complement the core accommodation offering. We explored how partnerships with local businesses, curated product packages, and convenient add-ons like airport transfers can significantly enhance guest satisfaction and profitability. Now, we pivot to a more advanced phase of revenue maximization: the art of upselling premium amenities and exclusive experiences. This isn't merely about offering more; it's about strategically identifying and catering to guests who are actively seeking an elevated and personalized stay, and who are willing to invest further to achieve it.

Upselling premium amenities and exclusive experiences moves beyond providing convenience to delivering a distinct level of luxury, personalization, and memorable moments. It taps into a segment of travelers who view their short-term rental not just as a place to stay, but as an integral part of their vacation narrative, a stage upon which to create cherished memories. These guests are often celebrating special occasions, seeking unique indulgences, or simply have a higher propensity to spend on comfort and exclusivity. The key here is to understand what constitutes "premium" for your target demographic and to artfully present these options in a way that resonates with their desires for an enhanced experience.

Let's delve into tangible examples of premium amenities that can be offered. For instance, consider the simple act of providing linens. While standard linens are expected, an upsell opportunity lies in offering a "Luxury Linen Package." This could include ultra-high thread count Egyptian cotton sheets, plush down or hypoallergenic alternative comforters, and a selection of premium pillows to suit various sleeping preferences. The perceived value is immense, transforming a basic necessity into a tactile luxury that directly impacts sleep quality and overall comfort. Clearly detailing the superior feel, breathability, and hypoallergenic properties of these linens in your marketing materials and pre-arrival communications can justify the additional cost. Imagine a guest arriving after a long day of travel, sinking into a bed adorned with sumptuously soft, cool sheets – this is a tangible upgrade they will appreciate and remember.

Another avenue for premium amenities is in the realm of in-room services that elevate the guest's relaxation and enjoyment. While many properties offer basic toiletries, an upsell could involve a "Deluxe Bath Experience" package. This might include artisanal, locally sourced bath bombs or salts, high-quality, richly scented soaps and lotions from a premium brand, plush spa-style robes and slippers, and perhaps even a selection of calming herbal teas or infused water. For properties with bathtubs, consider offering a "Romantic Bath Setup" that includes candles, rose petals, and a bottle of prosecco. These thoughtful touches create an atmosphere of indulgence and provide a spa-like experience within the privacy of their accommodation.

For those properties with kitchen facilities, a sophisticated culinary upsell could be the offering of a "Gourmet Kitchen Stocking" service. Beyond a basic welcome basket, this involves pre-stocking the refrigerator and pantry with high-end ingredients for specific meals or dietary preferences. This could range from organic produce and artisanal cheeses for a leisurely breakfast, to premium cuts of meat and accompanying sauces for a planned dinner, or even specific ingredients for baking or cocktail mixing. Guests who enjoy cooking or plan to entertain during their stay will find immense value in having these high-quality items readily available, saving them time and the hassle of grocery shopping.

Beyond physical amenities, the true power of upselling lies in offering exclusive local experiences that are curated and often inaccessible to the average traveler. This requires a deeper understanding of your locale and leveraging your network to create unique opportunities. For example, instead of just recommending a popular restaurant, you could arrange a private dining experience for your guests. This might involve a reservation at a restaurant during off-hours, a chef's table experience where they can interact with the culinary team, or even a private tasting menu focused on showcasing the best of regional cuisine. The exclusivity and personalized attention offered in such an experience command a premium price.

Consider the realm of cultural immersion. For guests interested in history or art, an exclusive guided tour with a local historian, art curator, or even the artist themselves could be an incredibly valuable upsell. Imagine arranging a private after-hours tour of a local museum, or a behind-the-scenes visit to an artist's studio followed by a personal meet-and-greet. These are not services easily booked through standard tour operators and offer a level of access and insight that creates truly unforgettable memories. The key is to build relationships with individuals who can offer these unique perspectives and experiences.

For the adventure-seeking guest, you might arrange a private, guided excursion that goes beyond the typical tourist trail. This could be a guided hike to a secluded waterfall with a gourmet picnic lunch prepared by a local chef, a private sailing trip along the coast with a stop at a hidden cove for swimming and snorkeling, or a personalized photography tour led by a professional local photographer to capture the most scenic spots. The "private" aspect is crucial here, as it guarantees dedicated attention and flexibility, catering directly to the guest's pace and interests.

For guests celebrating special occasions, such as anniversaries or birthdays, a "Celebration Package" can be an exceptional upsell. This could be a combination of premium amenities and experiences tailored to the event. Imagine a package that includes a bottle of premium champagne on arrival, a beautifully decorated cake from a renowned local bakery, a private chef to prepare a celebratory dinner in the accommodation, and perhaps tickets to a local theater performance or concert. The thoughtfulness and comprehensive nature of such a package, handling all the details for the guest, make it highly desirable and worth a significant premium.

Another area for sophisticated upselling is in the provision of personalized services that cater to specific needs or desires. For the business traveler, this might mean offering a "Productivity Boost Package" that includes a high-quality portable printer and scanner, a comfortable ergonomic office chair, and reliable high-speed internet with a dedicated secure network. For the wellness-focused guest, a "Rejuvenation Retreat" could be offered, featuring in-room yoga mats and guided meditation sessions, a selection of healthy organic snacks and beverages, and perhaps even a booking with a local massage therapist for in-house treatments.

The success of any upsell strategy hinges on how effectively these premium offerings are presented to the guest. It's not about being pushy, but about subtly highlighting the value and enhancing their perception of what a truly exceptional stay can be. This begins long before arrival, ideally during the booking process itself. Your direct booking website or platform should feature a dedicated section showcasing these premium upgrades. Use high-quality photography and compelling descriptions that evoke the feeling and experience of these offerings. Instead of simply listing "Luxury Linens," describe the "Silken Touch of Egyptian Cotton" and the "Deep, Restful Sleep" they promise.

When guests are in the confirmation stage or in the weeks leading up to their stay, a personalized email is an opportune moment to introduce these upsell options. Frame them not as mere add-ons, but as ways to "Elevate Your Experience" or "Craft Your Perfect Getaway." For instance, a pre-arrival email could read: "We're delighted to confirm your upcoming stay! To make your visit even more extraordinary, we'd like to share some exclusive options to enhance your experience, from a private chef dinner to a guided local wine tasting. Simply click here to explore and reserve your chosen indulgence."

It's also effective to segment your guests based on their booking behavior or stated preferences. If a guest has booked during a special occasion like Valentine's Day or a local festival, you can proactively suggest relevant premium packages. Similarly, if your property attracts a significant number of families, an upsell of a "Family Fun Bundle" that includes discounted tickets to local attractions, a curated selection of age-appropriate games and books, and perhaps a babysitting service can be highly appealing.

The pricing of these premium amenities and experiences requires careful consideration. It needs to reflect the added value, exclusivity, and often the direct costs associated with them. For services provided by third-party partners, you'll need to negotiate wholesale rates that allow for a healthy profit margin when you mark them up for your guests. For in-house offerings like luxury linens or curated food baskets, meticulously calculate all costs, including the premium products themselves, labor for preparation or setup, and any associated packaging. Your pricing should be perceived as fair by the guest, considering the convenience and the enhanced experience they are receiving. It's often beneficial to offer tiered packages, where a combination of premium elements might be priced slightly lower than if each element were booked individually, creating a compelling value proposition.

Operational efficiency is paramount to delivering these premium services flawlessly. If you're offering a private chef, ensure you have a reliable partner who understands your property's kitchen facilities and your guests' dietary needs. For in-house amenities, establish clear processes for inventory management, preparation, and timely delivery to the guest's unit. Train your staff thoroughly on how to present these offerings and handle any guest inquiries or requests related to them. Integrating these upsell processes into your property management system (PMS) can help automate bookings, confirmations, and billing, minimizing the potential for errors and ensuring a seamless guest experience.

Ultimately, the art of upselling premium amenities and exclusive experiences is about understanding your guests' desires and providing them with opportunities to indulge and create lasting memories. It requires a strategic approach to identifying value, a creative flair for crafting unique offerings, and a commitment to delivering exceptional service. By mastering these techniques, you can significantly increase revenue per booking, differentiate your property in a competitive market, and foster a loyal customer base that seeks out your listings for the extraordinary experiences they consistently provide. This move from basic accommodation to curated luxury is a hallmark of sophisticated short-term rental management.

Loyalty Programs and Repeat Guest Incentives

The consistent revenue stream that underpins a thriving short-term rental portfolio is not solely built on attracting new guests; it is profoundly strengthened by cultivating a base of loyal, returning clientele. In the dynamic landscape of hospitality, where choices are abundant and first impressions are critical, the art of fostering guest loyalty and incentivizing repeat bookings is a strategic imperative. This approach is not only more cost-effective than the perpetual pursuit of new customer acquisition – which often involves higher marketing spend and greater acquisition friction – but it also builds a more stable and predictable revenue model. By focusing on turning satisfied first-time visitors into enthusiastic advocates and consistent patrons, you establish a powerful competitive advantage and a foundation for sustained profitability. The core of this strategy lies in recognizing that a positive guest experience, coupled with tangible rewards for their continued patronage, is the most potent engine for long-term success.

At the heart of encouraging repeat business is the implementation of well-structured loyalty programs. These programs are designed to acknowledge and reward guests who choose to return, creating a sense of value and appreciation that goes beyond the transactional nature of a single booking. A tiered loyalty program is particularly effective, offering escalating benefits as guests reach certain milestones, such as the number of stays or total nights booked. For instance, a "Bronze" tier might offer a small welcome amenity or a complimentary late checkout on their second stay. As guests progress to "Silver," they could receive a percentage discount on future bookings or priority access to newly listed properties. The pinnacle, a "Gold" or "Platinum" tier, might unlock exclusive perks like complimentary upgrades to premium units, personalized welcome gifts reflecting their known preferences, or even invitations to special events hosted by your brand. The key is to ensure that the rewards are perceived as valuable and attainable, providing a clear incentive for guests to book with you again rather than exploring alternative options.

Beyond formal loyalty tiers, offering straightforward discounts for returning guests is a simple yet highly effective method to encourage repeat bookings. This can be communicated through personalized post-stay emails, often delivered a few weeks after checkout. The message can express gratitude for their stay and include a specific discount code or mention a special rate applicable to their next booking. For example, a "Thank You for Staying With Us – Enjoy 10% Off Your Next Visit!" message provides a direct financial incentive. It's crucial that this discount is genuinely beneficial and presented in a way that makes it easy for the guest to redeem. Integrating this into your booking engine or direct booking website is essential for a seamless experience. The perceived savings encourage guests to factor your property into their future travel plans, knowing they are receiving preferential treatment.

Personalized offers are another powerful tool for fostering loyalty. This involves leveraging data collected from past guest stays to tailor incentives that are relevant to their individual preferences and past behavior. If a guest has previously booked during a specific holiday season or expressed interest in a particular amenity or local experience, future offers can be designed around these insights. For example, a guest who frequently books family-friendly properties and previously inquired about local amusement park tickets might receive an early bird discount on a "Family Fun Package" for an upcoming summer season. Similarly, a couple who celebrated an anniversary at your property might receive a special offer for a romantic getaway package for their next visit, perhaps including a complimentary bottle of wine or a spa voucher. This level of personalization demonstrates that you understand and value their individual needs, transforming a generic discount into a highly relevant and appealing proposition.

Exceptional service throughout the entire guest journey is the bedrock upon which all loyalty initiatives are built. Even the most generous loyalty program or attractive discount will falter if the core guest experience is subpar. This begins with seamless booking and communication, extends through a meticulously clean and well-maintained property, and culminates in responsive and helpful support during their stay. Small gestures, such as remembering a guest's name, anticipating their needs (like providing extra towels if they are a family of four), or offering local recommendations based on their interests, can significantly elevate their perception of your service. When guests feel genuinely cared for and valued, they are far more likely to become repeat customers. This often translates into positive reviews, which, in turn, attract new guests, creating a virtuous cycle of growth.

Consider the power of proactive communication. Post-stay emails are not just for soliciting reviews or offering discounts; they are an opportunity to maintain a connection. A thoughtful follow-up message could include links to local events or activities that might be of interest for future visits, or even a brief mention of upcoming upgrades or new properties in your portfolio. This keeps your brand top-of-mind without being overly intrusive. Furthermore, recognizing significant dates, such as a guest's birthday or anniversary, with a personalized email or even a small token of appreciation during their next stay can create a memorable and emotionally resonant experience, solidifying their loyalty. These personalized touchpoints demonstrate a commitment to the guest relationship that extends beyond the confines of their booking period.

Leveraging technology can significantly enhance your ability to implement and manage loyalty programs and repeat guest incentives. Property management systems (PMS) and customer relationship management (CRM) tools can help track guest history, preferences, and booking patterns. This data is invaluable for segmenting your guest base and tailoring targeted offers. For instance, you can identify guests who have stayed multiple times but haven't booked in a while and send them a "We Miss You" campaign with a special incentive to return. Similarly, you can segment guests based on their spending habits or the type of properties they prefer, allowing for more precise and effective marketing efforts. Automation can also play a crucial role, ensuring that welcome emails, thank-you notes, and loyalty program updates are sent out consistently and on time, freeing up your operational resources to focus on delivering exceptional on-the-ground service.

The tangible benefits of fostering repeat business extend beyond predictable revenue. Returning guests are often more willing to try new offerings or upgrade their stays because they already trust your brand and understand the quality you deliver. This increased guest lifetime value is a critical metric for any successful short-term rental investor. Moreover, repeat guests often require less marketing effort and incur lower acquisition costs. Their word-of-mouth referrals, driven by positive experiences and loyalty rewards, become some of your most powerful and cost-effective marketing assets. They are your brand ambassadors, sharing their positive experiences with friends, family, and colleagues, thereby expanding your reach organically.

When designing loyalty programs, it's essential to consider the competitive landscape. Analyze what other properties or platforms in your market are offering. Your incentives should be attractive enough to stand out while remaining financially sustainable for your business. The perceived value of the reward is as important as the actual cost. Sometimes, non-monetary perks like early check-in, late check-out, or access to exclusive local experiences can be as appealing, if not more so, than a simple discount, especially for guests who prioritize convenience and unique experiences. The goal is to create a holistic program that fosters a sense of belonging and continued engagement with your brand.

Furthermore, integrating loyalty initiatives into your direct booking strategy can be particularly effective. By encouraging guests to book directly through your website rather than through third-party platforms, you can offer them exclusive direct booking benefits, such as a better price, a complimentary amenity, or entry into your loyalty program. This reduces your reliance on OTAs, which charge significant commission fees, thereby increasing your net revenue per booking. Communicating these direct booking advantages clearly on your website and in your pre-arrival communications is crucial. Emphasize that booking direct is the best way to access the full range of benefits and ensure a personalized experience.

Building a strong relationship with your guests, underpinned by thoughtful loyalty programs and personalized incentives, transforms them from one-time renters into a valuable asset for your business. It's about creating an ongoing dialogue and demonstrating a consistent commitment to their satisfaction. This approach not only secures repeat bookings and boosts revenue but also cultivates a resilient and thriving short-term rental business that can weather market fluctuations and stand out in a crowded industry. The investment in loyalty is an investment in the long-term sustainability and profitability of your enterprise, building a strong foundation of returning guests who appreciate and reward your dedication to their comfort and enjoyment.

Data Analytics for Continuous Improvement

The pursuit of enhanced revenue in the short-term rental sector is an ongoing journey, one that is significantly propelled by a rigorous commitment to data analytics. While building guest loyalty and refining operational efficiencies are foundational, it is the intelligent interrogation of performance metrics that allows for the continuous iteration and optimization of every facet of your business. This is not merely about collecting data; it is about transforming raw numbers into actionable insights that directly inform pricing, marketing, property management, and ultimately, profitability. By embracing a data-driven mindset, you move beyond intuition and assumption, grounding your strategic decisions in empirical evidence, thereby sharpening your competitive edge and maximizing the return on your investment.

At the core of any effective data analytics strategy for short-term rentals lies a deep understanding of your key performance indicators (KPIs). These are the quantifiable measures that reflect your business's health and progress. Among the most critical is the

occupancy rate. This metric, representing the percentage of available nights that are actually booked, provides a direct indicator of demand for your property or portfolio. A consistently low occupancy rate, even with competitive pricing, might signal issues with visibility, marketing, pricing strategy, or even the property's appeal. Conversely, an extremely high occupancy rate, particularly if coupled with a declining average daily rate (ADR), could suggest that you are leaving money on the table. Analyzing occupancy trends over different seasons, weekdays versus weekends, and in relation to specific local events allows for granular adjustments to your availability and pricing calendars. For instance, if you consistently see high occupancy the week before a major festival, but lower occupancy in the weeks immediately following, you might strategically increase rates during the festival week and consider offering promotional packages during the slower post-festival period. Furthermore, dissecting occupancy by booking source can reveal which channels are most effective in filling your calendar, enabling you to allocate marketing resources more efficiently.

Closely linked to occupancy is the

Average Daily Rate (ADR). This is calculated by dividing your total rental revenue by the number of paid rooms or nights occupied. ADR is a primary indicator of your pricing effectiveness. While high occupancy is desirable, it is ADR that truly drives revenue. Analyzing ADR in conjunction with occupancy is crucial. A common pitfall is to aggressively lower rates to achieve high occupancy, which can depress ADR and overall revenue. Conversely, setting rates too high can lead to low occupancy. The sweet spot lies in finding the optimal balance. Data analytics allows for sophisticated pricing strategies, such as dynamic pricing, where rates are adjusted in real-time based on demand, seasonality, local events, competitor pricing, and even booking lead time. For example, understanding that bookings for holidays often occur months in advance, you can implement premium pricing for those periods earlier in the booking window. Similarly, last-minute bookings might be priced differently, either at a premium to capture high-intent travelers or at a discount to fill unsold dates. Analyzing historical ADR data against competitor pricing data, which can be gathered through various market intelligence tools, provides invaluable context for setting competitive yet profitable rates.

The

RevPAR (Revenue Per Available Room) is another indispensable KPI that combines occupancy and ADR into a single, powerful metric. Calculated as ADR multiplied by the occupancy rate, or alternatively, as total rental revenue divided by the total number of available rooms (occupied or not), RevPAR offers a holistic view of your revenue-generating capability. By tracking RevPAR, you can benchmark your performance against the market and identify whether your property is maximizing its revenue potential relative to its availability. A rising RevPAR indicates that your pricing and occupancy strategies are working in tandem to boost overall earnings. Analyzing RevPAR by day of the week, season, or event presence can reveal which periods are most lucrative and which might require strategic intervention to improve performance. For example, if your RevPAR consistently dips on Tuesdays and Wednesdays compared to Fridays and Saturdays, you might explore offering mid-week discounts or packages to attract business travelers or event attendees during those less popular days.

Understanding your

booking sources is paramount for optimizing marketing spend and maximizing reach. Are your bookings primarily coming from direct bookings on your website, or are you heavily reliant on Online Travel Agencies (OTAs) like Airbnb, Booking.com, or Vrbo? Each channel has different commission structures and customer acquisition costs. By tracking which channels deliver the most bookings and, more importantly, the highest net revenue (after commissions), you can refine your marketing efforts. If data shows that your direct booking channel, despite lower volume, yields significantly higher net revenue due to zero commission fees, it becomes clear that investing in driving direct bookings through your own website, email marketing, and SEO is a high-priority strategy. Conversely, if a particular OTA consistently brings in a high volume of bookings at a profitable ADR, it warrants continued investment and potentially deeper integration with that platform. Analyzing the booking lead time from different sources can also inform your marketing calendar, helping you anticipate demand and adjust your promotional efforts accordingly. For instance, if you notice that bookings from corporate travel managers typically have a longer lead time than leisure travelers, you can initiate outreach to corporate clients earlier in the year.

Guest feedback is a treasure trove of qualitative data that, when systematically analyzed, can drive significant improvements in both guest experience and operational efficiency. Beyond generic star ratings, delve into the content of reviews. Identify recurring themes, both positive and negative. Are guests consistently praising the cleanliness of the property? That's a strength to maintain and highlight in your marketing. Are multiple guests mentioning the lack of a specific amenity, like a coffee maker or reliable Wi-Fi? That's a clear signal for an improvement that can directly impact future bookings and guest satisfaction. Sentiment analysis tools can help process large volumes of reviews, categorizing feedback into specific areas such as cleanliness, communication, location, value, and amenities. Understanding these sentiments allows you to address pain points proactively, enhance positive aspects, and refine your guest communication and expectations. For example, if guests frequently comment on the ease of check-in, document that process and consider featuring it in your booking confirmation. If, however, there are consistent complaints about noise from a nearby source, you might consider investing in soundproofing or clearly disclosing the potential for noise in your listing description to manage expectations.

Beyond these core metrics, consider the value of

cancellation rates. High cancellation rates can disrupt revenue forecasts, impact occupancy, and incur additional administrative costs. Analyzing the reasons for cancellations, if ascertainable (e.g., through post-cancellation surveys or by correlating cancellations with specific booking channels or times of year), can reveal underlying issues. Perhaps your cancellation policy is too restrictive, or maybe your booking confirmations are unclear. Tracking cancellations by booking source can also be insightful. If a particular OTA or promotional offer is associated with a disproportionately high cancellation rate, it may be a sign to re-evaluate that partnership or offer.

Guest demographics and booking patterns offer further layers of insight. Understanding who your typical guests are – their age groups, travel purposes (business, leisure, family), and booking frequency – can help tailor marketing messages and property enhancements. For example, if your data reveals a growing segment of business travelers, you might focus on providing enhanced amenities for them, such as a dedicated workspace, high-speed internet, and convenient access to business districts. Analyzing booking patterns, such as the average length of stay, the typical booking window, and the days of the week guests prefer to check in and out, can inform your availability management and pricing strategies. If data shows that longer stays are more profitable on a per-night basis due to lower turnover costs and a higher likelihood of repeat bookings, you might consider offering discounts for extended stays.

Website analytics are crucial if you have a direct booking channel. Understanding metrics like website traffic, bounce rate, conversion rate, and traffic sources can reveal how effectively your website is attracting and converting potential guests. High website traffic but a low conversion rate might indicate issues with the user experience, clarity of information, or the booking process itself. Analyzing user flow through your website can highlight where potential guests are dropping off, allowing you to make targeted improvements to the booking engine and content.

Furthermore,

channel performance analysis extends beyond simple booking volume and revenue. It should also encompass the cost of acquisition for each channel. By tracking marketing spend allocated to each OTA, social media campaign, or advertising platform, and then comparing it against the revenue generated and the commission fees paid, you can calculate the net profitability of each marketing initiative. This allows for a data-driven reallocation of marketing budgets, focusing resources on the channels that deliver the best return on investment. For example, if data shows that a particular Facebook ad campaign has a high click-through rate but a low conversion rate to actual bookings, you might adjust the campaign's targeting or messaging.

The process of data analytics is not a one-time activity but a continuous cycle. Regularly scheduled performance reviews are essential. This could involve daily checks of booking calendars and pricing, weekly deep dives into occupancy, ADR, and guest feedback, and monthly or quarterly comprehensive reviews of all KPIs and marketing channel performance. Establishing a rhythm for data analysis ensures that trends are identified promptly and that adjustments can be made proactively, rather than reactively. This iterative process of collecting data, analyzing it, implementing changes, and then measuring the impact of those changes is the engine of continuous improvement. By systematically leveraging data, you move from simply managing a short-term rental to strategically optimizing a high-performance asset, ensuring sustained growth and profitability in a competitive marketplace. This analytical discipline empowers you to make informed decisions that align with your financial goals and enhance the overall guest experience, creating a virtuous cycle of success.

Chapter Seven

Advanced Leverage and Exit Strategies

Building a MultiProperty Management Brand

The transition from managing a single property to overseeing a portfolio, and then to cultivating a distinct brand, represents a pivotal evolution in the short-term rental business. This strategic shift is not merely about increasing the number of doors you manage; it's about fundamentally transforming your operation from a collection of individual assets into a cohesive, recognizable entity that delivers consistent value to both guests and property owners. Building a multi-property management brand is about instilling confidence, establishing a reputation for excellence, and creating a scalable framework that can support substantial growth and, ultimately, offer robust exit opportunities.

At the heart of any successful brand is a clear and compelling identity. This begins with defining your unique selling proposition (USP). What sets your management company apart from the competition? Is it unparalleled guest service, cutting-edge technology integration, a focus on luxury properties, or perhaps a commitment to sustainability? Identifying and articulating this USP is the cornerstone upon which your brand will be built. This identity needs to be woven into every aspect of your business, from your company name and logo to your website, marketing materials, and even the way your team communicates with guests and owners. The name itself should be memorable, professional, and ideally, hint at the value you provide. A strong visual identity, including a well-designed logo and consistent color palette, will ensure your brand is easily recognized across all touchpoints. This visual cohesion is critical for building brand recall and projecting an image of professionalism and reliability.

Once your brand identity is established, the next critical step is the standardization of operational procedures. A multi-property management brand thrives on consistency. Guests expect the same level of quality, cleanliness, and service regardless of which property they book within your portfolio. Property owners, too, rely on predictable, high-quality management of their assets. This necessitates the development of comprehensive standard operating procedures (SOPs) for every facet of your operation. These SOPs should cover everything from guest check-in and check-out processes, cleaning protocols and quality control, routine maintenance and emergency repairs, to guest communication and issue resolution. For cleaning, for instance, an SOP might detail specific checklists for housekeepers, including the number of towels to be provided, the expected standard of dusting and vacuuming, and the inspection process by a supervisor. For guest communication, it might outline response time targets for inquiries, a script for handling complaints, and guidelines for personalized touches. These SOPs should be meticulously documented, easily accessible to your team, and regularly reviewed and updated. Training your staff rigorously on these procedures is paramount to ensuring consistent execution.

Implementing technology that supports these standardized operations is also crucial. Property management software (PMS) designed for short-term rentals can be instrumental in managing bookings, calendars, guest communications, cleaning schedules, and maintenance requests across an entire portfolio. Integrated channel managers ensure that your listings are consistently updated across all booking platforms, preventing double bookings and maintaining accurate availability. Smart lock systems can automate check-ins and outs, providing secure, contactless access for guests and allowing for easy management of access codes for different properties. Guest communication platforms can streamline messaging, automate responses to frequently asked questions, and help manage guest reviews. Investing in the right technology not only enhances operational efficiency but also reinforces your brand's image as a modern, professional, and tech-savvy management company.

Marketing strategies need to evolve as you transition to a brand-focused approach. While individual property listings on OTAs are still important, your brand marketing should aim to attract both guests who are searching for unique stays and property owners who are seeking professional management. For guest acquisition, focus on building a strong online presence that showcases your brand. This includes a professional website that features your entire portfolio, high-quality photography and videography of your properties, and compelling descriptions that highlight your brand's USP. Content marketing, such as blog posts about local attractions, travel tips, or guides to the properties, can drive organic traffic to your website and establish your brand as a trusted resource. Social media marketing can be used to showcase your properties, engage with potential guests, run targeted advertising campaigns, and build a community around your brand. Consider guest loyalty programs or referral incentives to encourage repeat bookings and word-of-mouth marketing, which is invaluable for brand building.

Crucially, your brand marketing must also target property owners. Many owners are looking for professional management services to handle the complexities of short-term rentals. Your marketing efforts should clearly articulate the benefits of partnering with your company. This includes demonstrating your expertise in maximizing revenue through dynamic pricing and optimized listings, your commitment to property maintenance and guest satisfaction, your transparent reporting and financial management, and your track record of success. Testimonials from satisfied property owners are incredibly powerful in building trust and credibility. Case studies showcasing how you have improved the performance of properties you manage can also be highly persuasive. Networking within the real estate community, attending investor conferences, and partnering with real estate agents can help you reach potential property owners. Clearly outline your management fees and the services included, ensuring transparency and building confidence.

Building a strong brand is an investment in long-term growth and profitability. A recognized and respected brand commands higher rates because guests are willing to pay a premium for the assurance of quality and reliability. It attracts more property owners, providing a consistent pipeline for portfolio expansion. This scalability is key.

With standardized processes and a strong brand, you can onboard new properties more efficiently and maintain service levels even as you grow. Furthermore, a well-established brand makes your business a more attractive acquisition target for larger management companies or investment firms. Investors often look for brands that have proven market appeal, a loyal customer base, and a scalable operational model. Your brand is your most valuable intangible asset, providing a competitive moat and significantly increasing the valuation of your business. It represents the sum of your reputation, your operational excellence, and your market presence, all working in synergy to create a sustainable and valuable enterprise. The ability to leverage this brand equity allows for strategic partnerships, preferential lending terms, and ultimately, a more favorable position when considering future exit strategies, whether that be a sale, a merger, or even an IPO in the larger management company space. It shifts the focus from individual property performance to the overarching strength and marketability of your management company as a whole.

Leveraging Debt and Equity for Portfolio Growth

The transition from managing a single property to overseeing a portfolio, and then to cultivating a distinct brand, represents a pivotal evolution in the short-term rental business. This strategic shift is not merely about increasing the number of doors you manage; it's about fundamentally transforming your operation from a collection of individual assets into a cohesive, recognizable entity that delivers consistent value to both guests and property owners. Building a multi-property management brand is about instilling confidence, establishing a reputation for excellence, and creating a scalable framework that can support substantial growth and, ultimately, offer robust exit opportunities.

At the heart of any successful brand is a clear and compelling identity. This begins with defining your unique selling proposition (USP). What sets your management company apart from the competition? Is it unparalleled guest service, cutting-edge technology integration, a focus on luxury properties, or perhaps a commitment to sustainability? Identifying and articulating this USP is the cornerstone upon which your brand will be built. This identity needs to be woven into every aspect of your business, from your company name and logo to your website, marketing materials, and even the way your team communicates with guests and owners. The name itself should be memorable, professional, and ideally, hint at the value you provide. A strong visual identity, including a well-designed logo and consistent color palette, will ensure your brand is easily recognized across all touchpoints. This visual cohesion is critical for building brand recall and projecting an image of professionalism and reliability.

Once your brand identity is established, the next critical step is the standardization of operational procedures. A multi-property management brand thrives on consistency. Guests expect the same level of quality, cleanliness, and service regardless of which property they book within your portfolio. Property owners, too, rely on predictable, high-quality management of their assets. This necessitates the development of comprehensive standard operating procedures (SOPs) for every facet of your operation. These SOPs should cover everything from guest check-in and check-out processes, cleaning protocols and quality control, routine maintenance and emergency repairs, to guest communication and issue resolution. For cleaning, for instance, an SOP might detail specific checklists for housekeepers, including the number of towels to be provided, the expected standard of dusting and vacuuming, and the inspection process by a supervisor. For guest communication, it might outline response time targets for inquiries, a script for handling complaints, and guidelines for personalized touches. These SOPs should be meticulously documented, easily accessible to your team, and regularly reviewed and updated. Training your staff rigorously on these procedures is paramount to ensuring consistent execution.

Implementing technology that supports these standardized operations is also crucial. Property management software (PMS) designed for short-term rentals can be instrumental in managing bookings, calendars, guest communications, cleaning schedules, and maintenance requests across an entire portfolio. Integrated channel managers ensure that your listings are consistently updated across all booking platforms, preventing double bookings and maintaining accurate availability. Smart lock systems can automate check-ins and outs, providing secure, contactless access for guests and allowing for easy management of access codes for different properties. Guest communication platforms can streamline messaging, automate responses to frequently asked questions, and help manage guest reviews. Investing in the right technology not only enhances operational efficiency but also reinforces your brand's image as a modern, professional, and tech-savvy management company.

Marketing strategies need to evolve as you transition to a brand-focused approach. While individual property listings on OTAs are still important, your brand marketing should aim to attract both guests who are searching for unique stays and property owners who are seeking professional management. For guest acquisition, focus on building a strong online presence that showcases your brand. This includes a professional website that features your entire portfolio, high-quality photography and videography of your properties, and compelling descriptions that highlight your brand's USP. Content marketing, such as blog posts about local attractions, travel tips, or guides to the properties, can drive organic traffic to your website and establish your brand as a trusted resource. Social media marketing can be used to showcase your properties, engage with potential guests, run targeted advertising campaigns, and build a community around your brand. Consider guest loyalty programs or referral incentives to encourage repeat bookings and word-of-mouth marketing, which is invaluable for brand building.

Crucially, your brand marketing must also target property owners. Many owners are looking for professional management services to handle the complexities of short-term rentals. Your marketing efforts should clearly articulate the benefits of partnering with your company. This includes demonstrating your expertise in maximizing revenue through dynamic pricing and optimized listings, your commitment to property maintenance and guest satisfaction, your transparent reporting and financial management, and your track record of success. Testimonials from satisfied property owners are incredibly powerful in building trust and credibility. Case studies showcasing how you have improved the performance of properties you manage can also be highly persuasive. Networking within the real estate community, attending investor conferences, and partnering with real estate agents can help you reach potential property owners. Clearly outline your management fees and the services included, ensuring transparency and building confidence.

Building a strong brand is an investment in long-term growth and profitability. A recognized and respected brand commands higher rates because guests are willing to pay a premium for the assurance of quality and reliability. It attracts more property owners, providing a consistent pipeline for portfolio expansion. This scalability is key.

With standardized processes and a strong brand, you can onboard new properties more efficiently and maintain service levels even as you grow. Furthermore, a well-established brand makes your business a more attractive acquisition target for larger management companies or investment firms. Investors often look for brands that have proven market appeal, a loyal customer base, and a scalable operational model. Your brand is your most valuable intangible asset, providing a competitive moat and significantly increasing the valuation of your business. It represents the sum of your reputation, your operational excellence, and your market presence, all working in synergy to create a sustainable and valuable enterprise. The ability to leverage this brand equity allows for strategic partnerships, preferential lending terms, and ultimately, a more favorable position when considering future exit strategies, whether that be a sale, a merger, or even an IPO in the larger management company space. It shifts the focus from individual property performance to the overarching strength and marketability of your management company as a whole.

As your short-term rental portfolio expands beyond a handful of properties, the financial strategies employed to fuel this growth become increasingly sophisticated. While initial acquisitions might have been funded through personal savings or conventional mortgages, scaling effectively necessitates a deeper understanding and strategic application of both debt and equity. This section delves into these advanced financial techniques, equipping you to accelerate your portfolio's expansion and maximize its long-term value.

The most accessible and common method for funding property acquisition is through debt financing. This involves borrowing money, typically from financial institutions, with the intention of repaying it with interest over time. For short-term rentals, the type of debt you

pursue can significantly impact your cash flow and overall profitability.

Secured loans are the bedrock of real estate investment financing.
These are loans where the property itself serves as collateral, offering
the lender a degree of security. A conventional mortgage, while often
associated with long-term residential properties, can also be adapted
for short-term rental investments. However, it's crucial to understand
that lenders often have specific requirements for investment properties, which might include higher down payment requirements and
different interest rates compared to owner-occupied residences. For a
burgeoning portfolio, exploring commercial mortgages or investment
property loans from banks, credit unions, or specialized mortgage
brokers can be more advantageous. These products are tailored to the
unique cash-flow dynamics of income-generating properties and may
offer terms that better align with the short-term rental business model.
For instance, some lenders may be more amenable to the fluctuat-
ing income streams of short-term rentals than traditional residential
lenders.

A significant advantage of using debt is the concept of leverage.
Leverage allows you to control a larger asset with a smaller amount
of your own capital. By borrowing money, you can acquire more
properties than you could with cash alone, thereby amplifying your
potential returns. If a property appreciates in value or generates rental
income that exceeds the cost of the debt servicing, the return on your
initial equity investment is magnified. However, leverage also amplifies risk. If property values decline or occupancy rates drop, the debt
obligations remain, potentially leading to negative cash flow or even
default. Therefore, meticulous financial modeling and a conservative
approach to debt utilization are paramount.

Beyond traditional mortgages, a crucial tool for agile portfolio growth is the Home Equity Line of Credit (HELOC) or a Home Equity Loan. If you own properties outright or have significant equity built up in your primary residence or existing investment properties, these instruments can provide a flexible source of capital. A HELOC functions like a credit card secured by your home's equity, allowing you to draw funds as needed up to a certain limit. This is particularly useful for bridging financing gaps, covering unexpected expenses, or making down payments on new acquisitions. Home Equity Loans, on the other hand, provide a lump sum of cash with a fixed repayment schedule. The flexibility and accessibility of HELOCs make them attractive for active investors, but it's essential to remember that you are using your home as collateral, so prudent management of these lines of credit is vital to avoid jeopardizing your primary residence.

Another powerful debt instrument for scaling is a portfolio line of credit. As your portfolio grows and demonstrates a consistent track record of profitability and loan repayment, you may qualify for a line of credit secured by the entire portfolio, rather than individual properties. This can provide significant borrowing power and greater flexibility, allowing you to draw funds for down payments, renovations, or operational expenses without needing to re-mortgage each individual property. These lines of credit are typically offered by larger financial institutions and require a well-established business and a strong financial history. They represent a more advanced form of debt financing, indicative of a mature and well-managed short-term rental operation.

When considering renovations or upgrades to enhance property appeal and increase rental income, construction loans or renovation loans are also vital debt options. These loans are specifically designed to fund the cost of construction or significant improvements. Some lenders offer combined financing packages that include the purchase price of the property and the renovation costs, simplifying the acquisition process. It's important to work with lenders who understand the short-term rental market and can structure loan terms that accommodate the project timeline and anticipated revenue increases post-renovation.

While debt financing is crucial for leveraging existing capital and borrowing for expansion, equity financing provides another powerful avenue for growth, particularly for acquiring larger or more numerous properties. Equity represents ownership in an asset. Raising equity means bringing in other investors who contribute capital in exchange for a share of ownership and potential profits.

Partnerships are a common way to raise equity. This could involve partnering with friends, family, or other investors who share a similar vision for your short-term rental portfolio. When forming a partnership, it is absolutely critical to establish a clear and comprehensive partnership agreement. This document should outline each partner's contribution (capital, time, expertise), ownership percentages, profit and loss distribution, decision-making authority, and exit strategies. A well-drafted agreement prevents future disputes and ensures that all parties are aligned. For example, one partner might contribute capital, while another brings operational expertise, and they agree to split profits 50/50 after covering all expenses and debt service.

Private equity, or private money lending, involves securing funds from individuals or private investment groups who are not traditional financial institutions. These investors often seek higher returns than those offered by more conservative investments and are willing to take on a degree of risk in exchange for that potential. Private lenders may be more flexible with their terms and can sometimes close deals more quickly than traditional banks, making them an attractive option for opportunistic acquisitions. However, private money typically comes with higher interest rates and fees due to the increased risk undertaken by the lender. Negotiating these terms carefully is essential to ensure the deal remains profitable.

Real estate syndication is a more sophisticated method of raising equity, particularly for larger acquisitions or portfolio purchases that exceed the capital capacity of a single investor or small partnership. Syndication involves pooling capital from multiple passive investors to acquire a significant asset or portfolio. A sponsor (you, in this case) manages the acquisition and operation of the property, while the passive investors contribute capital and receive a share of the profits. This structure requires significant expertise in deal sourcing, due diligence, financial structuring, and investor relations. A well-structured syndication involves a detailed offering memorandum that clearly outlines the investment opportunity, risks, projected returns, and the sponsor's experience. Legal and financial advice is indispensable when setting up a syndication.

When approaching potential equity partners or private investors, a compelling business plan is non-negotiable. This plan should clearly articulate your investment strategy, market analysis, projected financial performance (including revenue, expenses, and cash flow), management team expertise, and the specific deal you are presenting. Demonstrating a clear understanding of the short-term rental market, a proven track record of success, and robust operational procedures will instill confidence in potential investors. Transparency regarding all financial aspects, including fees, profit sharing, and reporting, is key to building long-term relationships.

Furthermore, it's important to understand the implications of equity financing on your ownership structure and control. When you bring in equity partners, you are essentially selling a portion of your ownership stake. This means future profits will be shared, and decision-making may become more collaborative, requiring consensus from your partners. It's a trade-off: you gain access to capital for faster growth, but you also dilute your ownership and potentially some control.

The decision to prioritize debt or equity, or to use a combination of both, depends on your specific financial situation, risk tolerance, and growth objectives. A conservative approach might favor a higher proportion of debt, provided that the cash flow from the properties comfortably covers the debt service. Conversely, if you want to limit personal liability and retain more operational control, or if debt markets are unfavorable, equity financing may be more suitable. Often, a balanced approach, utilizing both debt and equity strategically, offers the optimal path to accelerated portfolio growth. For example, you might use a conventional mortgage (debt) to acquire a property, then use a HELOC (debt) to fund renovations, and finally, bring in a private equity partner (equity) for a larger multi-unit acquisition that leverages your existing portfolio as a foundation.

The strategic deployment of both debt and equity is not merely about acquiring more properties; it's about acquiring them more efficiently and effectively, thereby maximizing your return on investment and accelerating your journey towards becoming a significant player in the short-term rental market. As your portfolio scales, so too should your financial acumen, enabling you to harness the power of leverage and investment capital to achieve unprecedented growth.

Asset Protection and Risk Mitigation

As your short-term rental portfolio expands, the inherent risks associated with property ownership and business operations escalate proportionally. What might be manageable with a single property can quickly become a significant exposure when you have multiple units, each with its own set of potential liabilities. Therefore, a robust strategy for asset protection and risk mitigation is not merely advisable; it is an absolute necessity for long-term success and the preservation of your hard-earned wealth. This subsection is dedicated to exploring the foundational pillars of such a strategy, ensuring that your investments are shielded from potential threats and that your business operates on a stable and secure footing.

One of the most fundamental and effective tools for asset protection is the strategic use of legal structures. For many short-term rental investors, forming Limited Liability Companies (LLCs) is a cornerstone of their protection strategy. An LLC creates a legal separation between your personal assets (like your primary residence, savings accounts, and other investments) and the assets and liabilities of your business. This means that if a lawsuit arises from a tenant's stay at one of your rental properties, such as an injury claim due to a faulty staircase or a slip-and-fall incident, the claimant can typically only pursue the assets held within the LLC. Your personal bank accounts, other properties not held within that LLC, and personal investments are generally shielded from such claims. When operating multiple properties, it is often advisable to create a separate LLC for each property or, in some cases, a holding company that owns the LLCs for individual properties. This tiered approach further compartmentalizes risk. If one property within a portfolio experiences a severe legal issue that exhausts the assets of its dedicated LLC, the other properties, even those within other LLCs, remain protected. While this adds complexity and administrative overhead, the peace of mind and financial security it provides are invaluable, especially as your portfolio scales. It is crucial to consult with a qualified attorney specializing in business and real estate law to determine the most appropriate legal structure for your specific situation and jurisdiction, as regulations can vary significantly.

Beyond the structural protection offered by LLCs, comprehensive insurance coverage is the next critical layer of defense. Standard landlord insurance, while necessary, is often insufficient for the dynamic nature of short-term rentals. You will need specialized short-term rental insurance policies that specifically cover the risks associated with frequent guest turnover, potential damage, liability claims, and business interruption. These policies typically offer broader coverage than traditional landlord policies, including:

General Liability Coverage: This is paramount and protects you against claims of bodily injury or property damage incurred by guests on your property. For instance, if a guest trips on an uneven step and sustains an injury, this coverage would help defend against potential lawsuits and cover medical expenses.

Property Damage Coverage: This covers damage to the physical structure of the property and its contents, whether caused by guests (intentional or accidental), natural disasters, or other covered perils. Look for policies that explicitly cover damage from guests, as this is a common exclusion in standard policies.

Loss of Income/Business Interruption Coverage: Short-term rentals can experience periods of vacancy due to unforeseen circumstances, such as property damage requiring extensive repairs or a public health crisis impacting travel. This coverage helps replace lost rental income during such periods, ensuring your cash flow remains stable even when the property is unoccupied.

Vandalism and Malicious Mischief Coverage: While guests are generally expected to treat your property with care, the risk of intentional damage or vandalism cannot be entirely eliminated. This coverage helps protect against such losses.

Guest Belongings Coverage: Some policies may offer limited coverage for guests' personal belongings in the event of fire, theft, or other covered incidents.

It is vital to review your insurance policies meticulously and understand the coverage limits, deductibles, and exclusions. Working with an insurance broker who specializes in short-term rentals is highly recommended. They can help you navigate the complex insurance landscape and ensure you have adequate coverage tailored to the unique risks of your business. Regularly reviewing and updating your insurance as your portfolio grows or as local regulations change is also essential. Do not assume that what was adequate last year is sufficient this year. The short-term rental market is constantly evolving, and so too should your insurance strategy.

The third pillar of asset protection and risk mitigation lies in the realm of robust contractual agreements. Every guest, every cleaner, every contractor, and every partner should operate under clearly defined terms and conditions. For guests, this means having well-drafted booking agreements and house rules that explicitly outline expectations regarding behavior, property use, and liability. These documents should clearly state that guests are responsible for any damages they cause beyond normal wear and tear, and they should include clauses regarding quiet hours, prohibited activities (like smoking or parties), and check-out procedures. While a house rule against smoking won't prevent a determined smoker, clearly stating it and potentially adding a fee for cleaning associated with smoke odor can provide a basis for recourse. Moreover, ensuring your booking platform agreements with OTAs (Online Travel Agencies) are understood and that your direct booking website has protective terms of service is crucial. These agreements form the legal basis for guest conduct and can provide recourse in cases of policy violations or damage.

In addition to guest agreements, it is imperative to have solid contracts in place with any third-party service providers, such as cleaning companies, property managers (if you are outsourcing), maintenance personnel, and even co-hosts or partners. These contracts should clearly define the scope of work, payment terms, performance expectations, indemnification clauses, and insurance requirements. For example, a cleaning contract should specify detailed cleaning checklists, quality control measures, and the required turnaround time between guests. It should also include an indemnification clause where the cleaning company agrees to hold you harmless from any liabilities arising from their negligence or actions. Similarly, if you partner with other investors or individuals, a comprehensive operating agreement or partnership agreement is indispensable. This document should meticulously detail ownership percentages, capital contributions, profit and loss distribution, management responsibilities, dispute resolution mechanisms, and exit strategies for each partner. A well-defined agreement prevents misunderstandings and disputes down the line, protecting both your financial investment and your professional relationships.

Risk mitigation extends beyond legal and contractual frameworks to encompass operational excellence and proactive planning. This involves implementing rigorous vetting processes for guests, where feasible. While instant booking is convenient, for higher-value or more unique properties, consider implementing stricter booking requirements, such as verified IDs, positive reviews from previous stays, or even direct communication with potential guests before confirming a booking. This allows you to gauge their suitability and identify potential red flags. For larger portfolios, investing in robust property management software (PMS) can also be a significant risk mitigator. A good PMS can automate many operational tasks, from managing bookings and guest communications to coordinating cleaning schedules and maintenance requests. This automation reduces the likelihood of human error, such as double bookings or missed cleaning turns, which can lead to guest dissatisfaction and negative reviews, thereby impacting your brand reputation and revenue.

Furthermore, a proactive approach to property maintenance is a critical risk mitigation strategy. Regular inspections and preventative maintenance can identify and address potential hazards before they lead to accidents or significant damage. This includes checking for loose railings, faulty wiring, plumbing leaks, or uneven flooring. Addressing these issues promptly not only ensures guest safety and enhances their experience but also prevents minor problems from escalating into costly repairs or serious liability claims. For instance, a small roof leak that goes unnoticed can lead to significant water damage, mold growth, and potential structural issues, all of which are expensive to rectify and can lead to extensive liability if a guest is affected by mold. Similarly, ensuring all safety equipment, such as smoke detectors, carbon monoxide detectors, and fire extinguishers, is regularly tested and up-to-date is a non-negotiable aspect of operational risk management.

The digital aspect of your business also presents unique risks that require mitigation. Data security and privacy are paramount. As you collect guest information, booking details, and payment information, you must ensure this data is stored and transmitted securely. Using reputable booking platforms and payment processors with strong encryption and security protocols is essential. Furthermore, protecting your online presence from cyber threats, such as phishing attempts or unauthorized access to your accounts, is crucial. Implement strong, unique passwords for all your online accounts, enable two-factor authentication wherever possible, and be wary of suspicious emails or requests for information. A data breach can not only result in financial losses but also severe damage to your brand reputation and potential legal liabilities related to privacy violations.

Finally, building a strong relationship with your local community and understanding local regulations is an often-overlooked but vital aspect of risk mitigation. Staying informed about zoning laws, short-term rental licensing requirements, and any upcoming regulatory changes can prevent costly fines or even the forced closure of your business. Engaging positively with neighbors and local authorities can foster goodwill and make it easier to navigate any potential issues that may arise. By treating your short-term rental operations with the seriousness of any other established business, and by proactively implementing these asset protection and risk mitigation strategies, you build a resilient foundation that can withstand challenges and support sustained growth and profitability in the dynamic short-term rental market. This diligent approach ensures that your investments are not only generating revenue but are also secured against the myriad of potential threats that can derail even the most promising ventures.

Developing an Exit Strategy Selling Your Business

The journey of a successful short-term rental investor doesn't end with maximizing occupancy and streamlining operations. True financial mastery involves a clear vision for the eventual realization of your investment's value. This means proactively planning for the exit, the strategic sale of your short-term rental business. Far from being a last-minute consideration, developing a robust exit strategy from the outset is a hallmark of sophisticated investing. It ensures that when the time comes to divest, you are not scrambling to organize finances or improve your business's attractiveness; instead, you are poised to capitalize on the value you have meticulously built. A well-executed sale can significantly amplify your returns, turning years of hard work and capital deployment into a substantial financial windfall. This chapter delves into the intricacies of preparing your short-term rental enterprise for a successful transition, covering everything from how to enhance its market appeal to understanding the valuation methods that will determine its price, and finally, identifying the most likely candidates to acquire your valuable asset.

The cornerstone of any successful sale is a business that is inherently desirable and easy for a potential buyer to understand and operate. Think of your business as a product you are preparing to place on the market. Just as a craftsman ensures their work is polished and functional before presenting it, you must meticulously prepare your short-term rental business for sale. This involves not only tidying up the physical assets but also refining the operational, financial, and legal aspects to present a compelling investment opportunity. One of the primary areas to focus on is the documentation and organization of your financial records. Buyers will conduct thorough due diligence, and having clean, transparent, and easily accessible financial statements is non-negotiable. This means having up-to-date profit and loss statements, balance sheets, and cash flow statements for at least the past three to five years. Ideally, these should be prepared by a qualified accountant, adding a layer of credibility. Beyond standard financial reports, maintaining detailed records of all expenses, including property maintenance, utilities, cleaning, insurance, taxes, and any software subscriptions, is crucial. This level of detail allows a buyer to understand the cost structure and forecast future profitability with greater accuracy.

Furthermore, the operational efficiency of your business will significantly influence its valuation and marketability. A buyer is not just purchasing physical properties; they are acquiring a revenue-generating system. Therefore, demonstrating that your business runs like a well-oiled machine is paramount. This includes having clearly defined standard operating procedures (SOPs) for every aspect of the business, from guest onboarding and communication to cleaning protocols, maintenance scheduling, and emergency response. Documenting these procedures makes it clear to a potential buyer that the business can be replicated or managed effectively, even without your direct involvement. For instance, detailed checklists for cleaners, a system for tracking guest reviews and responding to feedback, and a streamlined process for managing bookings and calendars all contribute to an attractive operational profile. If you utilize property management software, ensure it is well-maintained and that all data within it is accurate and comprehensive. This system itself can be a valuable asset to a buyer, especially if it integrates with multiple booking platforms and management tools.

The legal and regulatory compliance of your short-term rental business also plays a vital role in its saleability. Buyers will scrutinize your adherence to local zoning laws, licensing requirements, and any community regulations. Having all necessary permits and licenses in order, and being able to demonstrate a history of compliance, will significantly de-risk the transaction for a buyer. This includes having copies of all lease agreements (if applicable), permits, insurance policies, and any contracts with third-party vendors. If your business operates in an area with evolving or complex short-term rental regulations, providing evidence of your proactive engagement with these rules, such as attending community meetings or obtaining specific variances, can be a strong selling point. A buyer may be hesitant to acquire a business that faces immediate regulatory challenges or requires substantial effort to become compliant.

The physical condition of your properties is, of course, a critical component of your business's value. While you don't necessarily need to undertake extensive renovations immediately before selling, ensuring that all properties are well-maintained, clean, and presentable is essential. Buyers will conduct property inspections, and any deferred maintenance issues can lead to significant price reductions or even the collapse of a deal. Focus on the key areas that impact guest experience and safety: ensuring structural integrity, functional plumbing and electrical systems, updated appliances, comfortable furnishings, and appealing aesthetics. Curb appeal, even for short-term rentals, matters, as it's the first impression a potential buyer will have. A history of regular maintenance and upgrades, documented in a property log, can provide a buyer with confidence in the long-term viability of the assets.

Moreover, the financial performance and growth trajectory of your business will be at the forefront of any buyer's mind. Beyond just the current profitability, a buyer will look for evidence of consistent revenue growth and a stable or increasing profit margin. This is where the organization of your financial data truly shines. Presenting a clear picture of how your revenue has grown year-over-year, and how you have managed to control costs effectively, will build a strong case for the business's ongoing success. If you have implemented strategies that have demonstrably increased occupancy rates, average daily rates (ADRs), or guest satisfaction scores, be prepared to articulate these clearly. This might include the introduction of dynamic pricing strategies, enhancing your online listings with professional photography and compelling descriptions, or implementing loyalty programs for repeat guests. Any improvements made to the properties that have directly contributed to increased revenue or enhanced guest experience should also be highlighted.

When it comes to valuing your short-term rental business, several methodologies come into play, and understanding these will empower you to negotiate effectively. The most common approach is based on its earnings potential, often using a multiple of its Seller's Discretionary Earnings (SDE) or Earnings Before Interest, Taxes, Depreciation, and Amortization (EBITDA). SDE represents the total financial benefit available to a single owner-operator. It starts with the net profit and then adds back owner's salary, owner's personal expenses that are run through the business, depreciation, amortization, and any non-recurring or discretionary expenses that a new owner would not incur. For example, if your business generated $200,000 in net profit and you paid yourself a salary of $80,000 and incurred $10,000 in personal travel expenses through the business, your SDE might be $290,000. The multiple applied to SDE varies based on factors like industry stability, growth potential, the strength of your brand, the quality of your operations, and the overall economic climate. Short-term rental businesses, especially those with a strong track record and diversified booking channels, might command multiples ranging from 3x to 6x SDE, though this can fluctuate.

EBITDA, on the other hand, is typically used for larger businesses or those with more complex corporate structures. It is calculated by taking net income and adding back interest, taxes, depreciation, and amortization. The EBITDA multiple is generally lower than an SDE multiple because it represents earnings before financing and non-cash charges, making it a more standardized measure for comparing businesses. For a short-term rental portfolio, a buyer might also consider the value of the underlying real estate assets separately from the business operations. In such cases, the valuation might be a sum of the real estate value (determined by market comparables, capitalization rates, or discounted cash flow analysis) and the business value (based on SDE or EBITDA). A savvy buyer will likely perform their own valuation, so understanding your business's key financial metrics and being able to justify your asking price based on these metrics is crucial.

Another valuation method, particularly relevant for real estate-heavy businesses, is the asset-based valuation. This approach focuses on the fair market value of all the assets owned by the business, including the properties themselves, any vehicles, furniture, fixtures, and equipment. The liabilities of the business are then subtracted from the total asset value to arrive at a net asset value. While this method provides a floor for the business's valuation, it often fails to capture the intangible value of an established brand, loyal customer base, and optimized operational systems that contribute to the business's profitability. Therefore, it is often used in conjunction with earnings-based valuations. For instance, if your properties are located in high-demand areas and have significant equity, the real estate's intrinsic value will be a major component of the overall sale price.

When preparing to sell, it's also prudent to consider how to maximize the appeal of your business to a wider pool of potential buyers. Different buyers seek different things. Some might be individual investors looking to acquire a turnkey operation to manage themselves, while others might be larger investment firms or property management companies seeking to expand their existing portfolios. To attract a broader audience, consider optimizing your online presence and marketing materials. Professional photography and videography of your properties, along with a well-designed website or digital brochure that highlights the business's strengths, can make a significant impact. Clearly outlining your unique selling propositions (USPs) – what makes your business stand out from the competition – is vital. This could be your prime locations, exceptional guest reviews, unique property amenities, innovative operational processes, or a strong brand identity.

Identifying potential buyers is the next logical step. The most common buyers for short-term rental businesses fall into several categories. Individual investors, often experienced real estate entrepreneurs or those looking to transition from traditional rentals to the more lucrative short-term market, are a primary target. These individuals are often looking for a solid, income-generating asset that requires minimal upfront operational learning curve due to well-established systems. Strategic buyers, such as existing property management companies or larger hospitality groups, are another significant group. They might be looking to acquire your business to gain market share, access your established customer base, or integrate your properties into their larger operational infrastructure. Their motivation is often growth and synergy, and they may be willing to pay a premium for these advantages.

Brokers specializing in business sales or real estate can be invaluable in identifying and reaching out to potential buyers. They have established networks and understand the market dynamics, often having a list of pre-qualified buyers who are actively seeking opportunities like yours. When engaging with a broker, ensure they have specific experience in the hospitality or short-term rental sector, as this niche market has unique valuation and operational considerations. Alternatively, if you have built strong relationships within the industry, you might be able to identify potential buyers through your professional network. This can sometimes lead to more discreet and efficient transactions.

The process of selling a business, especially one with multiple physical assets and a revenue stream tied to guest experiences, can be complex. It involves careful negotiation, meticulous due diligence by the buyer, and the execution of legal agreements. To ensure a smooth transition, having a clear understanding of your own objectives and non-negotiables is important. Are you looking for the highest possible price, a quick sale, or a buyer who will continue to operate the business in a manner consistent with your vision? Clarifying these priorities will guide your negotiation strategy. A well-prepared business, with its financials in order, operations streamlined, and legal standing robust, is not only more attractive to buyers but also positions you to command a premium price and secure a truly rewarding exit from your short-term rental venture. This proactive approach to exiting is an integral part of scaling and achieving ultimate financial freedom through strategic real estate investment.

Licensing Your Brand and Management System

In the pursuit of scaling a successful short-term rental business, a common trajectory involves not just optimizing existing assets but also exploring avenues for expansive growth that leverage established success. While acquiring and managing more properties directly is a proven method, it inherently ties your personal time and capital to physical assets. A more sophisticated and potentially less capital-intensive approach to scaling lies in the strategic licensing or even franchising of your meticulously developed brand and operational management systems. This strategy allows you to replicate your winning formula across numerous markets and locations, not by physically owning more properties, but by empowering other entrepreneurs to operate under your established brand umbrella and utilize your tested methodologies. This is where the concept of licensing your brand and management system truly shines, transforming your hard-won expertise into a scalable revenue stream with reduced direct operational overhead.

The core idea behind licensing or franchising your short-term rental business is to package your entire operational blueprint – from the guest experience and booking process to cleaning protocols, vendor management, and financial reporting – into a sellable product. Think of it as creating a comprehensive "business in a box" that another entrepreneur can purchase the rights to use. This is not merely about lending your name; it's about transferring your proprietary systems, your refined operational procedures, and the brand equity you've painstakingly built. For potential licensees, this offers an incredibly attractive proposition: the opportunity to enter the profitable short-term rental market with a significantly reduced risk profile. They gain immediate access to a proven business model, a recognized brand, and a set of operational standards that have already demonstrated success, thereby bypassing the often-arduous and costly process of trial and error that new entrants typically face.

To effectively license your brand and management system, the first critical step is to meticulously document and codify every facet of your operation. This means moving beyond the informal know-how and creating a robust, replicable system. Your Standard Operating Procedures (SOPs) must be detailed to an almost granular level. For instance, the guest communication SOP should outline the exact sequence and content of pre-arrival messages, check-in instructions, mid-stay check-ins, and post-stay thank-you notes, including templates for common inquiries or issues. Similarly, cleaning protocols should be so specific that they can be followed by any cleaning team, anywhere. This might include checklists for each room, detailing specific sanitation procedures for high-touch surfaces, linen change protocols, and inventory checks for amenities. Vendor management, from vetting reliable cleaning services and maintenance personnel to negotiating contracts for utilities and supplies, needs to be clearly defined, along with criteria for selecting and managing these partners.

Furthermore, your pricing and revenue management strategies are a crucial component of the intellectual property you are licensing. This includes your dynamic pricing algorithms, your approach to setting nightly rates based on seasonality, demand, and local events, and your strategies for optimizing occupancy and average daily rates (ADRs). If you utilize specific software for revenue management, its role and how it's implemented within your system should be part of the licensed package. The guest experience itself, often a significant differentiator, needs to be articulated as a core part of the brand. This encompasses everything from the initial booking experience and the presentation of the property to the amenities offered, the communication style, and how you handle feedback or resolve issues. A strong, consistent guest experience is the bedrock of brand loyalty and positive reviews, which are powerful assets that licensees will want to replicate.

Once your operational framework is fully documented and standardized, the next step is to structure the licensing agreement itself. This is a legally binding contract that will define the terms under which a licensee can operate your business model. Key components of this agreement will include the scope of the license (what specific rights are being granted), the territory in which the licensee can operate, the duration of the license, and the financial terms. Financially, this typically involves an initial upfront licensing fee, often referred to as a franchise fee, which grants the licensee the right to use your brand and systems. In addition to this, a significant portion of the revenue will be generated through ongoing royalties. These royalties are usually a percentage of the licensee's gross revenue, ensuring that your income grows as their business grows. The agreement may also stipulate marketing contributions, where licensees contribute to a central marketing fund used for broader brand promotion.

Developing a comprehensive Franchise Disclosure Document (FDD) or a similar licensing disclosure document is often a legal requirement, especially if you plan to offer franchises in jurisdictions that regulate them. Even if not strictly required for a simple licensing agreement, it's best practice to provide a document that clearly outlines all aspects of the business opportunity, including your company's history, financial performance (if any), fees, obligations of both parties, and the territory. This transparency is crucial for building trust and ensuring that potential licensees are fully informed. The terms must be fair and clearly define the value proposition for both the licensor and the licensee.

A critical element that underpins the entire licensing model is the strength and recognition of your brand. Your brand is more than just a logo; it's the promise you make to your guests and the reputation you have cultivated. This includes your company name, logo, website design, social media presence, and the overall guest perception of your service quality. For a licensing strategy to be successful, your brand must be appealing and carry positive associations. If your properties consistently receive high ratings, generate positive word-of-mouth, and have a clear, attractive identity, this brand equity is what a licensee is paying for. They are buying into a proven concept that has demonstrated its ability to attract bookings and generate revenue. Therefore, continuous investment in brand building, marketing, and maintaining high service standards across your own operations is paramount, as this directly enhances the value of the license you offer to others.

The process of actually "selling" or granting these licenses requires a strategic approach to marketing your licensing opportunity. This might involve creating dedicated marketing materials that highlight the benefits of becoming a licensee, such as the proven business model, established brand recognition, operational support, and potential for profitability. You might advertise your licensing opportunities on business opportunity websites, through industry publications, or even by attending franchise expos. The selection process for licensees is also vital. You want to partner with individuals or entities who are not only financially capable but also share your commitment to quality and brand standards. This involves thorough vetting, including background checks, financial reviews, and interviews to assess their understanding of the business and their alignment with your brand's values.

Once a license is granted, your role transitions into that of a franchisor or licensor, providing ongoing support and oversight. This support is a key part of the value proposition for licensees. It can include initial training programs, which might cover everything from operational procedures to guest communication and revenue management. You would likely provide access to updated operational manuals, marketing collateral, and potentially centralized booking or management software. Regular performance reviews and ongoing support calls or site visits can help ensure that licensees are adhering to your standards and achieving their business objectives. The success of your licensees directly impacts your own revenue stream through royalties, so providing them with the tools and support they need to thrive is in your best interest.

This licensing model offers a powerful method for scaling your short-term rental business without the proportional increase in capital expenditure and direct management responsibilities that come with acquiring additional properties. It allows you to leverage your established success and brand recognition to fuel growth across new geographic markets. By franchising or licensing your proven operational systems and brand, you essentially build a network of independently operated businesses that contribute to your overall revenue through royalty payments. This diversification of your growth strategy can lead to a more robust and resilient business, capable of expanding its reach and impact far beyond what you could achieve solely through direct ownership and management. The key is to view your operational expertise and brand as an asset that can be effectively packaged and sold to other aspiring entrepreneurs, creating a win-win scenario where your proven success becomes the foundation for their new venture.

The financial implications of this licensing strategy can be substantial. Unlike direct property acquisition, which requires significant upfront capital for down payments, renovations, and furnishings, the primary investment for you as the licensor is in developing the documentation, legal agreements, and support systems. The revenue streams are primarily derived from initial franchise fees and ongoing royalties. If your model is highly sought after and your brand is strong, these royalties can represent a consistent and growing income stream, directly tied to the performance of your licensees. This can create a more predictable and scalable profit margin compared to the often-variable income from individual property rentals. For example, if your licensing fee is $30,000 and your royalty rate is 5% of gross revenue, and you have 10 licensees each generating $200,000 in annual gross revenue, your royalty income alone would be $100,000 per year, in addition to the initial franchise fees.

Consider the potential for market penetration. With direct ownership, you might acquire 5-10 properties in a given market over several years. Through licensing, you could potentially partner with 5-10 individuals or groups in that same market, or even across multiple diverse markets, within a much shorter timeframe. This accelerates your brand's presence and market share without the operational complexities of managing each individual unit. Furthermore, you become a central hub for best practices and innovation within your network of licensees, fostering a community that can collectively contribute to improving the overall system and brand.

The transition to a licensing model also changes your role from an operational manager to a brand steward and business developer. Your focus shifts to refining the licensing package, recruiting and supporting licensees, and ensuring brand consistency. This can be a more strategic and less demanding operational role, allowing you to focus on the high-level growth and development of your brand. However, it's crucial to understand that this does not mean an abdication of responsibility for maintaining brand integrity. A poorly performing licensee can damage your brand's reputation, so robust monitoring and enforcement of standards are essential. This might involve quality control checks, regular audits of financial reporting, and processes for addressing non-compliance, which could include issuing warnings or, in severe cases, terminating the license agreement.

When developing your licensing program, it's beneficial to research existing franchise models in related industries, such as hotels, serviced apartments, or even successful service-based franchises. Understanding their fee structures, support systems, and legal frameworks can provide valuable insights. However, the short-term rental market has its unique characteristics, particularly the dynamic nature of regulations, the reliance on online travel agencies (OTAs), and the direct guest interaction. Your licensing package must address these specifics and provide licensees with guidance on navigating these complexities. For instance, your operational manual should include strategies for managing OTA relationships, optimizing listings across multiple platforms, and developing a direct booking strategy to reduce OTA dependency and commission costs.

Ultimately, licensing your brand and management system represents a sophisticated evolution in scaling a short-term rental business. It transforms your operational expertise and brand equity into a powerful engine for growth, enabling you to expand your reach and impact significantly, while simultaneously creating a diversified and potentially more passive income stream. It's a strategy for those who have mastered the art of running a successful short-term rental operation and are ready to share that success, turning their proven model into a valuable commodity for other entrepreneurs seeking to enter the market with a competitive advantage. This approach not only amplifies your business's reach but also solidifies your brand's position in the market, creating a network effect that benefits all involved.

Chapter Eight

The Future of Short-Term Rentals and Continuous Growth

Adapting to Market Shifts and Trends

The landscape of short-term rentals is anything but static; it's a vibrant, ever-shifting ecosystem influenced by global economic forces, technological advancements, changing consumer preferences, and evolving regulatory environments. To not just survive but thrive in this dynamic market, a proactive and adaptive approach is not merely beneficial – it's essential. This means cultivating a keen awareness of emerging trends and understanding how to pivot your operations and offerings to align with these shifts. Ignoring these currents is akin to sailing a ship without a compass; you might stay afloat for a while, but you're unlikely to reach your desired destination efficiently, if at all.

One of the most significant recent transformations has been the blurring of lines between work and leisure, giving rise to the "work-cation" phenomenon. Driven by the widespread adoption of remote work policies, a growing segment of travelers are no longer confined to traditional holiday periods. They are seeking accommodations that not only offer comfort and local experiences but also provide the functionality to maintain productivity. This translates into a demand for properties equipped with reliable high-speed internet, dedicated workspaces (whether a separate office or a well-appointed desk in a quiet area), ergonomic seating, and ample power outlets. Hosts who proactively integrate these "work-friendly" features into their listings are tapping into a lucrative and expanding market. This might involve investing in a mesh Wi-Fi system to ensure seamless connectivity throughout the property, providing a comfortable desk and chair, ensuring good lighting, and even offering small amenities like surge protectors or portable chargers. Beyond the physical amenities, clear communication about these features in your listing description and marketing materials is crucial to attract this specific demographic. Highlighting your property as an ideal spot for a productive remote work retreat can significantly differentiate you from competitors who may only cater to traditional leisure travelers. The ability to seamlessly transition from a productive workday to enjoying local amenities or relaxation is a key selling point for this new breed of traveler.

Sustainability is another megatrend that is increasingly influencing travel decisions. Guests are becoming more environmentally conscious, seeking out accommodations that demonstrate a commitment to eco-friendly practices. This is not just about appealing to a niche market; it's becoming a mainstream expectation. From an operational perspective, this can involve a range of initiatives. Implementing water-saving measures, such as low-flow showerheads and toilets, can reduce utility costs and environmental impact. Energy efficiency is also paramount; switching to LED lighting, utilizing smart thermostats to optimize heating and cooling when the property is unoccupied, and encouraging guests to be mindful of their energy consumption can make a significant difference. Waste reduction is another critical area, which can be addressed through comprehensive recycling programs, providing reusable amenities (like water bottles or coffee cups), and minimizing single-use plastics. Furthermore, sourcing local and sustainable products for amenities or even for property maintenance can resonate deeply with environmentally aware travelers. Clearly communicating your sustainability efforts in your listing, perhaps through a dedicated section or a visible eco-friendly badge, can attract guests who prioritize these values and are willing to support businesses that align with their ethos. This commitment to sustainability not only contributes to a healthier planet but can also enhance your brand's reputation and attract a loyal customer base. Consider partnering with local eco-conscious suppliers for linens, toiletries, or even cleaning products to further bolster your green credentials.

Guest expectations are also constantly evolving, shaped by the broader hospitality industry and the experiences they have elsewhere. What might have been considered a luxury amenity a few years ago – like a Nespresso machine or a high-quality hairdryer – is now becoming standard. Travelers are also increasingly seeking personalized experiences and authentic local interactions. This moves beyond just providing a clean and comfortable space; it involves curating an en-

vironment that offers a sense of place. This could include providing
a curated list of local restaurants, attractions, and hidden gems, offering artisanal local products as welcome gifts, or even facilitating
connections with local service providers for unique experiences. The
rise of "experiential travel" means guests are looking for more than
just a bed; they want to immerse themselves in the local culture and
create memorable moments. Hosts who can anticipate and cater to
these evolving desires will find themselves ahead of the curve. This
might involve offering bespoke tours, partnering with local artisans
for workshops, or providing access to unique local events. Furthermore, in an age of digital connectivity, guests often expect seamless
self-check-in and check-out processes, intuitive smart home features,
and responsive communication via their preferred channels.

Staying ahead of these market shifts requires a consistent and systematic approach to market intelligence and adaptation. Firstly, continuous monitoring of industry publications, travel blogs, and trend
reports is crucial. Subscribing to newsletters from organizations like
the Short-Term Rental Owners Association, following influential figures in the travel and hospitality tech space, and engaging with online forums where hosts and travelers discuss their experiences can
provide invaluable insights. Pay attention to what features are being
highlighted in top-performing listings in your area and in aspirational
markets. Analyze booking data for patterns: are certain types of stays
(e.g., longer stays, mid-week bookings) becoming more prevalent? Are
there specific amenities that correlate with higher occupancy rates or
better reviews?

Secondly, actively solicit and analyze guest feedback. Don't just read
reviews; categorize the comments. Are guests repeatedly mentioning
the need for better Wi-Fi? Are they suggesting local experiences you
haven't considered? Use this feedback as a direct roadmap for im-

provements. Implement a structured system for collecting feedback, perhaps through post-stay surveys that ask specific questions about their experience and potential areas for enhancement. This direct line to guest sentiment is an underutilized goldmine for identifying emerging needs and preferences.

Thirdly, be willing to experiment and iterate. The short-term rental market rewards agility. Once you've identified a promising trend, don't be afraid to make small, calculated investments to test it out. If you're considering adding a dedicated workspace, start by reconfiguring an existing space and furnishing it modestly. If you're exploring sustainable practices, begin with low-cost initiatives like enhanced recycling and energy-saving reminders. Monitor the impact of these changes on your bookings, guest reviews, and overall revenue. If an experiment proves successful, you can then invest more significantly. If it doesn't, you can pivot without incurring substantial losses. This iterative process allows you to continuously refine your offerings and stay competitive.

Furthermore, understanding the competitive landscape is paramount. Regularly analyze what other successful hosts in your market are doing. What makes their listings stand out? Are they embracing new technologies, offering unique packages, or highlighting specific types of experiences? This competitive analysis should not lead to simply copying others, but rather to identifying gaps in the market that you can uniquely fill or areas where you can differentiate yourself by offering superior quality or a more compelling value proposition. For instance, if all listings in your area focus on budget-friendly stays, identifying an opportunity to create a premium, amenity-rich experience could be a winning strategy. Conversely, if the market is saturated with high-end properties, a well-executed, value-driven offering might capture a different segment of demand.

Regulatory changes are another constant factor that can significantly impact the short-term rental market. Local ordinances, tax laws,
and zoning regulations can change rapidly, and staying abreast of these
developments is critical for long-term viability. Missing a regulatory
update can lead to fines, operational disruptions, or even the inability
to continue operating. This means building relationships with local
authorities, joining industry advocacy groups, and subscribing to relevant government notifications. Understanding the legal framework
within which you operate allows you to adapt your business model
proactively rather than reactively. For example, if a city introduces a
new occupancy tax, you need to understand how it affects your pricing
strategy and ensure it's correctly implemented and communicated to
guests. Similarly, changes in zoning laws might affect where you can
operate or the types of properties you can offer, requiring careful
strategic planning.

In essence, adapting to market shifts and trends is an ongoing
process, not a one-time task. It requires a mindset of continuous
learning, a willingness to invest in understanding your market and
your guests, and the agility to implement changes effectively. By embracing the evolution of the short-term rental industry – from the
rise of remote work and the demand for sustainable practices to the
ever-increasing expectations of guests and the complexities of regulatory landscapes – hosts can position themselves for sustained success
and profitability. This proactive engagement with change ensures that
your short-term rental business remains relevant, attractive, and competitive in an industry that never stands still. It's about anticipating the
future and building a business that is resilient and ready to capitalize
on the opportunities that tomorrow's travelers will present.

Building a Community and Network

In the dynamic and often solitary pursuit of short-term rental success, the temptation to operate in a vacuum can be strong. Yet, as we navigate the future of this industry, one of the most powerful and underutilized assets at our disposal is the collective wisdom and shared experience of our peers. Building a robust community and a strong professional network is not just a supplementary activity; it is a foundational element for continuous growth, resilience, and innovation. This interconnectedness offers a vital counterbalance to the inherent challenges and uncertainties of the short-term rental landscape, providing support, knowledge, and opportunities that are difficult, if not impossible, to acquire in isolation.

The digital age has democratized access to information and connection, and the short-term rental world is no exception. Online forums and communities are veritable goldmines for those willing to engage. Platforms like Reddit, with subreddits dedicated to Airbnb hosting, property management, and real estate investing, offer a constant stream of real-time discussions, problem-solving threads, and candid advice from hosts at every stage of their journey. These spaces are invaluable for asking specific questions about anything from optimizing cleaning protocols to navigating complex tax implications, or even seeking advice on dealing with difficult guests. More experienced hosts often share their hard-won lessons, providing cautionary tales and practical solutions that can save you significant time, money, and stress. Engaging in these forums is not merely about passively consuming information; it's about active participation. By contributing your own experiences and insights, you not only solidify your understanding but also establish yourself as a valuable member of the community, which can lead to unexpected collaborations and reciprocal support.

Beyond the digital realm, the power of face-to-face interaction cannot be overstated. Local meetups and host gatherings, often organized by Airbnb itself or by independent host groups, offer a unique opportunity to connect with individuals who understand the specific nuances of your local market. These gatherings provide a chance to discuss hyperlocal issues, such as local zoning laws, tourist traffic patterns, or the presence of specific competitors, in a way that global online forums might not fully appreciate. The relationships forged in these settings can be incredibly strong. Sharing a coffee with another host who has just navigated a similar challenge, or discussing a new local regulation over dinner, builds a rapport that fosters trust and genuine support. These local connections can also lead to practical collaborations, such as sharing trusted vendor recommendations (cleaners, handymen, photographers) or even exploring joint ventures. For instance, a host with a property in a high-demand area might partner with a host in a complementary location to offer bundled packages or referral incentives.

Attending industry conferences and expos, while often requiring a greater investment of time and resources, offers a more structured and comprehensive avenue for networking and learning. Events like VRMA (Vacation Rental Management Association) conferences, industry-specific tech summits, and larger travel and tourism expos bring together property owners, managers, technology providers, and legal experts from across the globe. These events are curated to showcase the latest innovations in property management software, marketing strategies, guest experience technologies, and regulatory updates. The networking opportunities at these events are unparalleled. You have the chance to meet potential mentors, find collaborators for larger projects, and even discover investment opportunities or strategic partnerships that could significantly scale your business. The insights gained from expert-led workshops and keynote speeches can provide a strategic vision for the future, helping you anticipate industry shifts and position your business accordingly. Furthermore, these conferences are excellent places to connect with suppliers of goods and services, potentially negotiating bulk discounts or finding specialized providers that can enhance your operational efficiency and guest satisfaction.

The concept of mentorship, often facilitated through strong networks, is particularly crucial for accelerating the learning curve in the short-term rental business. A mentor, typically someone with more experience and a proven track record of success, can provide invaluable guidance, acting as a sounding board for your ideas and a source of constructive criticism. They can help you avoid common pitfalls, share strategies for overcoming obstacles, and offer personalized advice based on their own journey. Identifying a mentor doesn't necessarily require a formal program. It can emerge organically from building relationships within your network. Perhaps you admire a particular host's business acumen or their approach to guest relations; reaching out and expressing that admiration, and then asking for guidance on a specific challenge, can be the beginning of a valuable mentorship. The willingness of seasoned professionals to share their knowledge is often driven by a desire to see the industry grow and improve, and by the recognition that a rising tide lifts all boats.

Beyond individual mentorship, the collective knowledge sharing within a network allows for the rapid dissemination of best practices. When a new technology emerges that promises to streamline guest communication, or a novel marketing approach starts yielding results, word spreads quickly through well-connected communities. This allows you to adopt and adapt beneficial strategies much faster than if you were relying solely on independent research. It's about learning from the successes and failures of others, and then applying those lessons to your own operations. This collaborative intelligence is a powerful competitive advantage. It allows you to stay at the forefront of industry trends, constantly refining your offerings and operations to meet evolving guest expectations and market demands.

Furthermore, building a network fosters a sense of shared purpose and mutual support, which is essential for navigating the inherent stresses of the short-term rental business. There will be times when a difficult guest, an unexpected property damage, or a sudden regulatory change can feel overwhelming. Having a network of fellow hosts to turn to for advice, commiseration, or simply a listening ear can make a significant difference in your ability to persevere and maintain a positive outlook. This psychological support is as important as the practical advice. Knowing you are not alone in facing these challenges can significantly improve your mental well-being and your long-term commitment to the industry.

The future of short-term rentals is increasingly characterized by professionalization and a move towards more sophisticated business practices. Individuals and small businesses that embrace collaboration and continuous learning through community engagement will undoubtedly have an edge. This network effect amplifies individual efforts, creating a ripple effect of innovation and improvement across the entire industry. It transforms the competitive landscape into one where shared learning and mutual advancement are recognized as key drivers of success, ensuring that as the industry evolves, those who are part of a connected community are better equipped to adapt, thrive, and lead. This proactive engagement with a professional community is a direct investment in the future of your short-term rental enterprise, ensuring its continued relevance and profitability.

Maintaining Guest Satisfaction and Loyalty

The bedrock of any thriving short-term rental business isn't just about acquiring new bookings; it's about cultivating a loyal customer base. This loyalty is forged through an unwavering commitment to guest satisfaction, a continuous process of refinement that ensures every visitor leaves with a positive and memorable experience. We've touched on the importance of a strong network in navigating the industry, but the most potent network effect begins within your own properties, with your guests. When you prioritize their comfort, convenience, and overall enjoyment, you're not just providing a place to stay; you're creating an experience that guests will actively seek out again and recommend to others. This focus on guest satisfaction is a powerful engine for organic growth, transforming one-time visitors into repeat customers and brand advocates.

At the heart of maintaining this high level of satisfaction is crystal-clear and proactive communication. From the moment a guest books your property, establishing a consistent dialogue sets the stage for a smooth and enjoyable stay. This begins with a prompt and welcoming confirmation message, reiterating key details like check-in instructions, house rules, and contact information. During their stay, regular check-ins are crucial. A simple message asking if everything is to their satisfaction, or offering assistance with local recommendations, can go a long way. However, it's vital to strike a balance; too much communication can feel intrusive, while too little can leave guests feeling unsupported. The key is to be available and responsive without hovering. Many hosts find success in sending a mid-stay message, perhaps on the second or third day, to ensure everything is proceeding smoothly and to address any potential issues before they escalate. This also provides an opportune moment to offer additional services or local insights that might enhance their experience, such as suggesting a less-crowded time to visit a popular attraction or recommending a local eatery that aligns with their dietary preferences.

Anticipating guest needs is another cornerstone of exceptional hospitality. This goes beyond simply providing the amenities listed in your description; it's about thinking ahead and considering what might enhance their stay. For instance, if you know your guests are arriving late at night, perhaps a small, pre-packaged snack or a bottle of water in the refrigerator can be a welcome surprise. For families with young children, having a few basic items like a travel crib or high chair readily available (and clearly communicated as an option) can be a significant draw. Even anticipating common questions – such as where to find the nearest grocery store, the best local transportation options, or how to operate specific appliances – and proactively providing this information in a welcome guide can significantly reduce friction and enhance the guest's sense of being cared for. This guide can be a physical booklet or a digital document accessible via a QR code, offering a comprehensive resource for all aspects of their stay.

Consistently delivering on the promises made in your listing is non-negotiable. The photos and descriptions should accurately represent the property. Any discrepancies, however minor they may seem, can lead to disappointment and erode trust. This means ensuring that the amenities are in working order, the cleanliness standards are impeccable, and the overall ambiance matches what was advertised. If a hot tub is advertised, it needs to be clean and fully functional. If the listing highlights a fast Wi-Fi connection, it should indeed be reliable. Any unforeseen issues, such as a temporary closure of a community pool or a planned maintenance that might cause minor disruption, should be communicated to guests well in advance of their arrival, ideally with an explanation and perhaps a small gesture of goodwill.

Transparency and honesty in your listing and communications build a foundation of trust, which is essential for guest loyalty.

The power of positive reviews and word-of-mouth cannot be overstated in the short-term rental ecosystem. Happy guests are far more likely to leave glowing reviews, which in turn attract more bookings. These reviews act as social proof, influencing the decisions of potential guests who are researching properties. Beyond online platforms, satisfied guests become your most effective marketing channel. They will share their positive experiences with friends, family, and colleagues, generating organic referrals that are often more impactful than any paid advertising. Encouraging reviews, while always maintaining ethical boundaries and avoiding any form of coercion, can be as simple as a polite post-stay message thanking them for their patronage and mentioning that their feedback is highly valued. Some hosts even include a small, subtle prompt in their welcome guide or departure message, suggesting they consider leaving a review if they enjoyed their stay.

Furthermore, a focus on guest satisfaction translates into a higher occupancy rate and, consequently, increased profitability. Guests who feel valued and well-cared for are more likely to rebook with you, reducing the constant need to acquire new customers. This repeat business provides a stable revenue stream and allows for more accurate financial forecasting. It also means that you can potentially charge a premium for your well-managed and highly-rated property. When guests consistently experience excellence, they become less price-sensitive and more inclined to choose your property based on its reputation for quality and reliability. This creates a virtuous cycle: excellent service leads to great reviews, which leads to more bookings, which leads to greater revenue, allowing for further investment in enhancing the guest experience.

To truly embed guest satisfaction into your operational DNA, it's essential to have robust systems for collecting and acting upon guest feedback. This involves actively soliciting reviews, but also looking for opportunities to gather more qualitative data. Post-stay surveys, while sometimes overlooked by guests, can provide valuable insights into specific aspects of their experience. These surveys can be short and focused, asking about cleanliness, communication, amenities, and overall satisfaction. Analyzing this feedback, both the public reviews and any private responses, is critical. Identifying recurring themes, whether positive or negative, allows you to pinpoint areas of strength to reinforce and areas for improvement. For example, if multiple guests mention the comfort of the beds, this is a positive reinforcement. Conversely, if several guests note that the Wi-Fi signal is weak in a particular room, this is a clear signal for a technical upgrade or a repositioning of the router.

Implementing a system for addressing negative feedback constructively is just as important as celebrating positive feedback. When issues arise, and they inevitably will in any service-oriented business, how you respond can often turn a negative situation into a positive one. Prompt, empathetic, and solutions-oriented responses to complaints are crucial. Acknowledging the guest's experience, apologizing for any shortcomings, and outlining the steps you will take to rectify the situation or prevent recurrence can demonstrate your commitment to guest satisfaction. In some cases, a partial refund or a discount on a future stay might be appropriate. More importantly, use negative feedback as a learning opportunity. Each complaint is a chance to refine your processes, improve your property, and ultimately prevent similar issues from affecting future guests. This iterative approach to improvement, driven by guest feedback, is central to long-term success.

Beyond direct feedback, observing guest behavior and preferences can also offer insights. For instance, noting the types of local attractions guests frequently ask about might inform your future recommendations or even the types of amenities you consider adding. If many guests are families, perhaps investing in a few more child-friendly items or creating a dedicated play area could be beneficial. If your property is popular with business travelers, ensuring a well-equipped workspace and reliable high-speed internet becomes paramount. This kind of observational learning, combined with direct feedback, allows you to continuously adapt and tailor your offering to meet the evolving demands of your target market.

In the broader context of the future of short-term rentals, the emphasis on personalized guest experiences will only intensify. As the market becomes more competitive, hosts who can differentiate themselves through exceptional service and a deep understanding of their guests' needs will undoubtedly prosper. This means moving beyond a purely transactional approach and embracing a relational one. Building genuine connections with guests, even if brief, fosters a sense of hospitality that transcends the physical space. This might involve remembering a guest's preferred coffee type from a previous stay, offering a small personalized welcome gift based on their stated interests, or simply engaging in friendly conversation that makes them feel like more than just a booking number. These small touches of personalization can create a lasting impression and solidify guest loyalty in a way that generic service simply cannot.

Ultimately, maintaining guest satisfaction and fostering loyalty is not a one-time task but an ongoing commitment. It requires a proactive mindset, a dedication to continuous improvement, and a genuine desire to provide outstanding hospitality. By prioritizing clear communication, anticipating needs, delivering on promises, and actively seeking and acting upon feedback, you build a strong foundation for repeat business, positive word-of-mouth, and sustained growth in the dynamic short-term rental market. This focus on the guest experience is not merely a strategy; it's the essence of successful hospitality, ensuring that your short-term rental business thrives not just today, but well into the future. It's about creating an environment where guests feel not just welcomed, but truly valued, leading them to return again and again, and becoming your most vocal and impactful advocates in the process.

Financial Discipline and Reinvestment Strategies

As your short-term rental business matures and begins to generate consistent profits, the temptation to enjoy the fruits of your labor can be strong. However, true long-term success and expansion in this dynamic industry hinge on a disciplined approach to financial management and a strategic vision for reinvestment. Simply accumulating profits without a clear plan can lead to stagnation, leaving your business vulnerable to market shifts and competitive pressures. Prudent financial stewardship is not about depriving yourself of rewards; it's about strategically deploying capital to fuel further growth, enhance your existing assets, and build a more resilient and profitable portfolio for the future. This involves a conscious shift from simply managing income to actively building wealth through smart reinvestment strategies.

The cornerstone of this financial discipline is the creation of a robust financial plan. This isn't a static document but a living blueprint that evolves with your business. At its core, this plan should clearly delineate your income streams, operational expenses, and, crucially, your profit margins. Beyond basic bookkeeping, it requires a forward-looking perspective, forecasting potential revenue, anticipated costs for maintenance and upgrades, and identifying opportunities for expansion. One of the most effective ways to implement this is by establishing dedicated reserve accounts. Separate accounts for operational contingencies (like unexpected repairs or seasonal dips in occupancy), capital expenditures (for significant upgrades or property acquisitions), and a general profit reinvestment fund provide a clear framework for managing your finances. This compartmentalization ensures that funds allocated for growth are not inadvertently spent on day-to-day operations and vice versa, maintaining financial clarity and control.

Reinvesting profits wisely is not a one-size-fits-all strategy. The optimal allocation of funds will depend on your specific business goals, market conditions, and the current state of your properties. A common and highly effective strategy is to reinvest in property upgrades and enhancements. This can range from cosmetic improvements that boost curb appeal and guest satisfaction to functional upgrades that increase efficiency and desirability. Consider modernizing kitchens and bathrooms, investing in higher-quality linens and furnishings, improving Wi-Fi infrastructure, or adding desirable amenities like smart home technology, enhanced outdoor living spaces, or even dedicated workspaces for remote travelers. These investments directly impact your guest experience, justifying higher nightly rates, attracting a broader range of guests, and leading to increased occupancy and revenue. Moreover, well-maintained and updated properties tend to command better reviews, creating a virtuous cycle of positive feedback and bookings. The key here is to focus on upgrades that offer a tangible return on investment, either through increased revenue per booking or improved operational efficiency. This might involve data analysis to understand which amenities are most sought after by your target demographic or conducting a comparative analysis of similar properties in your market to identify competitive advantages.

Another critical avenue for reinvestment is the acquisition of new assets. As your existing properties become profitable and well-managed, leveraging that success to expand your portfolio can significantly accelerate your growth. This doesn't necessarily mean outright purchasing new properties immediately. It could involve exploring options like acquiring a neighboring unit in a multi-unit building, purchasing a property in a different, high-demand market, or even considering fractional ownership models. The capital generated from your existing successful rentals can serve as a down payment or provide the necessary capital for these acquisitions. When considering new properties, rigorous due diligence is paramount. This includes thorough market research, analyzing occupancy rates and average daily rates (ADRs) of comparable properties, understanding local regulations and zoning laws, and meticulously calculating potential operating costs and ROI. The goal is to acquire assets that complement your existing portfolio and offer similar or even greater profit potential.

Investing in marketing and brand development is also a vital component of a reinvestment strategy. While organic growth through positive reviews is invaluable, a strategic marketing push can accelerate your reach and attract a wider audience. This could involve enhancing your property listings with professional photography and compelling descriptions, investing in targeted online advertising campaigns on platforms like Google Ads or social media, collaborating with travel influencers or bloggers, or developing a strong direct booking website. Building a distinct brand identity – beyond just the property itself – can foster loyalty and differentiate you in a crowded market. This might involve creating a memorable brand name, a consistent visual aesthetic across all your communication channels, and a unique value proposition that resonates with your ideal guest. Allocating a portion of your profits to these marketing efforts ensures that your properties remain visible and appealing to potential guests.

Furthermore, reinvestment can extend to operational improvements and technology adoption that enhance efficiency and guest experience. This could include investing in property management software to streamline booking, communication, and cleaning schedules, implementing smart lock systems for secure and convenient check-ins, or utilizing dynamic pricing tools to optimize nightly rates based on demand. Exploring automation for routine tasks, such as sending pre-arrival and post-stay messages, can free up your time to focus on higher-value activities like guest relations or strategic planning. Investing in your team, whether it's hiring a reliable cleaning crew, a responsive maintenance person, or even a virtual assistant, can also be a crucial reinvestment that allows you to scale your operations effectively and maintain high service standards.

A key element of financial discipline is the establishment of clear reinvestment goals. Instead of simply distributing profits or making ad-hoc investments, define specific objectives. For example, a goal might be to acquire a second property within two years, to increase the average daily rate of your primary property by 15% through upgrades within one year, or to achieve a 90% occupancy rate across your portfolio. These SMART (Specific, Measurable, Achievable, Relevant, Time-bound) goals provide direction and a benchmark against which to measure your progress. Regularly reviewing your financial statements against these goals allows you to assess the effectiveness of your reinvestment strategies and make necessary adjustments.

Maintaining financial prudence also means understanding when not to reinvest aggressively. There may be times when market conditions are uncertain, interest rates are unfavorable, or your existing

properties require significant capital expenditures for essential maintenance. In such scenarios, it might be wiser to build a larger cash
reserve, pay down debt on your existing properties, or simply maintain
the status quo while waiting for more opportune conditions. Financial discipline is as much about knowing when to deploy capital as it
is about knowing when to conserve it. This requires a keen awareness
of macroeconomic trends, local market dynamics, and the financial
health of your own business. Regularly consulting with financial ad-
visors or experienced real estate professionals can provide valuable
insights and help you make informed decisions during these critical
junctures.

The long-term vision for your short-term rental business should
always include a strategy for scaling and diversification. Reinvestment
is the engine that drives this scaling. As your portfolio grows and your
profitability increases, you gain more leverage and financial flexibility.
This allows you to weather economic downturns more effectively, take
advantage of emerging market opportunities, and ultimately build a
more substantial and sustainable income stream. Diversification can
also be a form of reinvestment, spreading your risk across different
geographic locations, property types, or even entirely different investment classes, thereby building a more resilient financial future. The
discipline of setting aside profits and strategically reinvesting them is
not a short-term tactic; it's a fundamental principle for transforming a
successful short-term rental operation into a significant wealth-build-
ing enterprise that can provide lasting financial security.

Your Day Launch Success and Beyond

You've reached the culmination of this guide, a point where the
theoretical knowledge you've absorbed begins its exciting transition

into tangible reality. The journey from understanding the short-term rental market to actively participating in it can feel daunting, but the framework we've laid out is designed to make that leap not only possible but also remarkably achievable. Your 30-day launch plan is more than just a timeline; it's a meticulously crafted strategy to bring your first property online, optimized for bookings and guest satisfaction. This isn't about hitting an arbitrary deadline for the sake of it, but about instilling discipline, fostering momentum, and building the confidence that comes from execution. Within this initial 30-day period, you'll have navigated the essential steps: identifying your target market, sourcing the right property, preparing it for guests, setting up your listing on crucial platforms, and establishing your operational backbone for seamless check-ins and turnovers.

The success you achieve in those first 30 days is a powerful indicator of your potential and a solid foundation upon which to build. It's proof that with strategic planning and dedicated effort, the short-term rental landscape is accessible and profitable. This initial launch phase is your proving ground, where you'll encounter real-world scenarios, gather invaluable guest feedback, and begin to understand the nuances of your specific market from a host's perspective. Think of these first weeks as an intensive, real-time learning experience that complements everything you've read. The data you collect – occupancy rates, average daily rates, guest reviews, operational costs – will be the lifeblood of your future growth strategies. It's crucial to approach this initial period with an open mind, a willingness to adapt, and a commitment to continuous improvement. Don't be discouraged by minor hiccups; view them as learning opportunities that refine your processes and strengthen your business.

Beyond the initial 30-day launch, the true art of short-term rental investing lies in sustained growth and adaptation. The market is not static; it evolves with economic shifts, changing travel trends, and the emergence of new technologies and competitor strategies. Therefore, your approach must be equally dynamic. The immediate aftermath of your launch is the perfect time to analyze the performance data from your first month of operation. Dive deep into your booking calendar: which days of the week were most popular? Were there specific periods of high demand you could have capitalized on even further? Examine your pricing strategy. Did your chosen nightly rates align with market expectations and occupancy levels? Guest feedback, both positive and constructive, is a goldmine of information. What did guests consistently praise? What areas were flagged for improvement? This critical self-assessment is the bedrock of informed decision-making for the weeks and months ahead.

Your 30-day goal was to

launch, and you've achieved that. Now, the focus shifts to optimizing and scaling. This means continually refining your guest experience, streamlining your operations, and strategically expanding your reach and profitability. Consider how you can leverage the insights gained from your initial launch to elevate your property. If guests consistently mentioned the comfort of your bedding, perhaps it's time to invest in even higher thread counts or specialized pillows. If the check-in process was smooth, look for ways to make it even more welcoming, perhaps with a personalized welcome note or a small local amenity. Conversely, if any aspect received less-than-glowing feedback, prioritize addressing it. This iterative process of improvement is what separates mediocre hosts from exceptional ones.

The momentum generated by a successful 30-day launch is powerful and should be harnessed for continued learning and adaptation. The short-term rental industry is constantly evolving. New booking platforms emerge, guest preferences shift, and local regulations can change. Staying ahead requires a commitment to ongoing education. Subscribe to industry newsletters, follow leading short-term rental influencers and blogs, and actively participate in online communities and forums where hosts share insights and best practices. Understanding emerging trends – such as the rise of the "workcation," the demand for eco-friendly stays, or the increasing popularity of unique, experiential accommodations – will allow you to position your property to capture new market segments.

As you look beyond the initial launch, think about how you can enhance your property's appeal and revenue potential. This might involve strategic upgrades. Consider investing in amenities that differentiate your offering: a high-speed Wi-Fi upgrade for remote workers, a dedicated home office setup, enhanced outdoor living spaces for al fresco dining, or smart home technology for added convenience and security. Even small touches, like curated local guides, high-quality coffee makers, or artisanal toiletries, can significantly elevate the guest experience and justify premium pricing. The key is to invest in upgrades that have a demonstrable impact on guest satisfaction and booking conversion rates, aligning with the feedback you've received and your understanding of market demand.

Furthermore, the success of your first property opens the door to portfolio expansion. Once your initial venture is running smoothly and generating consistent returns, you can begin to explore opportunities to acquire additional properties. This could mean purchasing a second unit in the same building for economies of scale, acquiring a property in a different, high-demand market, or even exploring niche markets like glamping or unique dwelling rentals. Each new acquisition requires the same rigorous due diligence and strategic planning that guided your first purchase, but your experience now provides a significant advantage. You'll have a proven system for property selection, preparation, management, and marketing, allowing you to scale your business more efficiently and effectively.

Building a strong brand identity is another crucial aspect of long-term growth that should be considered early on. Your properties are more than just places to stay; they are experiences you offer. Developing a consistent brand aesthetic, a compelling narrative, and a memorable name can help you stand out in a crowded marketplace. This brand should be reflected in everything from your listing photos and descriptions to your guest communication and the physical presentation of your properties. A strong brand fosters guest loyalty, encourages repeat bookings, and can even enable you to command higher prices.

Your 30-day launch is a significant milestone, but it's merely the first step on a much longer and potentially more rewarding journey. The real opportunity lies in what you do next: in your commitment to continuous improvement, your willingness to adapt to market changes, and your strategic vision for growth. By consistently analyzing your performance, reinvesting wisely in your properties and operations, and staying informed about industry trends, you can transform your initial success into a thriving, scalable, and highly profitable short-term rental business. Embrace the ongoing learning process, stay agile, and never underestimate the power of a great guest experience. The future of your short-term rental empire is built on the discipline, insight, and proactive approach you cultivate starting today. Keep learning, keep optimizing, and keep growing.

Acknowledgements

I extend my sincere thanks to every guest who has chosen to stay with us. Your presence, your stories, and your thoughtful reflections have been the heartbeat of this project. The insights you shared not only enriched our understanding but also shaped the very essence of this guide. I am equally grateful to my family, whose patience, encouragement, and understanding have been unwavering throughout the many hours of research and writing. This work stands as a testament to the collective spirit, generosity, and support that made it possible.

About the author

As a seasoned Airbnb Superhost and short-term rental investor, Eric McDermott has a proven track record of successfully launching, scaling, and maximizing profits in the dynamic short-term rental market. Having generated over $1 million across multiple listings, Eric McDermott channels his passion for empowering others into guiding aspiring hosts through the intricacies of property acquisition, guest management, and operational efficiency. His expertise, honed through years of hands-on experience and continuous market analysis, forms the foundation of this practical guide. Eric McDermott is dedicated to sharing actionable strategies that demystify the process and pave the way for sustainable success in the STR industry.